The Aging Wisely Project

Endorsements

Dr. Ben Green, a veteran psychiatrist and psychoanalyst, and Scott Fisher, a career executive coach, take on the topic of aging in their new book, *The Aging Wisely Project*. In an increasingly greying population culturally reluctant to talk about getting old and dying, their thoughtful examination of the subject offers wisdom from a developmental, attachment, and neurocognitive point of view. Each chapter is carefully crafted to discuss a different psychological aspect of aging and offers solutions to curious readers who seek advice and a more profound understanding to enrich and cherish the meaning of this final stage of life.

Larry Mortazavi, M.D., CGP
President of Denver Psychoanalytic Society

The Aging Wisely Project is a tour de force, delving into the process and tasks of aging with great breadth and depth. The intimate descriptions of the lives of fifty-two elders left me feeling inspired and empowered to make the most of the last quarter of my life. This book is just packed full of wisdom!

David Nichol, M.D.
Psychoanalyst and Author of *The One-Minute Meditator*

The Aging Wisely Project is a marvelous book for those who find themselves, well, AGING. I recognize myself in many of the case studies. Ben and Scott clearly describe solid research findings so they are easily understandable, and this book is essential reading for anyone grappling with advancing years.

Rob Socolofsky
Retired Administrative Law Judge, State of Colorado,
Current Bassist, Luthier, Poet, and Brewmeister

Amongst the growing number of aging well books, *The Aging Wisely Project* is singular in how it weaves together psychological theory and personal anecdote. We're left with a sense of hope about growing old—provided we're ready to commit to continual learning and an adaptive attitude.

Cory Hines
Creative Adapter and Director,
Mount Washington (Massachusetts) Council on Aging

Why do some people grow old so well while others struggle? *The Aging Wisely Project* is a practical, smart guide for the person who wants to be intentional about growing older and setting the course to live life fully at every stage. I couldn't put it down!

Sharyl Johnson Harston
Retired Executive, Co-Founder of Adventures in Boomerland,
and Persistent Student of "Good Living"

The Aging Wisely Project incorporates contemporary developmental and relational research to augment and enrich concepts originally introduced by psychoanalyst Erik Erikson regarding psychological development throughout the lifespan. This scholarly work, particularly the focus on Elder Identity Revision, provides a valuable framework for clinical work, for students of human development, and for all of us interested in enriching our own developmental trajectories.

Esther Lowenstein, Psy.D.
Psychologist/Psychoanalyst, Faculty, The Denver Institute for Psychoanalysis

Forget the gold watch for the about-to-be-retired. Instead, give them *The Aging Wisely Project* by Ben Green and Scott Fisher to help them plan and live a happy, fruitful elderhood. And get one for yourself. The book features extensive interviews with fifty-two retirees and analyzes their successes and failures as they plan for their last years. Well-balanced between individual life stories and academic analyses, Ben and Scott have crafted a beautifully detailed path to successful aging.

Carol Tierney

The Aging Wisely Project is insightful, engaging, and full of concrete advice for people of all ages. The portraits of interviewed elders are fascinating—both in the life stories rendered and how the authors notice what goes unsaid. Their astute observations show how deeply the stories we tell ourselves shape our lives. This book is a thought-provoking and inspiring companion for all who seek to age wisely.

Lucy Marcus
Faculty, Borough of Manhattan Community College

Clear and comprehensive! A wonderfully unique, helpful, and insightful guide to rethinking the path of elder age in our present times.

Susie Carol
Elder Artist and Dabbling Musician

Frankly, I could not put *The Aging Wisely Project* down. I find it a true blueprint for aging wisely.

Judy Whitbeck
Mt. Washington, Massachusetts

The Aging Wisely Project is a compendium of powerful and revealing life stories of fifty-two elders that serve as a life-guide for better understanding and appreciating the many challenges and opportunities for living a meaningful and fulfilling life. The authors' research has resulted in the suggestion of a final stage (labeled Elder Identity Revision) to Erik Erikson's psychosocial development model to better explain their elderhood findings and conclusions. And finally, their book is enhanced by the authors' own humorous observations and wisdom from years of personal and professional experiences. Reading this book has provided a persuasive and actionable guide for my own pursuit and appreciation of the meaningful journey ahead!

James W. Spensley
Environmental Lawyer, Mediator, Adjunct Professor
University of Denver, Daniels College of Business and Sturm Law School

With *The Aging Wisely Project*, Ben and Scott have marvelously combined storytelling with an entirely new construct for how we can each become our best selves. Indeed, the two of them have created their own profound late-in-life stories. Read on. Let their wisdom add to yours.

Stephen Blum, Senior Director,
Strategic Initiatives Yale Alumni Association, Yale University

Whether we want or need direction, course correction, or confirmation about the later stages of our lives, *The Aging Wisely Project* provides an understandable, meaningful, and achievable path to live our best elder life. By analyzing poignant life stories juxtaposed with clearly delineated tasks of elderhood, the authors help us GRASP (Gratitude, Resilience, Active Practices, Self- acceptance, Purpose) intentional behaviors and attitudes that should enhance happiness and satisfaction in our final years. This is an important read on an often-ignored subject matter. Here's hoping you benefit from it as much as I did.

Andrew L. Braun, MBA

The Aging Wisely Project is engaging and informative. The interviews were the "glue" to understanding and navigating the aging process. The authors interconnected life and choices made into what can be expected in later life. All of us are affected by parents, childhood, and youth but an adaptive mindset and resilience can pave the way to a satisfying and productive adulthood and old age. The authors effectively combined real life stories with science. *The Aging Wisely Project* is a fascinating read.

Carmen Ashbaugh
Retired Mortgage Lender

The AGING WISELY Project

Forging Your Best Self in Life's Ultimate Stage

Ben Green, MD
Scott Fisher

NEW YORK

LONDON • NASHVILLE • MELBOURNE • VANCOUVER

The Aging Wisely Project

Forging Your Best Self in Life's Ultimate Stage

Published in New York, New York, by Morgan James Publishing. Morgan James is a trademark of Morgan James, LLC. www.MorganJamesPublishing.com

Proudly distributed by Publishers Group West®

Morgan James BOGO™

A **FREE** ebook edition is available for you or a friend with the purchase of this print book.

_____

CLEARLY SIGN YOUR NAME ABOVE

Instructions to claim your free ebook edition:
1. Visit MorganJamesBOGO.com
2. Sign your name CLEARLY in the space above
3. Complete the form and submit a photo of this entire page
4. You or your friend can download the ebook to your preferred device

ISBN 9781636984063 paperback
ISBN 9781636984070 ebook
Library of Congress Control Number:
2024941117

Cover Design by:
Rachel Lopez
www.r2cdesign.com

Interior Design by:
Christopher Kirk
www.GFSstudio.com

Morgan James is a proud partner of Habitat for Humanity Peninsula and Greater Williamsburg. Partners in building since 2006.

Get involved today! Visit: www.morgan-james-publishing.com/giving-back

To Paul Hudson Sangree and Jack Welner, grandfather and father-in-law,
respected ancestors who showed us their paths for aging wisely;
and
to Carol Green and Bev Michaels,
who travel that path gracefully, gratefully, and joyfully with us today.

Beautiful young people are accidents of nature,
but beautiful old people are works of art.
– Eleanor Roosevelt –

Table of Contents

Part Two: Minding Your Life Trajectory—GRASP

Foreword

As many of you probably know, I have strong opinions about ageism and how pervasive and damaging this bias toward older people is—for all of us. But it's time to move beyond age rage and explore more deeply what it means to be an older person these days.

With the dramatic increase in human longevity, I know there have been hundreds of books published on aging and retirement. (A lot of them are on my bookshelf.) They cover a wide range of topics, like health and wellness, financial and estate planning, senior lifestyles. Good, basic stuff. But what's largely missing in these times is a deeper and much-needed exploration of aging from a psychosocial perspective.

That's why I was so gratified—delighted—when I met Scott Fisher and Ben Green, co-authors of *The Aging Wisely Project*, in late spring of 2023. We met at our Fiftieth Yale Reunion, where they gave a presentation outlining the book's basic themes. Since that time, I've been engaged in an ongoing conversation with these two men, which resulted in their appearance on my podcast *45 Forward*.

Scott and Ben, who have enjoyed a fifty-year friendship, bring considerable expertise to this subject matter. Scott spent four decades as an organizational psychologist, corporate leader, and executive coach. Ben spent those same forty years, first as a psychiatrist and then as a psychoanalyst, treating patients and training other clinicians. When you speak with them, you can tell that they have honed the skills (and art) of listening and discerning the underlying feelings, as well as the hopes, insecurities, and fears, of a wide variety of individuals—including older folks, who often believe they're overlooked, undervalued, and largely invisible.

What I really appreciate is the authenticity of these two men. Like me, they're in their seventies, but they remain deeply curious about life, always thoughtful, continually searching and learning. They're hopeful about our potential to experience happiness, fulfillment, and personal growth in our last years. At the same time, they acknowledge the vulnerabilities and the humbling realities of aging. It's a brave exploration. As Bette Davis famously said, "Getting old ain't for sissies." Neither is aging wisely.

What I've discovered from Ben and Scott is a powerful, systematic, and immensely useful approach to help propel our understanding of aging forward—especially at a time when public perceptions about "old people" and their mental competence are often badly misinformed. The book proposes an important premise: because of longer and healthier lifespans today, and because there are many more choices now available to elders, a new and distinct developmental stage of elderhood has emerged. They call this final stage "Elder Identity Revision." It's a reworking of our identity as it evolves in our elder years, with an interesting parallel: these are the same issues we faced in adolescence. Who are we? What do we stand for? What do we really want out of life?

During this stage, we're forced to cope with changes in our bodies and minds, changes in how and where we live out our daily lives. In the first part of their book, Scott and Ben identify five critical psychological tasks, challenges we face during this period, such as dealing with the loss of control over our lives and the competencies we have acquired during our lives, and especially the loss of connection to intimate partners, family, friends, and community groups. In the book's second part, the authors provide an extensive compendium of skills and attitudes (they call them "Healthy Habits") to address these challenges. They're represented by the acronym, GRASP: Gratitude, Resilience, Active Practices, Self-Acceptance, and Purpose. By appreciating and strengthening these Healthy Habits, they explain, we can make a substantial difference in how we experience this stage of life.

Interspersed in the book are Scott and Ben's personal stories, as well as the in-depth life stories of numerous *Aging Wisely* elders. Together, these elements comprise a compelling journey into old age, where understanding the psychological tasks that await us in elderhood can bolster our hopes and expectations for improved health and happiness—a meaningful journey, a life well-lived, despite the inevitable setbacks.

Like Scott and Ben, I believe that knowledge and intention are the keys to fulfillment in life's ultimate stage. And as the world continues to age, *The Aging*

Wisely Project will become an invaluable guide to elderhood—one that requires an understanding of our essential humanity.

Not just being smart. Wiser.

Ron Roel
VoiceAmerica and Podcast Host, *45 Forward*
March 2024

PART ONE

HOW WE BECOME WHO WE ARE

Introduction:

Rethinking Elderhood

L aura Carstensen admits that, at age twenty-one, she was a typical young adult. Although her father was a university professor, she passed on going to college herself—she was focused on dating, enjoying music, and hanging out with friends. That all changed in a flash when a drunk driver sideswiped the car she was in and flipped it off the road. Laura broke more than twenty bones and came perilously close to losing her life. Although she survived, it took four months before she was able to leave the hospital.

During this period of convalescence, several life-altering events occurred. First, her priorities radically changed—she immediately lost all interest in meeting new people or in discovering hot, leading-edge bands—she just wanted to be with family and old friends. As she regained her strength, she was struck by this sudden shift in priorities. Second, she got to know the mostly elderly women who were also hospitalized on her inpatient rehabilitation unit. Although she had harbored the usual stereotypes about elders being boring, slow, tired, and depressed, what she discovered was, in reality, quite the opposite. Certainly, like others in their age group, these senior citizens had lost some ground, both mentally and physically. Nevertheless, they were remarkably lively, interesting, and content with their lives. How could this be?

Laura was curious and driven by this new mission. She completed a correspondence course in psychology and liked it well enough to go on to earn a Ph.D. in psychology. She became a university professor and eventually founded the Stanford Center for Longevity. During the 1990s she was one of the pioneers in the study of the psychosocial aspects of aging. Carstensen's work anticipated by several decades

3

the current surge of interest among aging Baby Boomers and subsequent generations in prolonging longevity and sustaining youthfulness. As Carstensen learned,
and as you will soon read, there is much to look forward to in elderhood.

Like others in her field, Laura Carstensen took particular note of the 2007
research findings of economist David Blanchflower.[1] Gathering data about personal
happiness from 132 different countries—large and small, rich and poor—Blanchflower generated a U-shaped happiness curve, with those at either extreme, both the
youngest and the oldest, being the happiest; and those in the middle, in their late
forties, being the least happy.

Sifting through these and other data, Carstensen and her colleagues concluded
that the advantages of youth, such as cognitive processing speed and physical prowess, mattered considerably less with regard to happiness than did the superior coping
strategies of elders.[2] Two major coping mechanisms in particular were identified.
First, it is well documented that stimuli evoking fear or rage easily capture the attention of younger people, as provocative journalists and political demagogues figured
out long ago. Conversely, as several of Carstensen's publications have elucidated,
elders preferentially seek out and remember happy faces and upbeat images—a tendency she called the 'positivity effect.' The perceptual bias of young adults tends to
make them easily upset or angry, while the inherent inclination among older people
brings them relative comfort and contentment.

Second, Carstensen also discovered how the proximity of one's 'time horizon'—
the imagined or anticipated time left in your life—has a huge effect on your preferences and choices. Elders entering their final years (or anyone with a short time to
live) will choose to spend time with familiar people, visit favorite places, and select
menu items that they already know and enjoy. This was exactly what Carstensen had
personally experienced after her near-fatal car accident. People with an uncertain or
foreshortened future do not want to risk wasting time by making bad choices. By
contrast, those with the expectation of a lot of time ahead of them tend to explore
new possibilities and take some calculated risks. (Similarly, economic theory asserts
that investment risk-taking yields greater rewards for those with more time to har-
vest the benefits.)

Although slower processing speed, physical weakness, and a shorter remaining
life span are not desirable attributes, it is welcome news that the typical coping strategies of elders can significantly enhance happiness and wellbeing. This rigorous and
persuasive work by Carstensen and others can inspire a more hopeful and optimistic
attitude about the final decades of life. These insights contradict the pervasive and

insidious effects of the prejudicial ageism prevalent in Western cultures, particularly in the youth-driven American society.

These attitudes are important. Becca Levy, a psychologist at Yale, devised the Stereotype Embodiment Theory (SET) which proposes that the internalized (and often unconscious) attitudes that we hold about aging become self-fulfilling prophecies.[3] For example, longitudinal research has found that young adults with negative stereotypes about elderhood are twice as likely to have major cardiovascular events after age sixty. Those with positive attitudes about aging live longer, healthier lives, in part because they are more committed to health-promoting practices.

This brings us to the recurring themes of our book: it is essential to learn about aging from a biopsychosocial perspective and to understand the challenges and Tasks that await us. Understanding bolsters our hopes and expectations for elder health and happiness. And, by strengthening the Tools (skills and attitudes) at our disposal, which we call 'Healthy Habits,' we can make a substantial difference in how we experience this stage of life. These insights, translated into strategies and goals for aging wisely, help us to become more intentional about how we move forward in our lives. This is why we have spent much of the last six years researching the work of others, interviewing our own wonderful and diverse group of elders, and writing about our journey in *The Aging Wisely Project*. And it is why we are glad to be able to share with you what we have learned.

Let us describe briefly how we came to initiate *The Aging Wisely Project*. As we, Scott and Ben, approached our seventieth birthdays, the challenge of aging well and wisely loomed ever larger. We were both on the verge of retirement, our children were up and out, and our bodies were increasingly insistent that things were changing. We were not as proficient as we used to be at multi-tasking, and our facility for instant recall had receded considerably. We used to be proud of our physical strength and stamina, but no more. Sometimes we find ourselves becoming short of breath after even minor physical exertions. Our memories of being college champion intramural swimmers together offer only faint comfort.

Oh, yes—and there is that 'mortality thing.' Both of us had known people who had reached their eighties and nineties with enduring vitality and joie de vivre. On the other hand, we had also known family members and friends who seemed to have just given up on life. They just dwindled away—not due to age, specifically, but because some essential flame was sputtering out. We were curious about these divergent paths, so we decided to work together to figure out what kept some elders going strong, while others lost interest, or drive, or both. Each of us is enjoying relatively good health and we are committed to maintaining it. But we each have our own challenges—Scott is losing his hearing and Ben his eyesight. We are determined to learn as much as possible about how to make our elder years as satisfying and fulfilling as possible.

Our fifty-year friendship has been close and gratifying. We had supported each other through a variety of personal and professional challenges over the years, but we had never actually worked on a major project together. We wanted to educate ourselves and perhaps help others as well. We were both semi-retired, so we had some time to work with. We also figured that this would be a good way to stimulate our brains and it would give us another reason to get out of bed in the morning. Maybe this was our current-day substitute for the shared youthful fantasy of buying a couple of Harley Davidsons and hitting the open road. (When shared with our wives, this cherished teenage fantasy was met with much eye-rolling and head shaking.)

Both of us enjoy the benefits of a great education—we first met as freshmen roommates at Yale in 1968—and we continue to feel an enduring debt of gratitude to that fine university for the generous scholarships that enabled our middle-class families to send us to such an elite school. We went on to enjoy reasonably successful careers, and both endured the vicissitudes of marriage, divorce, and then second marriages. Happily, we both eventually found our life partners. And, barring catastrophe, we would not run out of money if we were prudent. Compared to many people, we have a lot going for us. We are both grateful for the many advantages and privileges that we have enjoyed and we are mindful that there are many who—because of systemic prejudice, familial dysfunction, unfortunate individual choices, and other conditions—have not been so fortunate.

We brought considerable vocational expertise to bear on this project. Scott had spent four decades as an organizational psychologist, corporate leader, and executive coach. He learned to interview people, connect with them, assess their capabilities, and figure out how to motivate and guide them. Ben, first as a psychiatrist, and then as a psychoanalyst, spent those same forty years listening intently to his patients to hear their words, and the unspoken feelings and urges behind the words. Both of us had patiently honed the art of listening carefully to discern the underlying feelings, motives, and traits, along with the hopes, insecurities, and fears, of a wide variety of individuals.

We began by reading the available literature on aging, some of which was terrific (see Suggested Reading). Most of these publications were heavy on statistics and superficial generalities, but weak on a deeper exploration of the psychological dynamics and relationship phenomena of individual lives. And there was a disappointing lack of persuasive, actionable guidance that we had hoped to find. We were seeking insights that could make a real difference in our lives and the lives of others.

Our next step was to interview a demographically diverse group of fifty-two individuals, from seventy to ninety-six years of age. As is evident from the *Life Stories* you are about to read, we were enchanted and captivated by the breadth and depth of the lives that were shared with us. Each of these varied life trajectories was shaped by the unique interaction of genetic inheritance, family relationships, and adult experiences. In addition to appreciating this robust individualism, we were also able to examine these lives collectively, and identify several organizing patterns and some fundamental truths about aging well. We look forward to sharing these insights with you.

As a result of our research, we came to appreciate the importance of understanding both the challenging Tasks facing us in old age, and the essential Tools needed to meet those challenges. Our happiness, fulfillment, and personal growth during these final years or decades can be significantly enhanced by understanding how to modify our lifestyles. Making fundamental changes requires self-reflection and robust intentionality. To do this, we need to find within ourselves a motivating vision of who we want to be, to prioritize specific goals, and to dig deep to find the discipline to persevere.

If you would like to move beyond the status quo, there is much worthwhile work to be done. This is not for the faint of heart. We welcome you to join us on this journey to age wisely.

1

Listening to Lives—
The Stories and The Storytellers

W e want to introduce you to Ella, seventy-seven years old, and one of the elders interviewed for *The Aging Wisely Project*. As with all the individuals we interviewed, her name has been changed, along with other identifying details, to protect her anonymity.

Ella had been raped twice by the time she was eight years old. At three, she was attacked by a neighborhood teenage boy. At eight, the predator was one of her uncles. When the family blamed her mother for the first violation, she abruptly abandoned Ella and the family. Ella's father could not protect her very well—he suffered from serious mental illness, probably schizophrenia, and was hospitalized repeatedly during Ella's childhood. Not a storybook start to life, with trauma and insecure parental attachments dragging her down.

Fortunately, there were better days ahead. Several aunts from Ella's extended African-American family stepped in. Also, her grandfather, a charismatic and kind Native-American healer, listened deeply to Ella and nurtured her sharp intellect and self-confidence. Hearing Ella's story, we were persuaded, as we were by the stories of several others, that when the nuclear family cannot provide the secure attachment that a child needs, the extended family can sometimes offer the requisite trust and safety. This alternative pathway, however, is not without complications.

Despite facing early adversity, Ella enjoyed many successes in school and in her career. She went on to graduate from law school and became an attorney for a prominent western legal firm. She established herself as a mentor, especially for young

9

female attorneys, and achieved success in a male-dominated practice specialty. She even became a trusted confidant to the senior members of her firm. Ella described herself in these consultative situations as having adopted her beloved grandfather's calm, reflective presence. She eventually expanded her teaching mission by becoming a law school dean—she loved working with the next generation of lawyers. While doing all this, she raised two ambitious and hard-working children, both of whom have remained close to her.

Although our *Aging Wisely* sample size is relatively small, at fifty-two elders, we noticed that individuals raised by extended families, rather than by one or two primary caregivers, tended to have performed better in their careers than in their marriages. Is this because there is a lingering insecurity, a sense of not having been lovable enough as a child to keep birth parents from leaving? Does this early loss of parenting figures result in a more fragile self-esteem, especially when it comes to adult relationships? Could such conditions tend to focus an individual on extrinsic and vocational success in hopes of filling self-esteem and security needs? There are also theoretical questions about the depth of a child's attachment to a group of caregivers, rather than to one or two primary attachment figures. While 'the village' may help raise a child, it may do so with some limitations.

Beebe and Lachmann's fascinating research with infants and their mothers decisively demonstrates that the precursors of a child's attachment security can be detected as early as four months of age.[4] Like a well-practiced jazz duo, the communication between a securely attached infant and its mother (or father) displays an astonishing alignment of movement and gaze, tempo and intensity, and even (pre-verbal) vocalization. All this attests to a profound, visceral connection between them. When one initiates, the other responds, and vice versa. In resonant harmony, both mother and child feel known, understood, and loved, at a deep emotional level.

Later in life, this capacity for intimately knowing another human being plays a powerful role when looking into the eyes of a lover. Are you convinced that you know who they really are, and that you can trust them with your innermost thoughts and feelings? Do they make you feel safe? Can you allow yourself to be at your most vulnerable with them? The answers to these questions heavily influence the decision to connect intimately with someone and whether to commit to a long-term partnership. Although even the most securely attached adults can make poor relationship choices, the ability to look beyond superficial characteristics is critically important when choosing a mate or life partner. We suspect this capacity may be less likely to develop, or mature fully, when a child has numerous and shifting caregivers.

Ella, for instance, seems to have received sufficient childhood love and support to allow her to succeed in school and as an attorney, yet she ended up choosing two husbands who both cheated on her. The second of these men not only abused her physically for years, but also found a way to manipulate her and to divert most of her retirement savings to himself. These men each had some superficial attractiveness: the first was on his way to a doctorate and the second was a deacon at her church. Certainly, many high-functioning people get divorced, but Ella's choices got worse with experience, not better.

Did the childhood traumas come back to haunt her as insecurity and as a loneliness-driven impulsivity? Ella was at least partially aware of some of these tendencies—she described herself as 'a people pleaser,' which may have served her better in her professional relationships than in her personal life. Although few of us have had to deal with traumatic abuse comparable to Ella's, many of us can see connections in our own lives between poor partner choices in adulthood and adverse childhood experiences.

Unfortunately, even Ella's stellar professional career was derailed at age seventy, after she took a tragic fall down a flight of stairs at work. Ella sustained cerebral trauma and other serious injuries. Suddenly, her life trajectory veered wildly off course. She lost her ability to speak for a year and was forced to retire abruptly from the law school. Ella did not give up but embarked upon a grueling year of rehabilitation therapies to regain her speech and mobility. But then, just as she was beginning to recover, her caretaker daughter decided to move the family across the country to a small semi-rural community. This sudden relocation took Ella away from her professional, church, and social relationships and situated her in a place where her academic credentials and her Colorado license to practice the law were irrelevant.

As we had with several of our *Aging Wisely* elders, we scheduled a follow-up interview with Ella a year later. She told us a hair-raising story about being stranded alone in the new house, without electricity, during a blizzard. Fortunately, an alert neighbor stepped in to rescue her. This was the first of several important new relationships. Ella is working hard to establish herself in her new community, and she has started doing some volunteer work through the church she recently joined. Now well into her eighth decade, Ella remains grateful for what she has, and she is determined to fashion a life of Purpose and meaning, despite the obstacles.

We hope Ella's story was as engaging for you as it was for us. The detailed *Life Stories* that follow, and the accompanying in-depth analyses of the storytellers, are what sets *The Aging Wisely Project* apart from other books of this genre. Most of the publications on aging have been written by journalists, who are superb storytellers, but lack a professional background in psychological development or relationship dynamics. The writings of academic psychologists, on the other hand, tend to emphasize data from questionnaires and the statistical analyses of narrowly focused rating scales. Still other publications, by medical practitioners, focus on the biomedical aspects of aging.

Although we will also include some statistics and numerous biomedical considerations, our primary focus will be the exploration of the fascinating individuality of our *Aging Wisely* elders. From the outset, we were determined to let each of them tell us how they saw their own lives, and how they made sense of it all. Yes, we were keen to identify patterns and cause-and-effect relationships, but we wanted these inferences to emerge organically from the data, rather than arbitrarily imposing any theories, top-down, on the data. To do this, we kept in mind several different conceptual perspectives, and let the *Life Stories*, whenever possible, speak for themselves.

Consider this first chapter an orientation to our case study and research methodology, as well as a primer on several foundational psychoanalytic principles that support and inform our conclusions. For some readers, these concepts may seem new and somewhat off putting. Please bear with us. We are committed to making these theories both commonsensible and explanatory.

Project Framework

As noted, to open our minds to different perspectives and methodologies, we began *The Aging Wisely Project* by reviewing the available literature. Our next decision was a momentous one: we committed ourselves to completing a considerable number of intensive interviews with a diverse sample of elders aged seventy and older. We wanted to hear from them, first-hand, their *Life Stories*. Because conducting and analyzing so many in-depth interviews would require hundreds of hours from highly experienced interviewers, this component is consistently missing from comparable investigations. We also made the decision to study people who were not within our professional spheres. Although both of us had learned a great deal in our careers from working with numerous over-seventy individuals, we realized that there were several reasons that we could not utilize the stories of the people we already knew.

First, as is evident in books written by other psychotherapists, these authors' descriptions of their patients' lives had to be restricted to brief fragmentary vignettes to protect confidentiality. By contrast, we wanted to describe the entire developmental arc of our elders' lives and to do so in vivid detail. Another reason was that we wanted to avoid any sort of situational bias. Scott saw clients who were working in a particular employment context—this heavily influenced what was said and the nature of the interaction. Ben's observations were colored by the complications of the dynamics of the physician-patient relationship. Virtually all of Ben's patients walked into his office with a particular mindset. Some craved his approval, others sought to prove that they did not really need any help, and a few especially provocative patients persistently tried to pick a fight. For the purposes of *The Aging Wisely Project*, we wanted to talk with people in a neutral situation that minimized bias, expectation, or relationship drama.

To accomplish this, we assembled a group of heterogeneous elders who were neither Ben's patients nor Scott's clients and promised them anonymity. (We diligently collected a sample of elders that closely approximated the proportions of the U.S. subgroup population with regard to race, ethnicity, and sexual/gender orientation—see the Appendix for demographic statistics.) Each elder signed an informed consent and we promised to disguise their identities. Although we were concerned that our interviewees would be reluctant to share intimate details about their lives, we were pleasantly surprised with their openness and candor. To complicate matters, the COVID-19 pandemic struck just a few months after we had begun meeting with people. The ensuing restrictions required us to conduct some of our interviews using a remote video platform. While not ideal, this approach did offer the advantage of providing a recording that could be reviewed afterward.

During the interviews, we tried to put each elder at ease by simply asking them to tell us the story of their lives. After an hour or so, we asked a standard set of questions, skipping areas already covered. Most of what has been written about elderhood has focused on how the individual was doing around the time of the evaluation. As noted, however, we were convinced that the distinctive individuality of our *Aging Wisely* elders could only be fully appreciated by hearing the complete developmental arc of their lives. Accordingly, we sought to understand things as far back as they could remember. We wanted to know about their early childhood, their parents and siblings, and their experiences at school. What had been their reputation among their schoolmates? What about their adolescent and early adult romantic relationships? Later, how about their career successes and setbacks? Had they had any children, and, if so, what had it been like to be a parent? We then focused on their current lives—we asked if they had someone they could reliably depend upon in a crisis. What were their current joys and fears? What gave their life meaning right now? Did they have any persistent regrets, or people that they just could not forgive? And our final question was: How close are you to being the person that you want to be? (See the Appendix for the interview protocol and questions.)

Ella is one of fifty-two elders, aged seventy to ninety-six, whose *Life Stories* we listened to for at least two hours. We took careful notes and recorded these sessions. As mentioned, sometimes there were follow-up interviews. Both of us had spent our careers interviewing people, so we knew how to listen carefully to what was said, how it was said, what was implied, and what was *not* said. Immediately after each interview, we independently scored the interviewee on the thirty variables that we had deemed important (see Appendix). We later compared scores, and when necessary, sifted through the interview data together to reconcile any highly discrepant impressions. Two sets of eyes and ears, and two experienced minds, were invaluable for improving the reliability and validity of our assessments. Our blended formulations covered not only the content of the *Life Stories*, but also the manner in which the stories were told, which revealed much about the psychological dynamics of the storyteller. We know of no other book on aging that delves into individual psychological profiles in such granular detail.

Making sense of these multifaceted *Life Stories* required the scaffolding of an overarching theoretical structure. While we deeply respect the uniqueness of each elder's *Life Story*, we also hoped to identify some common patterns and generalizable similarities. After our review of the relevant literature, we concluded that no conceptual framework could compare with the broad sweep and intuitive genius of Erik Erikson's comprehensive psychosocial development model. Erikson's thinking was shaped not only by his personal experiences, and his psychoanalytic practice, but also by his participation as a researcher with the Berkeley Guidance Study.

The work of George Vaillant, one of Erikson's intellectual disciples, provided a resounding confirmation of the wisdom, validity, and applicability of Erikson's model. For more than three decades, Vaillant was the primary investigator for the Harvard Study of Adult Development, an incomparable longitudinal study that collected massive data files on 268 undergraduates. Begun in 1938, this Study continues to track these individuals—and now their kids and grandkids. To make sense of this ocean of data, Vaillant also chose Erikson's developmental model, finding it to be both insightful and inclusive. Erikson's model continued to hold up well, even when Vaillant added two other larger cohorts (one of boys from blue-collar families, one of public school, high-IQ girls), as described in his landmark publication, *Aging Well: Surprising Guideposts to a Happier Life.*

With the honorable exception of Vaillant's work, most of the books about the psychology of aging are either disappointingly superficial or obscured by esoteric jargon or off-putting statistics. One of our goals has been to make many of the illuminating insights from psychology and psychoanalysis more accessible to a general readership. Although the psychoanalytic perspective is often dismissed, or even vilified, we are heartened by the words of Noble Prize-winning neuroscientist Eric Kandel: "Psychoanalysis still represents the most coherent and intellectually satisfying view of the mind." More recently, Mark Solms, founder of the International Neuropsychoanalysis Society, has written extensively about how modern neuroscience consistently validates the basic assertions and paradigms of psychoanalysis. So how does a psychoanalytic perspective shed light on how one hears, and understands, *Life Stories*?

Life Story Analysis

Analyzing *Life Stories* requires navigating and assessing several layers of complexity. The first layer pertains to the difference between the actual 'historical truth' and the so-called 'narrative (personal) truth.' The former would be a video recording, while the latter is how a human mind perceives an event and then constructs a story to explain it. Fundamental to the psychoanalytic perspective is the assumption that, to protect our self-image (how we see ourselves) and our self-esteem (how we feel about ourselves), human beings *selectively* perceive and remember the events of their lives.

Our memories, especially about emotionally charged matters, comprise a blended mix of objective and subjective elements. (If you are skeptical about this assertion, ask a group of friends or family members to all write down, independently, a detailed description of a recently witnessed evocative event, and then compare notes.) Although it offends our proud belief that we are fully in control of our minds, and that we perceive the world without any filters, there is profuse evidence that humans are routinely influenced by unconscious forces. (In the 1930s, it was Freud's nephew who launched an advertising campaign to convince Americans that, before taking on a 'manly' day of work, one needed meat and eggs for breakfast. This sly appeal to masculine pride changed the eating habits of our nation.)

It is humbling to accept that unconscious forces can undermine and redirect even our most earnest attempts to be purely logical and rational. (Surprisingly, human beings cannot even generate random numbers without revealing an unconscious bias.) Many influential thoughts and feelings, many memories and urges, are kept out of our awareness—especially if they are embarrassing, shocking, or distressing. So, when our elders were asked to tell us their *Life Stories*, many of them experienced some conflicts about how much they truly wanted to reveal. And this invariably reflected just how honest they routinely were with themselves as well. Mature, well-adjusted individuals cultivate the mental habit of honestly reflecting upon themselves and others. They cannot help but notice the good and the bad, the admirable and the shameful, in their own thoughts and behaviors. Others, however, habitually redact and edit to create a version of reality that pleases them.

A high degree of self-awareness engenders an ongoing *Life Story* that is authentic and accurate—it rings true. Each of our healthier elders, in their own idiosyncratic way, has woven together the various strands of their *Life Story* to fashion a coherent personal narrative. When we heard this sort of finely wrought autobiography, we silently applauded this as an admirable human achievement. We will describe this later as Self-Integrity (in this chapter and in detail in Chapter 10).

Conversely, there are those who cannot bear to remember past traumas or to acknowledge shameful aspects of their lives—they construct a narrative that is distorted and self-serving. Because they have not been able to honestly reflect upon themselves, and to accept their mistakes and limitations, their story comes across as sanitized, whitewashed, and as shallow as a cardboard cutout. Whereas those with an authentic, balanced personal narrative are usually comfortable sharing it with others, those with an embarrassing *Life Story* face a considerable quandary. (Erving Goffman's book, *The Presentation of the Self in Everyday Life*, captures this situational dilemma precisely.)

A slew of psychological motives for distorting, embellishing, omitting, and even intentionally altering certain facts arise when communicating your autobiographical narrative to another person. Although scientifically imperfect, the lie detector test, or polygraph, is based on the principle that most people (who are not chronic liars) experience some physiological distress when not telling the truth—and this is revealed by changes in heart rate, breathing, or sweating. Something similar happens when people start to tell a *Life Story* that is intolerably overstimulating, embarrassing, traumatic, or associated with unresolved conflicts. In such circumstances, there are likely to be confusing inconsistencies, irrelevant tangents, or even outright contradictions. Moreover, in addition to problems with the content of the story, typically there are significant disturbances in the form and structure of the language as well. This might include the choice of words, phrases, metaphors, verb tense, syntax, pronoun consistency, and degree of detail. Because the story is not being told in a simple, honest manner, the storyteller is attempting, frantically, on the fly, to edit, reconfigure, and rewrite a more pleasing alternative.

This process greatly taxes the storyteller's cognitive capacities, especially when the elements threatening to break through are upsetting and distracting. It is no surprise that mistakes are made. Researchers who have studied this phenomenon in exacting detail have coined the term 'narrative coherence': the degree to which the content and the form of the story are relatively congruent and devoid of contradictions, intrusions, discontinuities, irrelevant deviations, or disturbances of language. We will provide specific examples of high and low narrative coherence in several of the case studies.

As interviewers, in our effort to discriminate the more honest and accurate accounts from those significantly modified or misrepresented, we listened with what psychoanalysts call 'the third ear.' We listened intently to notice when elders minimized or avoided certain topics or periods of their lives, while over-emphasizing others. We were attentive to when our elders shamefully avoided important details, or defensively rationalized certain choices, or attempted to distract us with charming digressions. We were constantly assessing when a narrative seemed genuine or when it seemed revised, embellished, tangential, cluttered, or distorted. Often, we felt like detectives, sifting through the clues to uncover and to understand the story *and* the character of the storyteller.

Given that the communication of a life's narrative is complex and layered, it was invaluable to have two veteran interviewers involved. With some of our elders, we found that our impressions of them were strikingly similar. With others, however, there were significant discrepancies. This required us to return to our detailed transcripts and notes for additional analysis to determine where and how our perceptions had diverged so markedly.

Returning to Ella's *Life Story*, both of us were moved by her courage, her candor, and her determination. She had overcome so many obstacles—with new ones still presenting themselves—and yet she tenaciously held onto her hope for a better future. Ella was taken away from old friends but immediately started making new ones. And the form of her story inspired confidence that she was simply and honestly telling us the pleasant and the unpleasant, the laudable and the cringeworthy. We heard about her career successes and her flawed marriages. Her children were thriving, but she herself was struggling. We were duly impressed when we heard that she had graciously reached out to help her dying ex-husband, despite his mistreatment of her. She practiced the Christian charity that she preached.

Observations and Conclusions

Ella's narrative structure was relatively simple and straightforward, with no discernable defensive evasions. This is only possible when a person has come to terms with the good, the bad and the ugly in their life, and has thought about and processed it enough to weave it into a relatively seamless narrative. Narrative coherence strongly correlates with Self-Integrity and with a well-consolidated personal Identity. And, although we have described narrative coherence in somewhat technical terms, most listeners can intuitively recognize the characteristics of this sort of communication, even if they are not quite sure how they know it.

The response evoked in others is telling. Individuals with narrative coherence and Self-Integrity tend to be perceived as dynamic and likable—they speak with personal authority and convey, both verbally and non-verbally, that they are trustworthy. Those lacking in Self-Integrity, by contrast, typically come across as confused and unpredictable. As we will describe later, of all our scored variables, Self-Integrity was the most highly correlated with the global *Aging Wisely* score (see Appendix).

In subsequent chapters, we will describe the fundamental psychological elements that give rise to character, motivation, social connection, and Identity—and how these foundational structures and capacities determine how each of us responds to the developmental Tasks of elderhood. In addition, we will identify the specific behaviors and attitudes—the Tools—that we can cultivate to age wisely during this culminating and ultimate stage of life.

2

Attachment—
The Foundation of Relationships

T he study of infant-caregiver attachment—how human beings learn to bond
with and trust others and to become trustworthy as well—began in earnest
in the late 1930s. John Bowlby, an English psychiatrist, trained to become
a psychoanalyst under the direction of one of Freud's most distinguished disciples,
Melanie Klein. However, upon graduation, he found that Freud's elegant theories
of psychosexual development, in and of themselves, did not serve him well in his
attempts to understand the delinquent adolescent boys he was treating.

After getting to know these teenagers in depth, Bowlby increasingly became
convinced that abandonment by their fathers, and pathological relationships with
their mothers, were primarily responsible for their stunted development and their
anti-social behaviors. These clinical experiences inspired Bowlby to explore paradigms from across wide-ranging disciplines, such as embryology, anthropology, and
ethology. This effort led him to develop what we now know as Attachment Theory.
Although Bowlby's insights about the critical importance of infant-parent bonding
may seem obvious to us today, they were so controversial at the time that he was
almost expelled from the British psychoanalytic community. Needless to say, Klein
was deeply disturbed that one of her students had gone so wrong. But time proved
Bowlby right.

Subsequent to Bowlby's first publications, three generations of rigorous
researchers have resoundingly validated the fundamental assertions of Attachment
Theory. There is now virtually universal agreement that an infant's attachment to

caregivers who are available, sensitive, and responsive is foundational to how he or she develops, grows, and thrives. In fact, overwhelming empirical evidence clearly demonstrates that these intimate connections provide the support, validation and love needed for health and happiness, not just during childhood but throughout the entire life cycle. One of the factors that Vaillant identified as protecting against premature illness, depression, and death is having a stable late-life partnership.

Our *Aging Wisely* interviews underscored the critical importance of early positive and secure attachments in several important ways. Secure attachment propels us into adulthood feeling good about ourselves and open to trusting others, which are both essential for building and maintaining good relationships. This solid foundation enables us to succeed with teachers and peers, to choose suitable romantic partners, to thrive in the workplace, and then to nurture and to foster healthy children of our own. The absence of a secure childhood attachment makes it qualitatively more difficult in adulthood to establish the loving intimacies and trusting peer relationships necessary for thriving in personal and professional spheres.

Happily, however, several of our interviewees did unequivocally demonstrate that it is possible, later in life, to overcome childhood relationship deficits and even extreme traumata. This sort of compensatory psychological growth can be achieved through decades of healthy socializing and intensive relationship-focused psychotherapy. Or, most frequently, by choosing a steady, loving life-partner. Although these 'late bloomers' might regret the wasted years and the people that they may have hurt along the way, such success in changing their life trajectories is nothing short of inspirational. Stories like these provide us all with hope: it is never too late to improve the quality of your relationships and to create a more positive *Life Story*.

We would hasten to add that there are no rigid prerequisites for healthy human relationships. The range of *Life Stories* that we heard in these fifty-two interviews expanded our awareness about the possible range of non-traditional pathways leading to healthy adult attachments. Ella's is one such story (Chapter 1) but there are numerous others to consider.

We will now present the lives of two more women we interviewed, both from ethnic minority communities. Both are bright, well-educated, thoughtful, physically and socially active, and are happily married. Each of their fathers owned and operated a business. Their parents were stably married, intelligent, and hard-working. Both families placed a high value on the education of their children: the two interviewees and all their siblings were successful in school and in their careers. But the attachment patterns of these two women—first with their parents and, later, with their husbands, siblings, and children—were strikingly divergent. And that appears to have made all the difference.

Gloria's Life Story of Secure Attachment (75 years old)

As far as attachment goes, Gloria held the proverbial golden ticket. She was the youngest of six and her father's favorite. Her older sisters doted over her and pampered her like a little doll. Gloria proudly told us the story of her Mexican parents and grandparents, all of whom were hard working, ambitious, and devoutly Catholic. For Gloria, adherence to Catholic doctrine was not so much a burden or an obligation as simply another dimension of her commitment to family, her loyalty to her heritage, and her contribution to community cohesion. She was unabashedly grateful for her ancestors and proud of her siblings, all of whom had strong careers and long marriages (several of them, like her, have been married for more than fifty years).

Gloria spoke only Spanish until she entered first grade, but she quickly picked up English. She was an excellent student, popular with peers, and involved in student government. Her values and strong work ethic did not waver; she neither drank nor smoked, and her virginity was "sacrosanct" and saved for marriage. She required that her fiancé ask for her hand by honoring the ancient traditions: his parents had to meet first with her parents to initiate the process. At college, she prepared herself for a career in teaching by majoring in secondary education. Immediately after the marriage, she found work as a substitute teacher.

However, before she could be assigned a classroom of her own, she discovered that she was pregnant. So, she threw herself into the roles of wife and mother. She stayed home for twenty years to raise her five children and remained there until her youngest child was in fourth grade. She and her husband also took care of Gloria's mother, who suffered from Alzheimer's disease, for the last eighteen years of her mother's life. They even remodeled their home to create an additional bedroom for her.

Gloria knew all along that she wanted eventually, in her words, to "spread her wings" in a career, but she waited patiently until the time was right for her family. (As the Bible instructs, "For everything, there is a season.") Her husband, as one might expect from a lifelong Catholic, urged her to teach in a parochial school. Gloria, however, saw her teaching as a kind of ministry and she wanted to work with the most needy and impoverished children—those who were in the local public schools.

Once back in the classroom, Gloria earned immediate recognition as an unusually talented teacher with leadership potential. Soon she was asked to give educational presentations to more experienced teachers. Her principal recommended her for the school district's Leadership Academy, which placed her on a career path to become a school principal. Upon graduation, she audaciously accepted the position as principal at a school that had been placed on administrative probation due to its chronically poor test performance and low student and teacher morale. It took several years, but with her announced credo of "It's all about the kids," she was able to inspire and motivate her students, their families, and her faculty.

Her school progressed so much that it met the stringent requirements to qualify as a Title I School, which garnered it additional funding and resources. Gloria stayed in that leadership role for twenty years. Eventually, however, the ten-hour workdays convinced her that it was time to retire. She was so beloved by her staff that they gave her an expensive charm bracelet, with one charm for each of the departments that she had supervised. Now, many years later, she still wears that bracelet every day. It serves as a proud reminder of her vision, her values, and her significant career accomplishments.

However, tragedy can visit even the most charmed lives. While Gloria was still working at her school, her youngest child, who was just twenty years old, developed a severe infection—which was repeatedly misdiagnosed by their family doctor. Shockingly, this otherwise healthy, active young woman developed a raging septicemia, a bacterial infection of the blood, and died. The entire family was stunned. Understandably, Gloria was rocked to the core. Yet, after only a short bereavement leave of absence, Gloria returned to her job. She later admitted that this had been very difficult, but that her work had felt like a kind of therapy.

For the next year, she cried every day on the drive to work, pulled herself together for the school day, and then cried all the way home. She struggled to regain her equilibrium. Despite working so hard throughout her life to resist anger or to seek vengeance, Gloria found herself consumed by homicidal fantasies towards this negligent physician, who had also been a long-time family friend. After this doctor died, she went to his gravesite, spit on it, and screamed curses at him. The conflict she felt about her un-Christian-like anger was so deep and persistent that, ultimately, for the first and only time in her life, she sought out psychotherapy.

Fortunately, the psychotherapy worked. Even here, her strong childhood attachments had made a substantial difference—her basic trust in the world, and in the supportive people around her, allowed her to believe in her psychotherapist. She had been profoundly let down by her daughter's physician, but she did not allow this mistrust to carry over to other health care providers. She also tenaciously held onto her lifelong belief that, if she did what she was supposed to, things would work out for the best. And they did—she got herself back on track. Gradually, in addition to her job, she was able to refocus on her marriage, her children, and her grandchildren. She resolved her anger at God for his not having saved her daughter—she concluded that "God's not a bellboy." Bad things do indeed happen to good people, but God is always there, afterward, to comfort and console, and to help one move forward. Soon thereafter, she and her husband took on a leadership role in a local parent bereavement group.

Ten years after her daughter's death, Gloria decided to retire. After a year of relatively inactive retirement and decompression, she launched into volunteer work with a variety of religious and philanthropic organizations. Today, she is an associate nun at her church, a volunteer coordinator for hospice, a participant in an interfaith immigration council, and a board member for a national charitable organization.

The loss of a child is one of the greatest blows a parent can sustain, and Gloria was staggered by the loss. Nevertheless, she mustered the necessary resilience to persevere, returning to her job through her tears, and continuing to function effectively within her multi-generational family. Over time, she found spiritual insight and meaning, which made her even wiser and stronger. (Chapters 5 and 6 discuss this 'post-traumatic growth.') Gloria's secure attachments helped her to weather the storm and strengthen her resilience, without giving up on herself, or God, or on relationships in general.

Attachment Theory: Looking Deeper

Having a stable and secure childhood attachment to one's parents (or other caregivers) is, in the most fundamental sense, the gift that keeps on giving. Gloria felt loved and lovable from the very beginning. A securely attached individual, upon meeting someone new, will assume that they will like this person and be liked in return ("What's not to like about me?"). If the relationship with this person does not work out, it may be painful, but it does not rock their world. They will still believe in themselves and have high hopes that things will go better with the next person they meet.

Attachment styles can be detected as early as twelve to eighteen months of age. Bowlby's principal collaborator, Mary Ainsworth, developed the so-called Strange Situation procedure in the 1970s to identify individual differences in attachment styles. From this work, infant attachment categories were delineated. Later on, other researchers described related adult attachment styles, which, confusingly, have different names.

The Strange Situation procedure entails a series of eight separation and reunion events between the infant, the mother (or father), and a stranger (the researcher). The child's reaction to these various situations indicates their degree of security, and the specific type of attachment bond that they have with this caregiver.

Securely Attached children freely explore the playroom during the experiment—they show a little distress when mom leaves the room, but then quickly recover when mom returns. Most of these kids will grow up to become Secure and Autonomous adults. They have the capacity for sustained intimacy, but also for strong, independent functioning.

There are three main forms of insecure attachment, based on the infant's coping strategy when dealing with separations and reunions. It may seem implausible that such young infants are sophisticated enough to have developed a coping strategy, but these reactions to relationship distress are the psychological equivalent of a child learning to pull their hand away from a hot stove. These attachment styles represent the infant's best effort to cope with the caregiver's ability to make them feel safe. Infants and young children are extremely dependent on their caregivers. When a securely attached child—who is being cared for by an attentive, sensitive, and responsive caregiver—cries out, they have every expectation that they will be helped. Not so with insecurely attached kids, who have to resort to alternative strategies to get their needs met.

Insecure Ambivalent (Resistant) infants and toddlers seem too fearful throughout the Strange Situation to explore the playroom, and then they fall apart emotionally when their mom leaves the room. When she returns, they cling to her, but also fight with her—they are both needy and angrily combative. Typically, this attachment style develops when the caregiver is distracted or ambivalent about parenting. To get their needs met, these kids adapt by 'turning up the volume' to force a parental response. They stay close to mom just in case they need to prompt her again to pay attention to them. This restricts the child's healthy exploration of the environment, which stunts learning and psychological development. If there are no major changes in their families, these children are most likely to grow up to become adults classified as Insecure Preoccupied. These adults are desperate to find someone they can depend upon, but also so insecure that they repeatedly demand reassurances: "Do you really love me? How can I be sure?" Unfortunately, this neediness often sabotages the very relationships that they crave.

By contrast, Insecure Avoidant children seem coldly indifferent to their mom leaving, and they give her a chilly reception when she returns. This pattern is associated with parents who criticize, or even punish their children for being too demanding or dependent. Whereas Insecure Ambivalent children try to change their caregiver's behavior by clambering for attention, Insecure Avoidant children try to adapt by changing themselves—by repressing their anxieties and needs. They bravely try to act as if they do not really need their caregivers. Such children just stop asking—but their chilly reaction to mom's return conveys an underlying hostility that reveals how they actually feel about this arrangement.

Not surprisingly, Insecure Ambivalent children tend to grow up to become hyper-independent adults, who are classified as Insecure Dismissive. These adults dismiss the need for close relationships and systematically suppress their feelings about relationships. They are not conscious of the normal human need for closeness or support—but there is laboratory evidence that they do show physiological agitation (elevated heart rate, blood pressure, and respirations) in response to psychological prompts about separations and losses. The body keeps score—they do have strong feelings about attachments, but they are masters of denial. Many of these adults are quite successful in their careers, but their obliviousness to their partner's relationship needs often dooms their romantic lives. (Many marital therapists write about the goal of teaching such individuals to notice and respond to their partner's desires for closeness, sensitivity, and empathy.) They often seek psychotherapy when their confusion and dissatisfaction become unbearable—they are blind to the absence of true affection or intimacy in their lives. No amount of money, prestige, power, adrenalin, sex, drugs, or rock-and-roll can fill such a relationship void.

Insecure Disorganized children are the most deeply disturbed of all. They do not seem to have any organized strategy for making themselves feel safe or secure. In the Strange Situation, they act confused, frozen, or even dazed when their mother leaves and then returns. Bizarrely, their arms may reach out for their moms while their legs are carrying them away from her. They appear to be seized by a raging internal conflict between approach and avoidance. Many children in this category have been subjected to severe neglect or abuse—as adults, these individuals are the most likely to develop major psychiatric difficulties. Their relationships tend to be chaotic, confused, volatile, and indiscriminate. Such adults are classified as Insecure Disorganized-Unresolved.

Although childhood attachment styles do not always predict adult attachment patterns, unless major changes, good or bad, occur in the caregiving environment, the child's predominant attachment strategy is likely to persist. Fortunately, as mentioned, some people do find a way to alter their capacity for intimate relationships later in life.

Gloria felt secure in her loving attachments from infancy onward. This engenders what Erik Erikson called Basic Trust and Hope, a bias toward trusting others and an optimistic hope that the world is mostly a safe and rewarding place. Gloria developed age-appropriate competencies as she grew up, and she was also quite sure that, should her own coping strategies fail her, there would be others there to help. Throughout her life, Gloria had a high degree of confidence that she would be successful, that she could be a good leader, and that, whenever she found herself in an interpersonal conflict, she and that individual would find a way to resolve their differences. Insecurely attached individuals are not so lucky, which brings us to Natasha's *Life Story*.

Natasha's Life Story of Insecure Attachment (77 years old)

Natasha was an attractive, well-dressed woman who looked considerably younger than her chronological age. After introducing ourselves, we explained our project and asked her simply to tell us the story of her life. Curiously, this seemed to distress her—she asked what the "focus" was and informed us that she had not expected such an unstructured format. It was as if she had anticipated a series of narrowly focused questions, with multiple-choice response options.

Pushing through her initial confusion, Natasha gamely stumbled ahead. She began with a description of some of the extreme hardships that her parents and older siblings had experienced in a Russian labor camp prior to her birth. Even prior to this, her parents, as children, had endured multiple separations and rejections from their own families. Curiously, while describing all this, there were two separate points, within the interview's first several minutes, when Natasha blurted out that her parents possessed no parenting skills. She then jumped ahead to elaborate other manifestations of her family's dysfunction. One older sister hated Natasha from the beginning and, later as an adult, cut her off from the sister's children and grandchildren. (Vaillant's longitudinal study found that the relationship between adult siblings was highly predictive of overall social success.)

Natasha's childhood family culture emphasized remaining silent and not expressing oneself. Up until early adulthood, she had been unable to recall any childhood memories prior to age seven (which is quite unusual). It was only when she took a memoir writing course in college that she was able to recover a trove of dissociated and repressed childhood memories. Even with this, there were still sizable gaps in her knowledge of her family's history. Decades later, at some reunions of her extended family, Natasha learned many surprising facts about her parents and grandparents. Shockingly, she learned her father had been born out of wedlock, and because of this, he had never been fully accepted by the rest of his family. She also discovered that her mother, as a young girl, had been abandoned by her own mother for five years.

Abruptly, at this point in the interview, Natasha had an intrusive memory that her father had attended all of Natasha's track meets in high school, where she excelled—but that her mother had never come to any of them. (If this had been psychotherapy, the therapist could have pointed out to Natasha the associative connection in her mind between her mother's childhood abandonment and her later shortcomings as a parent. Natasha seemed completely unaware of this linkage.) She then added that she was able to go to college on a track scholarship. (In the flow of the conversation, the happy memory of the scholarship took her away from talking about the painful unavailability of her mother—just as going to the out-of-state college took her away from her hurtful family. Parallel escapes from her mother, one in the present, one in the past.)

The content of Natasha's story vividly depicts multi-generational insecure attachments and emotional traumas. The form of her story illustrates how, in such circumstances, the mind struggles to fashion a coherent narrative. Pent up feelings and memories repeatedly erupted as intrusions and tangents that disrupted the smooth chronological flow of her story. And this material was too highly charged emotionally for her to pause and hear for herself what she seemed to be struggling with. In general, such upsetting memories are simply too painful to tolerate or to mull over long enough to weave them into a sensible and coherent autobiographical narrative. This gives rise to a *Life Story* that is fragmentary and poorly integrated, which prevents the consolidation of a personal Identity. This might explain why Natasha had hoped for an interview with multiple-choice answers to our questions.

Insecurity might seem unlikely for a bright, athletic, hardworking, and strikingly attractive woman like Natasha, who went on to have a successful career in sales and as a corporate executive. But her personal life was plagued by demons. As is often the case, the sins and traumas of the previous generation are visited upon their descendants. Her father and mother, as noted, both came from chaotic families and their political missteps in early adulthood resulted in exile to a Siberian labor camp, where Natasha's brother and twin sisters were born. At the end of World War II, the family somehow was able to make its way to America. They settled in California, where Natasha was born. In stark contrast to the pride that Gloria felt about her family and her Mexican and Catholic roots, Natasha's family seemed determined to distance themselves from all things Russian. They spoke only English at home, they never socialized with other Russian immigrants, there was no mention of extended family, and she and her siblings had exclusively American-born friends.

Natasha's high school track prowess earned her an athletic scholarship at a small southern California college, but she dropped out after her sophomore year to follow a boyfriend to Seattle. Once there, she married the boyfriend and worked several menial jobs while completing her degree requirements at a local community college. Unprompted during the interview, she denied being sexually harassed by her bosses. Upon graduation, she was hired for an entry-level clerical position at Starbucks and was later promoted to a management position.

Natasha and her husband had three children, a boy and two girls. At some point, her husband lost his job and Natasha divorced him, reportedly because she thought he had become "lazy." There was no further explanation offered for this seemingly abrupt change in his character. We were unsure if Natasha was consciously withholding some explanatory details about this divorce, or whether she just could not bear to dwell on it.

After the divorce, Natasha moved back to her hometown in California with her three children. Although she hoped to receive some support—emotional and financial—from her parents, little was forthcoming. Fortunately, she did find employment fairly quickly. Regarding her family life, it was striking to us how Natasha's description of her children, and the experience of parenting them, was emotionally impoverished. There were no details about happy trips, holidays, challenges, adversities, or of her children's successes or setbacks. There were no details offered about the temperaments, idiosyncrasies, or personalities of her children. It was as if Natasha had seen parenting as a job, and she had done what she had to do without love or joy.

Only years later did Natasha learn that her son had begun to sexually abuse his two younger sisters during this period. Could her emotionally disconnected parenting style have contributed to her not noticing this abuse? There was a striking parallel between her arms-length childhood relationship with her own parents, and, decades later, her impersonal style with her own kids.

To her credit, all of Natasha's children did well in school, earned college degrees, and are now stably employed. In recent years, Natasha remarried, this time to a kind and supportive husband who had a solid career and financial resources. Almost as an afterthought, at the end of the interview, Natasha tersely mentioned that she has been completely alienated for more than a decade from her son and her older daughter. Again, no details were offered about how this came about or what impact this has had upon her. She was quick to add, however, that she calls her younger daughter several times a week and that they visit each other periodically. She has no grandchildren. Also, she has had virtually no contact with her siblings for more than thirty years, and they have cut her off from their families. To complete the picture of her relational world, Natasha did briefly mention some current friendships, but did not describe any specific individuals or events or activities. Her comments about them were devoid of emotional content.

Our Innate Need for Relatedness

Interpersonal relatedness is baked into our DNA; the fundamental orientation towards other human beings is evident from the very beginning of life. As if compelled by a mysteriously inborn image, newborns fixate on a picture of the human face—but only if it has the correct arrangement of eyes, nose, mouth, and hairline. Also, just a few hours after birth, infants will imitate the facial gestures of their caregivers. The drive for interpersonal connection and alignment seems almost innate. How is this possible?

Earlier we introduced the remarkable research of Beebe and Lachmann (Chapter 1). Their slow-motion recordings of four-month-old infants with caregivers demonstrated that, using the language of facial expression, pre-semantic verbalization, head position, and eye contact, children and their parents carry on a lively back-and-forth dialogue. At four months of age! This involves precise timing: an initial excited utterance by the infant, maybe accompanied by a head tilt and arm raising, is followed by a brief pause to 'switch speakers' and then the mother (or other caregiver) responds with a paired vocalization or gesture. This is the precursor of adult conversational turn-taking. And the rapidity of these interactions is breath-taking. The mom responds to the infant (on average) in one-sixth of a second and the infant responds back in one-third of a second. Human beings are hardwired to be social creatures.

One apparent function of these early interactional exchanges has to do with the critical importance of emotional regulation. *Homo sapiens* have a comfort zone regarding the intensity of our feelings. Whether it be sadness, fear, or anxiety—or even positive emotions such as excitement—distress arises when emotional intensi-ties fall outside of the comfort zone. With maturity, most of us learn to cope with strong feelings, maybe by turning on some music, going for a jog, or calling a friend. Infants and young children, on the other hand, are exquisitely dependent on their caregivers to keep emotions within a tolerable range. A securely attached child has come to trust that their caregiver will be available, sensitive, and competent. The caregiver provides comfort when the child is sad or scared, engages with them when they are lonely or bored, and reassures or distracts them when they are in pain. An insecurely attached child, by contrast, has repeatedly experienced adults who are not paying attention, do not know how to interact, are annoyed by the child's demands, or who simply are not around.

From the outset of the interview, Natasha was compelled to complain repeat-edly that her parents had no parenting skills. She described her parents, especially her mother, as uncaring and unavailable. Natasha remembered her psychotherapist telling her that it was hopeless to try to repair these "toxic relationships." Growing up, her parents had shown little interest in her feelings or relationships. The consis-tent focus was on externalities—her obedience and compliance, her scholastic and athletic achievements. She was raised to keep her feelings to herself and to manage them on her own.

The mutual sharing of intimate feelings represents a fundamentally important aspect of the parent-child relationship. Emotion is at the core of human subjectivity. Learning about feelings in oneself and others, getting comfortable with a wide range of feelings, and learning how to communicate them reciprocally—these are crucial aspects of psychosocial development. When a securely attached child is engaged with a parent, there is an intense exchange of feelings back and forth. They carefully watch each other's facial expressions and listen intently to discern the emotional tone of the voice, in addition to the meaning of the words. Even young children can detect patterns in these communications and notice how each caregiver has their own style of emotional expression. From infancy onward, they learn volumes about perceiving and sending emotional signals. When a child is insecurely attached, it is likely that these two-way communications will be carelessly rushed, irritable, incomplete, or misperceived.

At their most primitive level, emotions can be experienced as part and parcel of the actions that they provoke: you are angry, so you hit; you are scared, so you run. Much of psychotherapy is often directed at helping a patient slow the process down and notice feelings before they are acted upon. This requires pausing, stepping back from the urgency to act, and then reflecting upon the feeling itself. This capacity for self-reflection opens up new possibilities for exercising good judgment and for developing greater self-control. Looking before you leap. With securely attached children and their caregivers, this emotional education begins in early childhood. Ultimately, the development of a robust capacity for self-observation and self-reflection is one of the crowning maturational achievements of a lengthy, multi-step interactive process between a child and their caregivers.

Iconic pediatrician-turned-psychoanalyst D.W. Winnicott identified some of the first steps in this developmental progression. He observed that infants 'find themselves' in the eyes of their mother. When a secure attachment exists between child and mother, there is a sensitive and harmonious connection between them. It is powerful when a mother reflects back to the child his or her own excitement—about, for example, walking for the first time. At such a moment, the child feels their own visceral thrill of accomplishment as well as, simultaneously, the external validation and amplification of that feeling by their parent. The mother's facial expression and tone of voice give shape and substance to their own emotional reaction. Their feeling has been externally validated—it is real, not just a fleeting shadow passing over them. For these fortunate children, feelings become one more reality in the world that must be considered and understood.

Similarly, at times of disappointment, the mother's face and tone of voice reflect back to the child their own sadness. The mother is soothing the child and also teaching them about the nature of different feelings. She is communicating, "This is what sadness feels like to you and what it looks like in me. But do not worry, you are not alone, and I'll help you deal with this." With each subsequent repetition, the child becomes more familiar with various feelings and more confident about dealing with them. Eventually, securely attached children become more competent in regulating most emotions on their own. Developing in parallel with this is a growing self-awareness. The child is beginning to map out their internal world, and this contributes substantially to their nascent, developing personal Identity.

Still later, the sensitive caregiver teaches the child the names for different emotions, which greatly facilitates the sharing of subjective experiences with others. Emotional self-awareness and the ability to communicate about feelings are foundational aspects of emotional intelligence. Such an awareness also enhances the self-regulation of emotion, by providing the individual with an internal language to facilitate making sense of themselves and others. A secure attachment to caregivers greatly accelerates all of these maturational processes.

Natasha, growing up in a family rife with insecure attachments, got none of these benefits. She was judged by externalities: her grades, her athletic achievements, her appearance, and her submission to authority. There was little interest shown in her internal, subjective self, which made her less curious herself about her internal world. There was no practicing within the family about how to identify or share emotional states. This sort of parenting stunts the development of the ability to understand either yourself or others deeply. Later in life, when choosing a friend or romantic partner, having access to your own intimate feelings, and to those of others, is crucially important. There is no substitute for developing the capacity, and the desire, to look deeply into someone's eyes and to connect with them in such a way that each of you feels known, understood, desired. Sensitive, stable, loving caregivers gift this capability to their children.

By contrast, shallow and defensively restricted relationships in the childhood family tend to produce adults ill-prepared for either marriage or parenthood. First, such an adult may choose a partner impulsively based on superficial characteristics, such as physical appearance or career prospects. Second, when problems inevitably arise in the partnership, such adults may lack the tools to understand or to manage such difficulties. The partners may have neither the words to explain how they are feeling, nor the interpersonal skills needed to resolve deep-seated conflicts. Natasha and her family members all appear to have suffered from variations of the Insecure Dismissive attachment style—they dismissed the importance of intimately knowing others (or themselves) and denied the need for having people in their lives that they could depend upon.

Seen from this perspective, it is no surprise that Natasha was so evasive and superficial during the interview. She could only bear to briefly acknowledge her family's trauma in Russia, her pervasive conflicts with her parents, her painful alienation from her siblings, her divorce, and her tragic estrangement from her two elder children. The discussion of each of these situations begged for some explanatory details or a few illustrative vignettes. Most importantly, we would have expected to see and hear some heartfelt expression of feeling from her about these crucial aspects of her history. Instead, Natasha hastily skipped over all these pivotal events. By systematically avoiding any exploration of her feelings or her relationships, Natasha repeated the very tendencies of her parents that she had complained so bitterly about.

Happily, Natasha has now been married to a stable, financially successful, caring, and loving man for more than twenty years. She is close to her younger daughter. Belatedly, she is surrounding herself with trustworthy people. Natasha also claims to have a circle of friends but says that she likes to take them in "small doses." She sees herself as a work in progress.

Implications for Aging Wisely

As we scan the *Life Stories* of our fifty-two elders, those with secure childhood attachments have a high probability of late-life health and happiness. Conversely, those with blatantly insecure childhood attachments rarely made it into the top tier of our *Aging Wisely* scoring system. As noted, however, some individuals were able to change their relationship patterns in later life, which made a decisive difference. In our sample, having at least one dependable attachment relationship—a person that you know you can trust in a crisis—is as important in adulthood as it is in childhood.

The current principal investigator with the Harvard Study of Adult Development, Dr. Robert Waldinger, concludes that having a dependable adult attachment is the single most important requirement for aging well. Inevitably, we all come to realize that there are limits to our ability to take care of ourselves, if not at present, then certainly as the full effects of aging set in. Reliable relationships help prevent the excessive triggering of that 'fight-or-flight' neural mechanism that we are wired to mobilize in times of threat. Feeling alone and unsupported can predispose individuals to a persistent, exhausting, and unhealthy state of hyper-arousal.

Chronically high levels of stress hormones, such as cortisol or epinephrine, and elevated inflammatory elements in the blood strongly correlate with a wide variety of medical afflictions. Natasha, for instance, has multiple food allergies, high blood pressure, and a mixed connective tissue disorder. She also had a recent severe gastrointestinal infection. Her degenerative arthritis is painful enough to limit walking, exercising, or playing golf. And she experiences only limited relief from corticosteroids, two different pain medications, physical therapy, acupuncture, and aroma therapy. A lifetime of poorly developed interpersonal skills and conflicted relationships have severely compromised her immune system.

Warning: Statistics!

If you have an aversion to math, feel free to skip this section and subsequent statistical interludes (although we will simplify this material as much as possible). As noted, we independently scored thirty variables for each of our fifty-two interviewees. The analysis of this data did augment, in some instances, some of our subjective formulations. For those with a deeper interest in numerical analysis, supplemental material appears in the Appendix.

Three of our measured variables are conceptually associated with attachment: Reliable Adult Attachment, Social Connection, and Healthy Grieving. To determine how important each of the thirty variables was to an individual's successful aging, we calculated each variable's correlation with our comprehensive *Aging Wisely* score (and then squared it to determine the variance). The higher the variance, the more influence that particular variable had on the overall *Aging Wisely* score. It turns out that all three of these attachment-related variables had variances in the top third of all the variables, and Healthy Grieving had the second-highest variance score of all. Also, all three of these variables correlated strongly with each other, which confirmed their inter-relationships.

Regarding Healthy Grieving, it may seem counter-intuitive, but those with stable, loving relationships also grieve in the healthiest manner. They are devastated, of course, by losing a loved one, but they also have the Resilience, the confidence, and the social skills to reorganize their lives and to make the most of what they have left. (Although the older literature on grieving used words like 'recover,' people really never go back to where they were, so 'reorganize' is a more apt descriptor.) The net effect of this data is to strongly support our assertions about the importance of secure attachments.

Observations and Conclusions

How might you understand the effects of secure or insecure attachments in your own life, starting with your childhood? Did you develop into a teenager who generally trusted others? Did you experience the world as a safe and welcoming place?

How open and trusting is your current relationship with a spouse or partner? Do your early relationships still influence you? Are those influences serving you well, or do you need to consider working through some lingering issues? (If you would like to explore these matters more deeply, refer to the journaling prompts in the Self-Assessment exercise in the Appendix.)

Even those of us in happy partnerships, with friends aplenty, can still resort to unhealthy relational patterns during stressful times. Those with Insecure Dismissive tendencies may default to an 'I don't really need anyone' posture. Asking for help when we need it is increasingly important as we age. Those with a more Insecure Preoccupied style may make excessive demands of others, as if to test the reliability of their love for us. This can stress partners and friends. Being aware of these tendencies allows you to catch yourself and respond differently. As the philosopher Santayana warned, "Those that know not history are doomed to repeat it."

In concluding this chapter, the authors acknowledge having some significant deficits in their own early attachments with parents. Some of those deficits were mitigated by loving and supportive grandparents and other extended family members. Despite that, both authors made poor choices regarding early adult partners, which we have remedied with much stronger second marriages. We invite our readers to reflect a bit about their *own* attachment histories, and to think about what might be needed going forward to strengthen intimate relationships and social networks.

Finally, this chapter's focus on how we form close and trusting relationships with others sets the stage for understanding how we develop into unique individuals through a series of unfolding developmental challenges across the sequential stages of our lives. Elderhood is just the final and ultimate stage of this developmental process, as we will describe in the next two chapters.

3

The Development Model— Growth and Maturity

E rik Erikson's story is the stuff of legend, especially in the straitlaced world of psychoanalysis. Raised in the early 20th Century in the tightknit Jewish community of Frankfurt, Germany, he was teased by schoolmates because of his tall, blonde, Nordic appearance. Outside his community, he was subjected to the pervasive antisemitism of the mainstream German culture. He must have felt confused about just where he belonged. It was not until Erikson was a teenager that he learned that his mother, Karla Abrahamsen, prior to her marriage to Theodor Homburger, had been impregnated, probably by a member of the Danish royal family. This confusing paternity no doubt exacerbated young Erik's struggle to find himself as an adolescent. This was, we suspect, one of the major influences that led him, later in life, to coin the phrase 'identity crisis,' which later became one of the seminal psychological concepts of our culture.

Over time, he even changed his last name, reinventing himself as 'Erik, son of Erik.' Erikson also defied his parents' expectation that he attend medical school. In fact, after just a year of studying art, he dropped out of school and began wandering around Europe as an itinerant artist. Eventually he was hired by a friend to serve as an art teacher for the children of psychoanalysts living in Vienna. Anna Freud, the daughter of Sigmund, quickly recognized his extraordinary intuitive and interpersonal gifts, and offered to train him as a psychoanalyst. Given that Erikson lacked even a college degree, this was extraordinary: these training positions were reserved almost exclusively for graduates from medical schools. The wisdom of Anna Freud was born out, however, when Erikson went on to distinguish himself as one of the preeminent psychoanalysts of his generation.

Of all the models of human development available to us as a research frame-work, we chose Erikson's because of its intuitive genius and its real-world relevance. Subsequently, there was a large body of empirical evidence that further validated the inclusiveness and utility of Erikson's model. Most impressive, perhaps, was its util-ity in helping to make sense of the voluminous longitudinal data gathered for the Harvard Study of Adult Development (described in Chapter 1). Erikson's writings integrate the scholarly insights of psychoanalysis with his own unusually diverse, multicultural life experiences. Most notable in this regard is his abiding appreciation for the pervasive influence that culture and ethnicity have on parental attitudes, childrearing practices, and early personality development.

In his iconic book, *Childhood and Society*, Erikson proposed eight developmen-tal 'Tasks' that he believed constituted the essential challenges and opportunities for psychosocial growth and maturity. These Tasks, sometimes referred to as 'ages' or 'stages ,' were presented as emerging in a sequential, age-appropriate manner. (We selected the term 'Tasks' because, among these options, it is the most action-able.) However, although each Task has a particular developmental period during which it is the primary focus, Erikson was emphatic that a person engages each of these eight Tasks throughout their life cycle. As novelist William Faulkner put it, "The past is never dead. It's not even past."

Unlike Sigmund Freud, who described adulthood, prior to senescence, as a plateau, Erikson proposed that there are significant shifts, and changing priorities, throughout the adult years. Also, while Freud explained development in terms of 'psychosexual' stages, Erikson shifted the emphasis to a more relational model, hence 'psychosocial' stages. Erikson saw the unfolding of human development as influenced by the com-plex interaction of biology (genetic inheritance) and experience, especially interpersonal experience (nature *and* nurture). Although he does not invoke Attachment Theory by name, Erikson shared many assumptions and paradigms in common with Bowlby about the foundational importance of intimate relationships, especially regarding the nurturing of children. Their two theoretical models are highly compatible, for instance, the convergence of Erikson's Basic Trust with Bowlby's Secure Attachment. We will draw upon these two conceptual models liberally in the pages that follow.

Given the declared scope of this manuscript, we will focus primarily on the develop-mental Tasks of late adulthood and elderhood. However, because of our commitment to understanding elderhood in the context of the entire life cycle, we will briefly consider all of Erikson's Tasks, both as they first manifest themselves at the time of their age-appro-priate ascendency and also as they reemerge and are renegotiated in elderhood.

ERIKSON'S PSYCHOSOCIAL STAGES OF DEVELOPMENT

STAGE	BASIC CONFLICT	VIRTUE	DESCRIPTION
Infancy 0-1 year	Trust vs. Mistrust	Hope	Trust (or mistrust) that basic needs, such as nourishment and affection, will be met
Early Childhood 1-3 years	Autonomy vs. Shame/Doubt	Will	Develop a sense of independence in many tasks
Play Age 3-6 years	Initiative vs. Guilt	Purpose	Take initiative on some activities—may develop guilt when unsuccessful or boundaries overstepped
School Age 7-11 years	Industry vs. Inferiority	Competence	Develop self-confidence in abilities when competent or sense of inferiority when not
Adolescence 12-18 years	Identity vs. Confusion	Fidelity	Experiment with and develop identity and roles
Early Adulthood 19-29 years	Intimacy vs. Isolation	Love	Establish intimacy and relationships with others
Middle Age 30-64 years	Generativity vs. Stagnation	Care	Contribute to society and be part of a family
Old Age 65 onward	Integrity vs. Despair	Wisdom	Assess and make sense of life and meaning of contributions

SOURCE: McLeod, Saul (January 12, 2024). www.simplypsychology.org/erik-erikson.html. Simply Psychology.

Traditionally, the focus with each of the developmental Tasks has been on the desired outcome. For example, the preferred outcome of the first Task, Basic Trust vs. Mistrust, is Trust—toward the world and the people in it. Erikson's binary formulation invites us to consider the dialectic tension between Trusting and Mistrusting. A healthy individual does not stake out a fixed position along this continuum; they move up and down it depending on the moment-to-moment situation they find themselves in. A high-functioning individual trusts their partner and their friends, but they would not indiscriminately trust a high-pressure salesperson. Similarly, for each of the eight developmental Tasks, there is an important psychological benefit to the so-called 'negative' pole of the dialectic.

Toward the end of his own life, Erikson, along with his wife, Joan M. Erikson, and Helen Q. Kivnick, asserted that, in the final years of elderhood, all the previous Tasks are renegotiated again. And they warn that the negative poles of the various dialectics become more prominent in late elderhood. This was the essential message in his final two publications, *The Life Cycle Completed* (extended version) and *Vital Involvement in Old Age*.

While we will consider Erikson's psychosocial Tasks in their original order, it is helpful to appreciate that this is a cumulative model. Each Task drives the individual's development toward the achievement of what Erikson called a 'basic strength'— for the Task of Basic Trust vs. Mistrust, for instance, the strength is Hope. The acquisition of each successive strength prepares us to take on the challenges of the developmental Task to come. Conversely, lack of success in one of the Tasks can compromise the individual's capacity to tackle later Tasks in the sequence. However, such developmental difficulties are reversible—there is always the possibility of compensatory 'catch-up' growth.

I. Basic Trust vs. Mistrust

Erickson's words leap off the pages of *Childhood and Society*, vivid and visionary. In contrast to other Freudians of his generation, Erickson unambiguously affirmed the crucial importance of relationships, beginning with the sensitive, trustworthy care by parents (or others). The quality of this caregiving depends, in turn, on the parents' own trust in themselves, which is powerfully influenced by the parenting they themselves received as children. It is essential that parents have a conviction that what they are doing is 'good enough.' Early on, the infant's Basic Trust is manifested in the ease of the child's feeding, the depth of their sleep, and the relaxation of their bowels. Over time, this Trust will facilitate the development of intimate relationships, the assurance of inner goodness and consistency, and a broader sense of belonging to the community. Again, we hear Bowlby echo this in his description of a secure attachment.

However, to ensure fundamental safety and self-protection, it is essential to imbue a child with a healthy Mistrust of dangers, such as sharp objects, steep flights of stairs, and busy streets. On the other hand, overemphasizing danger and prohibition can give rise to a preponderance of Mistrust—which is associated with physiological dysregulation, parent-child conflicts, and later, alienation from society. In Erikson's worldview, there is an organic inseparability of one's attitudes toward body, self, family, and culture. Successful adaptation to this Task results in a strength called Hope—the belief that one can be safe while navigating a sometimes-hazardous world, as long as we have the help of loving caregivers.

Elder Reworking

Given that elders must revisit all the earlier Tasks, let us consider the dialectic of Trust vs. Mistrust. As bladders leak, joints ache, hearts flutter, erections fail, vaginas dry up, and vision and hearing decline, it is a considerable challenge to sustain Trust in ourselves and the world. When new living situations are thrust upon us, and cherished people die, it can feel like we are losing control of our lives, which can engender global Mistrust. Elders are especially vulnerable to Mistrust if they have not anticipated the inevitable losses of aging. Many retreat into irritable curmudgeonhood, having stubbornly assumed that they would continue to enjoy the robust functionality of a youthful body indefinitely. It takes wisdom indeed to find stability and serenity in a situation roiled by change and loss.

On the flip side, however, elders must exercise an appropriate degree of Mistrust to protect themselves from situations involving internet scams or fraudulent salespeople. Elders have lost large sums to unscrupulous con artists because of naive gullibility. Elders that indulge in wishful thinking that everything is okay, that they can impulsively find a trustworthy new romantic partner, or that everyone is telling the truth, make themselves easy marks. Solid critical thinking skills can help us evaluate specific situations and decide where we need to be on the Trust vs. Mistrust continuum.

II. Autonomy vs. Shame and Doubt

With the flowering of muscular strength and coordination, a child can walk and grab and climb. There can be a thrilling exuberance in experiencing that power and agency. However, unregulated by conscientious caregiving, these new developmental acquisitions can lead to reckless risk-taking and painful consequences. After such missteps and transgressions, a child may be stricken with Shame, which may be accentuated by punishment, verbally or physically, by caregivers. If this is a recurrent experience, children may come to Doubt themselves.

Similarly, successful toilet training allows the child to take their rightful place in the social world. However, there is no escaping the ever-present threat of a toileting accident, which would subject them to embarrassment and ridicule. Optimally, there develops a harmonious balance between the freedom to exert one's independence, and compliance within the limits and expectations imposed by their specific cultural milieu. In the healthiest of individuals, these limits and expectations are internalized and come to feel quite natural and self-imposed. Mastering this Task involves developing control over internal urges, learning to exercise age-appropriate assertiveness, and feeling good about exercising one's Will to influence the world.

On the other hand, some cultural anthropologists have suggested that our negative attitude about Shame is a distinctly Euro-American cultural phenomenon. Because we value individuality so highly, we do not want to hold our children back by making them feel bad about themselves. Several Asian and other cultures, by contrast, believe that Shaming represents an important cultural tool to enforce compliance and to enhance group cohesion. In such cultures, there is no compunction about strongly discouraging individualistic attention-seeking.

Elder Reworking

In comparing childhood with elderhood, of course, we know that the developmental progressions are moving in opposite directions. However, the challenge is similar: how to preserve a sense of dignified self-determination while avoiding shameful *faux pas* and embarrassing failures. In elderhood, episodes of incontinence or falling in public loom as shameful and hazardous possibilities. As one's dependency needs escalate, the elder is well-advised to learn to accept help gracefully, and to do so without exaggerated Shame or feelings of failure.

In Mitch Albom's book (also a fine movie) *Tuesdays with Morrie*, Morrie admits that being wiped by someone else after a bowel movement was one of the most Shameful aspects of his deterioration. However, there is also an adaptive utility to Shame and Doubt: elders need to continue to be sensitive to the needs and rights of others. Particularly with individuals who are prone to self-centeredness and disruptive behaviors, feeling embarrassment and Self-Doubt may motivate them to get along better with others. This is especially important if they live in a communal setting.

III. Initiative vs. Guilt

With the consolidation of earlier achievements and new ones added, children begin to notice opportunities to be 'on the make,' to become 'movers and shakers,' with a newfound capacity to influence, to create, and to possess. However, they may also begin to realize that others have gotten there before them. Dad already has mom, and mom has dad. Older siblings and peers have possessions and privileges that they covet but cannot yet have ("Why can't I have a cell phone—I'm almost six!"). If these strivings can be redirected towards refining their own social and psychological skills, children can feel proud of proceeding down the path toward honorable maturity. If, however, the expression of these competitive and acquisitive drives is too raw, and not moderated by social norms and sensitive caregivers, there can develop bitter rivalries, intractable jealousies, and a deep-seated Guilt about their hostile and voracious desires.

Healthy development in this Task results in the strength of Purpose and the establishment of a promising place in a rapidly expanding world. As with Shame and Self-Doubt, Guilt is known as a 'social emotion' because it helps to socialize children by hastening the internalization of moral and interpersonal standards of behavior. Someone who is Shameless and impervious to Guilt is in danger of becoming perniciously antisocial.

Elder Reworking

Even elderhood can present opportunities to start a new organization, a discussion group, or a romantic relationship. Some elders seem to initiate and to assert themselves naturally, with easy confidence, while others may watch from the sidelines with barely contained jealousy or a burning sense of inferiority. In such circumstances, their hostility may be most overtly directed at others, but this is invariably accompanied by Guilty self-recriminations associated with their own shortcomings and their ugly jealousies. This is particularly likely in those with unmet partnership needs.

As in childhood, the threat of feeling Guilty helps many elders to behave in more considerate ways towards others. Those who are immune to Guilt run the gamut from the carelessly self-centered to the ruthlessly exploitative.

IV. Industry vs. Inferiority

This is the developmental stage when children go to school and enter into the world outside the family. To be successful, they must be able to temporarily set aside their immersion in imaginary play and their childish expectation of unconditional approval. They must master the rules, the tools, the technologies, and the new social roles of an environment that demands focus, diligence, perseverance, and productivity. The domains of these challenges range from academics to athletics, art, music, and the social sphere. If they are successful, self-esteem will surge as they begin to find their place in the wider world. If they struggle to master these new competencies, or feel defeated, they may withdraw back into the family or into themselves via fantasy and isolation.

The challenge during this development Task involves building the strength of Competence. But the benefits of experiencing inferiority, in small doses, should not be overlooked. Failing at something can strengthen one's determination to succeed, can build resilience, and can teach empathy for those less well-endowed or for those from disadvantaged circumstances.

Elder Reworking

Some of our elders were shining successes in academia, science, art, or business. Entering elderhood, they faced the difficult decision of whether to persist with their careers or to transition to a qualitatively new life as a retiree. The choice to persist risks burnout and diminishing competitiveness, especially in vocational fields that demand long hours, a youthful vitality, or creative new ideas. Those that chose retirement face the daunting prospect of creating an alternative life structure with a new sense of Purpose, a radically transformed daily schedule, and a reimagined personal Identity. It takes creativity to envision new ways of being relevant and useful, and humility to become a beginner, after so many years of being a respected expert. Stepping out of your vocational silo can confront you with many unfamiliar technological and organizational challenges that make you feel incompetent and Inferior.

Those individuals who worked in menial, tedious, or physically taxing jobs tend to be profoundly relieved to retire. However, the challenge of filling their unscheduled days with people, meaning, and Purpose can be daunting. Many are tempted to give up on Industriousness altogether, but this would put them on the fast track to early disability, dementia, and death. Use or lose it.

V. Identity Consolidation vs. Confusion

(In 1950 Erikson labeled this Task 'Identity vs. Role Confusion' because of the considerable emphasis placed at that time on occupational and familial roles. We renamed it, as above, because of our culture's shift away from more stable external roles to the more fluid, and internal, sense of personal Identity.)

In adolescence, given all the bodily, sexual, cognitive, familial, and peer relationship changes underway, it is no surprise that the self-image, the fundamental sense of who someone is, becomes diffuse and fragmented. Erikson emphasized how teenage love, with or without sexuality, is intensely conversational, because there is a powerful need for self-expression and a relentless curiosity to find out how others see you. There is also a powerful tendency to battle with authority figures and to define oneself by joining a conformist group with high entry standards to meet, and barriers to entry for outsiders. Whereas Erikson focused on the primacy of finding a vocational Identity, today's teens face the daunting challenge of discovering and declaring their sexual preferences, clarifying gender identities, expressing their musical and stylistic choices, and choosing their attitudes toward drugs and alcohol. Their loyalties to celebrities, groups, athletic teams, and political movements evolve as they labor to figure out exactly who they are, and what they believe in. There is a quest to establish Fidelity—a strong allegiance to their true self—as soon as they can clarify what that is.

Confusion about one's Identity, as painful as it is, prevents the premature closure of Identity formation and allows for healthy trial-and-error experimentation with different selves, different pathways. When considering the success of adolescent Identity Consolidation, the optimal stance is captured by the 'Goldilocks Principle': not too early, not too late; not too rigid, not too vague; just right.

Elder Reworking

It is our assertion that, because of longer and healthier life spans for many more elders today compared with prior generations, and because there are many more choices available to elders today, there is an additional, ultimate stage of development. We call it Elder Identity Revision™ (EIR) and we will describe it in detail in Chapter 4. In many ways, EIR is the reworking in elderhood of the same issues we faced in adolescence: who are we? What do we stand for? What do we really want out of life?

Just as in adolescence, tolerating a certain amount of Identity confusion in elderhood allows for more exploratory behavior and reflection. This may allow for the consideration of more options, and result in better decisions, and superior outcomes. Moderate degrees of uncertainty and doubt create an 'open space' for imagination and creativity. Especially for those prone to linear, 'left-brain' thinking, there is a risk that emotional and relational factors, which can be somewhat amorphous and ineffable, will be overlooked when making major life decisions.

When the work of EIR is completed satisfactorily in elderhood, this culminating life Task can deliver peace and contentment, a sense of completion and fulfillment. In such felicitous circumstances, it can seem that one's life has been a meaningful journey, a life well-lived, despite the inevitable setbacks and mistakes.

VI. Intimacy vs. Isolation

A reasonably consolidated Identity in adolescence allows individuals, in early adulthood, to risk temporarily losing themselves in the merger of sexual and emotional Intimacy. Optimally, a shared ethical trustworthiness safeguards the mutual vulnerability implicit in this intimate commitment. The alternative pole, Isolation, describes the fate of those defensive individuals who resist interpersonal union, perhaps because they could never fully trust another or, indeed, trust themselves. The goal for this developmental Task is Love.

On the other hand, temporary Isolation can allow for contemplation and self-reflection. Rather than making the same relationship mistakes repeatedly, a period of withdrawal and reconsideration—with or without a therapist or trusted confidant—can be extremely beneficial. This is only true, however, if it is followed by a renewed effort to find connection and Intimacy. Over the long haul, all but the most extreme introverts need the sustenance that only other humans can provide.

Elder Reworking

As mentioned, having a loving and dependable partner in late life is one of the most powerful protective factors possible. Especially when surrounded by children and grandchildren, such a couple embodies the essence of a rich, full, productive life. This is a remarkable human achievement that deserves our respect. Even after one spouse dies, many widows and widowers remain Intimate and faithful to their deceased partners for the remainder of their lives.

In stark contrast, some elders enter their final decades with the distressing suspicion that they have never truly loved or been loved. According to hospice workers, this is one of the most searing of deathbed regrets. Other elders may choose to engage in late-life romances. Some of these relationships seem authentic and heartfelt, others appear to be pale imitations, wannabes, of prior partnerships. It is probably rare for someone to find deep intimacy for the first time in later life, but the great neurologist and author Oliver Sachs describes just such an occurrence in his autobiography, *On the Move: A Life*. It took Sacks many years to overcome his generation's homophobia. One might also expect this late-life awakening in someone who had spent several decades in a monastic, celibate community.

Just as in early adulthood, temporary periods of Isolation can serve as productive opportunities to reset and to reconsider. However, as we will describe later, prolonged social isolation, experienced as loneliness, significantly increases the risk of depression, dementia, and premature death. Maintaining Intimate connections with family and friends is vitally important for sustaining a sense of Purpose, meaning, and wellbeing for the vast majority of people. Not all people require pair-bonding: some find adequate engagement with a close circle of friends or in a close-knit community.

There are some curious exceptions to the notion that Intimacy is indispensable. For example, the Hindu belief about life stages (ashrams) includes both the penultimate phase of the hermit forest-dweller (who still functions as a teacher) and the final stage of the wandering ascetic. Even in India, however, the number of individuals today who follow this path is estimated to be less than one person per 20,000.

Let us examine how Erikson's first six psychosocial Tasks are addressed through the lives of two of our *Aging Wisely* elders: first you will meet Frank, who exemplifies a 'stay the course' life trajectory; then you will read the *Life Story* of Tony, whose considerable strengths are perpetually undermined by his unresolved psychosocial conflicts in what might be described as a 'fragile success' trajectory.

Frank's Life Story (91 years old)

Frank was singled out by the nuns at his parochial school as a particularly well-groomed and well-behaved youngster. Born into a large, cohesive family, he has been an unquestioning, devout, and obedient Catholic his entire life. In matters large and small, his engagement with the world exudes Trust and hope. His self-sufficiency and can-do attitude leave no doubt about his confidence in his own Autonomy and Initiative. At school, and later at work, he always did his best and maintained a cheerful, eager-to-please attitude towards authorities, peers, and customers. At every stage of his formal education and employment, he strove for and demonstrated Industry and competence.

His sense of Identity during adolescence was strong and stable. He grew up during the Great Depression and came of age during World War II. He was proud of his father's success running a building maintenance company that was awarded contracts by some of St. Louis's leading businesses. His father died when Frank was just fifteen. His mother sold the company and he, like his six siblings, had to find his own way. Frank was forced to leave his elite Catholic high school for a tuition-free public school, but he did not miss a beat. He continued to do well academically, played on the football team, and met his future wife in typing class. His Identity was cohesive and steady. Throughout the interview, he was eager to tell us how well he had done and how steadfast he was on his path.

He intermittently interjected throughout the interview how his Catholic faith has made his seventy-year marriage rock solid, how he always remained close to his siblings, and that "God is a reality!" Frank indisputably demonstrates impressive fidelity to his beliefs and commitments. He clearly mourned his father's death, but he took to heart his father's advice that he should do his best at every job and remember that each one might be a steppingstone to something better. And that is exactly how things played out. He progressed from door-to-door salesman to store clerk, then to realtor, and finally, to owner and manager of one of the larger real estate brokerage firms in the area. He and his wife raised a half dozen children, and now enjoy numerous grandchildren and several great-grandchildren. Even when he experienced tragedies or adversities, such as his father's early death, or when one of his sons was born disabled, he accepted these as "God's will." There can be no doubt that he succeeded with regard to the early adult Tasks of Intimacy and love.

Tony's Life Story (70 years old)

Tony grew up in a family riven by multi-generational stress and dysfunction. His Italian grandparent immigrants were harsh, critical, and pessimistic. The Great Depression thwarted Tony's father's desire for a college education, so he supported his young family as a career blue-collar employee for the City of Boston. His fiery, volatile temper intimidated the entire family and Tony still attributes his low self-esteem and anger management issues to his father's influence. Tony's mother protected herself by receding into the background, and Tony was critical of her for not shielding her children from her husband's brutality. Tony evidenced no bond with, or empathy for, his mother having been, like him, a victim of his father's rage. There was a great deal of yelling in their family. Once Tony's older brother had grown into a muscular adolescent, he began to physically challenge their father and their home became an even more dangerous battleground.

Tony characterized himself as small, quick, and easygoing as a kid. At the time of his birth, the family lived in a low-income, poor part of the city. Tony acknowledged having been threatened there by neighborhood toughs. He engaged in some shoplifting escapades but got off easy, something he now attributes to "white privilege."

During the interview, Tony delivered his information in a flat, well-rehearsed manner, almost as if he was talking about someone else. There was no subjective context provided, no evocative vignettes, no retrospective commentary of what it had felt like to him at the time. The cliches continued: he was a star math student and chess player, but lousy at sports. He was guiltily conflicted about masturbation and went on to develop chronic difficulty with sexual performance as an adult. (Note: to maintain a comfortable relationship with our interviewees, our consistent policy was not to ask about sexuality unless this information was volunteered spontaneously.)

When he was offered a spot in the elite Boston Latin High School, Tony readily accepted, only to find that, once there, he was no longer the smartest kid in the class. A self-described nerd at the time, he had no close male friends and he never was able to muster the courage to ask a girl out. Then, because his class ranking had fallen at his new school, he had to settle for admission to a second-tier college.

Looked at through the lens of Erikson's developmental Tasks and challenges, Tony grew up in a threatening and emotionally impoverished environment that was neither safe nor supportive. He had good reason to Mistrust others and the world and there was little reason for hope. His Insecure attachment was inevitable and debilitating. He apparently did not have the opportunity to safely exercise his age-appropriate willful Autonomy, nor to express his innate curiosity or creativity. He doubted his capacity to take the Initiative and was Guilty about his sexuality. Socially and athletically, he felt humiliated and defeated. Although his academic success represented a significant bright spot, even here his Industriousness was criticized, as when a teacher faulted him for reading too much (perhaps to escape from reality?). And then his intellectual self-esteem took a major hit when he moved into a school filled with highly competitive peers, many of whom were accepted by the very universities that had turned him down.

Tony's adolescent Identity consolidation was off to a rocky start. He felt much Shame about himself physically, athletically, socially, and sexually, and now even his intellect had fallen short of his aspirations. Once in college, Tony tried to invest himself in his classes, but his motivation faltered. Desperate for connection, he forced himself to ask ten women out on dates, one after the other, but was turned down ten times. He acknowledges, with reluctant self-awareness, that he probably came across like a "jerk with few social skills." He only made a couple of male friends—although two of them did become lifelong buddies.

Tony dropped out of college and, over the next ten years, worked a variety of entry-level, blue-collar jobs. He sought consolation in the fantasy that maybe he could be a writer, like Hemingway, but he could not sustain any serious literary efforts. He described feeling more comfortable with the "real people" working menial jobs, rather than with those individuals who populated high-pressure academic or corporate work environments. (This seemed like a flimsy rationalization.) At this point in his life, Tony's vocational path had become strikingly similar to that of his detested father, but Tony seemed unaware of this similarity.

Unfortunately, his dysfunctional life trajectory persisted. Tony became increasingly depressed and despondent. He was prescribed several different psychiatric medications and engaged in intensive psychotherapy for more than five years. Even with all this support, he struggled with chronic suicidal urges. Then, seemingly by chance, while perusing the shelves of a used bookstore, Tony picked up an introductory text in accounting. He was transported back to memories of his natural affinity for mathematics. Flushed with newfound hope, he decided to apply to one of Boston's community colleges, was accepted, and ultimately graduated with highest honors.

With undisguised pride, Tony told us that he was accepted by the Wharton School of Business, one of the top graduate schools in the country. However, the absence of his family at his college graduation was somewhat deflating. A couple of years earlier, Tony had written a harshly critical letter to his father, and the family broke off all communication with him for an extended period. Only a solitary aunt showed up to see him receive his diploma.

As his interviewers, we were struck by the lack of any softening of Tony's attitude toward his parents. We heard none of the usual adult revision of childhood memories. He saw himself only as having been unfairly punished and deprived by angry and unloving parents. For example, he expressed no real gratitude for his parents, long ago, having moved across town to be closer to his new high school. Later in the interview, when we asked about how he had dealt with the deaths of family members, Tony talked only of the relief he had felt. His mother died first; he went to her funeral but felt no grief. Next, his brother died, and Tony remarked to us that his brother had been a "pain in the ass." Finally, after his father died, Tony said to himself, "Now I can get on with my life."

Off Tony went to graduate school, where he once again excelled academically. This led to an impressive job offer at one of the top national accounting firms. Tony carved out a solid career as a corporate tax specialist, although ultimately, he was denied partnership, reportedly because he had been too anxious and indecisive. However, he later made partner at a smaller, regional firm.

It was only when Tony was well established, professionally and financially, that he began having some success romantically. He married and had three daughters. In an offhand manner, however, he told us that the same violent temper that had plagued his father and brother had also surfaced in his marriage. This was said as if he bore no responsibility for this character flaw. In fact, he had been shocked when his wife abruptly demanded, after one of his outbursts, that he move out immediately. Moving into a sparsely furnished rental, his adult success with Intimacy veered precipitously towards Isolation. Now, although he claims that he continues to care about his three daughters, he lacks a strong connection with any of them.

So how might we understand how Tony dealt with the tasks of adolescent Identity Consolidation and early-to-midlife adult Intimacy? His *Life Story* offers an example of a singular outstanding intellectual strength standing alongside much fragility and a globally stunted developmental profile. He came perilously close to ending his life prematurely in his mid-twenties, but then was saved by a chance reminder of his almost-forgotten mathematical talents. Building upon his educational and career success, he was, belatedly, able to marry and start a family. But then, mostly because of a hot and hurtful temper, and a lack of the emotional maturity needed to regulate it, his family fell apart.

Of course, there were forewarnings of marital discord: Tony also mentioned that he often had trouble tolerating his wife's messiness and lateness, and he also complained about how she spent money. These seemed to him to be good reasons to absolve himself of responsibility for the marriage break-up. He added that they stopped having sex after their last child was born and tried to justify this by saying that their lives had just been too busy. This was said in a half-hearted manner, as though even he did not really believe it.

Observations and Conclusions

One can appreciate that Frank and Tony dealt with very different genetic capacities, as well as drastically dissimilar family dynamics. Readers also may have noticed the similarities between Tony's *Life Story* and our earlier descriptions of Ella and Natasha. All three of them had difficulties establishing secure and safe attachments to parental caregivers. All three had significant intellectual gifts that ultimately served them well in their professional careers, even as they struggled to establish trusting and intimate relationships with marital partners. The pervasive influence of an insecure attachment style is substantial, but not insurmountable. Natasha now appears to be happily married and Ella is close to her children and she seems to be content making friends and contributing to her new community.

In Chapter 4, we will continue examining Erikson's psychosocial development Tasks from mid-adulthood through old age. We will explore these ideas through the *Life Stories* of these same two elders and we will describe the additional developmental stage of EIR as it became clear to us through our interviews and data analysis.

4

Elder Identity Revision— Completing the Life Cycle

W e can now examine Erikson's final two psychosocial Tasks, those that most concern elders, and the addendum suggested by George Vaillant, one of Erikson's intellectual disciples. These Tasks describe the fundamental challenges of elderhood and set the stage for our proposed extension to Erikson's model, a ninth developmental stage we call 'Elder Identity Revision' (EIR).

VII. Generativity vs. Stagnation (Late Adulthood)

Generativity pertains to caring for and investing in the next generation as a parent, grandparent, teacher, supervisor, mentor, or coach. The alternative pole in this dialectic, Stagnation, is characterized by a pervasively impoverished self-absorption. Generativity requires that one move beyond narrow narcissistic pursuits to support, nurture, and guide the young. It entails the sort of generosity of spirit that motivates people to plant trees under whose shade they themselves will never sit.

A reasonable addition to Erikson's model was suggested by George Vaillant, who, as noted previously, directed the Grant Harvard Study of Adult Development for more than three decades. Vaillant suggested adding to Erikson's theory the late adulthood Task of Guardianship, which is similar to Generativity but focuses on inanimate entities rather than people. This might involve preserving and enhancing important institutions, organizations, structures, collections, or archives.

Aging Wisely elders were serving on the governance boards of local nonprofit organizations or were engaged in educational, artistic, social, or political initiatives.

Guardianship also can be focused on more personal and family projects. For example, several of our elders spoke lovingly of their determination to organize and to catalogue family photographs, to research ancestors and genealogies, or to write memoirs for children and grandchildren. 'Caring' is the preeminent strength characteristic of Generativity and Guardianship. (Note: for the sake of brevity, we will consider Guardianship to be a subsidiary part of Erikson's Task of Generativity.)

VIII. Self (Ego) Integrity vs. Despair (Early Elderhood)

This Eriksonian Task focuses on *Life Review* and life integration. An individual's level of Self-Integrity is evident in the degree to which they authentically feel that their life has been well-lived, that they have been productive and fulfilled—that, despite the inevitable disappointments and losses, they can accept, with some degree of serenity, that their one and only life cycle is approaching its end. Such a psychological state can be achieved only through a diligent self-reflection that has integrated in their minds their strengths and their weaknesses, the good and the bad in their lives. If we can do all that and give due consideration to our place in history and the universe, then we can rightfully claim to have acquired some measure of elder Wisdom.

These two developmental strengths—Caring and Wisdom—are crucially important, and we will illustrate their relevance in several of our case studies. However, our *Aging Wisely* interviews led us to conclude that an additional developmental Task could be identified. Curiously, Erik and his wife, Joan M. Erikson, arrived at this same conclusion toward the end of his life, but they settled for restating the same eight developmental Tasks already proposed. In the second version of *The Life Cycle Completed*, they reiterated that all the previously described psychosocial Tasks of the various ages/stages are being renegotiated perpetually, especially during the final years and decades of life. They also warned that the unhealthy negative tendencies of each Task loom more threateningly as elderhood progresses.

Based on our interviews, our data analysis, and our own lives, we identified the emergence of a distinct ninth and final stage that we believe is even more helpful and explanatory: Elder Identity Revision (EIR). To be consistent with Erikson's developmental framework, we have entitled this Task as 'Adaptive Coherence vs. Dysfunction.' As profound and inclusive as Erikson's model was in 1950, we concluded that elders today inhabit a radically different world and, therefore, have additional adaptive tasks to accomplish. The pace of cultural change continues to accelerate. To be our best selves, tenacity, self-awareness, and effortful intentionality are required so that we can constantly rebalance our sense of Identity. Otherwise, our internal Coherence will suffer and Dysfunction will ensue.

IX. Elder Identity Revision: Adaptive Coherence vs. Dysfunction (Late Elderhood)

Compared to older Americans decades ago, many elders today enjoy not only a longer life span, but also an extended 'health span.' In addition, many individuals and couples now have significantly more discretionary income, earlier retirements, and many more choices regarding housing, travel, recreational sports, adult education programs, and entertainment. In 1950, a much smaller proportion of seniors lived past eighty, and most of those who did tend to stick with their long-established homes, communities, and social roles.

Today, a dizzying array of possibilities and choices confront elders. There are numerous communal living environments created exclusively for those aged fifty-five or older. In these sheltered enclaves, the drinks are inexpensive and the band starts playing at 5:00 p.m.—and then packs up by 9:00 p.m. And there still are occasional outbreaks of venereal disease. In fact, there is now significant relationship instability during elderhood. The so-called 'grey divorce' rate (involving those over the age of fifty) increased more than 100 percent between 1990 and 2015; By comparison, during that same period, the divorce rate for those in their forties increased by only 14 percent.[5] Also, cohabitation rates for unmarried individuals over fifty rose by 75 percent between 2007 and 2017.[6] Elder lifestyles are changing rapidly in the 21st Century.

Laura Carstensen's work, discussed in the Introduction, helps make sense of these trends. Your 'time horizon' (your perceived proximity to the end of your life), significantly influences your preference for novelty vs. familiarity. More time to work with promotes a greater interest in exploration, like trying out new things and taking some chances—maybe a new relationship, an unconventional living situation, travel to exotic places, or some sexy lingerie. However, if you perceive that your time is limited, you will want to make the most of your few remaining opportunities. You will choose 'sure things'—like the people, the restaurants, and the vacation spots that you already know you like. (This phenomenon was also detected among younger adults with foreshortened futures, such as those with a terminal illness, or those residing in Hong Kong just prior to its absorption by mainland China.)

Much has been written about the 'paradox of choice.' It is widely assumed that people prefer to have as many choices as possible. Actually, a number of replicated investigations have found that facing too many options can be highly distressing. This is particularly true for those elders with poorly defined Identities. For them, facing an overwhelming range of choices in today's world may remind them (unconsciously) of the uncomfortable confusion of adolescence.

The EIR Task focuses on the challenge of constructing and maintaining a personal Identity that is consolidated and coherent, but also adaptive to changing circumstances. Identity is an underlying psychological structure that, like the bones of our skeleton, determines our fundamental shape and provides a scaffolding upon which other structures are connected. Identity is a complex composite that includes both conscious and unconscious elements, and which combines the ways that we see ourselves as well as how others see us—which we then internalize and make our own. A healthy Identity gives us a sense of direction and provides guardrails for our behavior. Using Freud's formulation, it is intrinsic to the fundamental human endeavors: to love and to work. As the more experience-near component of our character, Identity is something that evolves over a lifetime. The concept of EIR, however, asserts that, in addition to changes in elders' bodies and minds, there is currently a qualitative acceleration in the evolution of the cultural milieu.

As one of our wisest elders told us, "My friends and I have come to realize that we have to constantly pivot to maintain our equilibrium and our sense of wellbeing." A carefully revised Identity enables elders to respond in a coherent manner to the situations and decisions they face every day: Who are you now? Who do you want to be with? What are your values and priorities? What do you really want to be doing? Where do you want to be? Is this the right time to make a change? Most of our parents and grandparents, we suspect, were not challenged nearly so much by these questions. But for our generation, this represents both a threat and an opportunity.

Listening to the *Life Stories* of our *Aging Wisely* elders, it became clear to us that the functionality and adaptability of different Identities vary widely. There are five characteristics of Identity that seem most important. Across the board, the optimal range for each of these variables is in the middle ground characterized by the 'Goldilocks Principle': not too much, not too little, just right.

The five primary Identity characteristics follow:

1. A healthy Identity should be fairly stable, integrated, and durable—but also flexible. Someone with a diffuse or fragmented Identity will be unstable and will make unwise decisions. Those with a fragile sense of self can be

overwhelmed by even minor adversities. At the other extreme, people with an overly rigid Identity may stubbornly resist noticing or responding to opportunities for new discoveries, adventures, or relationships.

2. One's Identity should strike a balance between a focus on self and a focus on others. Excessively self-absorbed individuals lack empathy and make poor friends. Alternatively, those who are so busy trying to please others may neglect their own needs and appear to lack a personality of their own.

3. There is a natural tension between one's ideal self and one's perceived actual self. Too much self-satisfaction leads to narcissistic blindness. On the other hand, an overly harsh self-appraisal gives rise to low self-esteem, demoralization, even depression.

4. Currently, there is much emphasis on mindfulness and 'the power of now.' Although it is healthy to ground oneself strongly in the here-and-now, it is also important to feel integrated with your past self and thoughtful about your future self.

5. A healthy self-awareness allows one to learn and adapt. Being oblivious to your coping strategies and relationship patterns can doom you to repeat past mistakes, while being overly self-conscious can lead to self-recrimination, inhibition, and paralyzing insecurity.

Informed as we have been by our elders' *Life Stories*, we have determined that EIR entails five developmental Sub-Tasks, 'the 5 C's': Control, Competence, Connection, Continuity, and Consciousness. As you review the following descriptions, note both the challenges each Sub-Task presents, and the opportunities for adaptation.

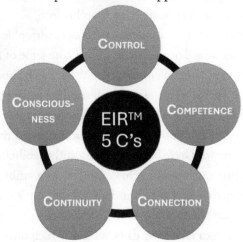

EIR Sub-Task: Control

From infancy onward, in addition to seeking a secure attachment, human beings work extremely hard to gain a sense of mastery and control over their bodies and the world around them. This begins with learning how to control head and limb movements then, later, bowel and bladder functions. We learn how to grab, crawl, and feed ourselves. We learn how to comprehend and produce language.

With the acquisition of each new developmental skill, children experience an expanding sense of safety, comfort, and self-confidence. Mastering these basic skills reassures them that they are finding their niche in the world, and that they will increasingly 'belong' within the human community. Genetic or acquired deficits in any of these key areas are likely to cause major complications in the maturational process and in the consolidation of a healthy, robust sense of Identity.

For elders at the other end of the life cycle, the loss of one or more fundamental capacities can trigger panic, a fear of being forced back towards an infantile-like state of helplessness. The loss of vision or hearing or becoming a post-heart attack 'cardiac cripple' can be devastating. The prospect of urinary or fecal incontinence in public is mortifying. A stroke can deprive you of the ability to walk or talk. A diagnosis of malignancy or dementia may evoke hopelessness. Elders may be stricken by another sort of out-of-control feeling after losing someone dear to them—a spouse, child, sibling, or best friend. It is a terrible blow to our sense of agency that we cannot protect the ones we love. This may cause some to wonder if life is still worth living.

And there are other sorts of threats to our sense of being in control. Not being able to recall a word or name is disturbing, as is the momentary loss of balance climbing stairs, or the inattentive tripping over absolutely nothing. (Thank you, Bev, for occasionally reminding Scott to pick up his feet!)

We observed a wide variety of responses to these catastrophic threats and losses in our *Aging Wisely* interviewees. For some elders, their core sense of Identity was destabilized—they were depressed, shut down, and left without much hope. Some even seemed to have given up. Others, however, reacted with startling equanimity and philosophic acceptance—these individuals were inspirational. Those of us who have been fortunate enough to have dodged such catastrophes, so far, know that our time will come.

Especially for elders who have become significantly debilitated, the wish to have more control can come out sideways; for example, as a stubborn insistence on a rigid TV-watching schedule or a petulant demand that one's sandwich be prepared 'just so.' Experienced caregivers often allow elders to exert control over trivial matters—for instance, when to take their daily walk or which outfit to wear—to enlist their cooperation in other less-negotiable matters, such as taking medications on time. Similarly, for many years, surgeons were convinced that they had to put their post-operative patients on rigid 'every six-hour' opiate regimens to prevent drug overuse. Surprisingly, research shows that when patients are allowed to self-administer their medications, they used not more, but less than before. More control, fewer pain meds.

Frequently, we associate one loss emotionally with other losses. An elderly woman in marital therapy became agitated when her husband casually suggested that they could combine 'his' and 'hers' checking accounts at the bank. The therapist initially was confused by the ferocity with which this woman opposed this seemingly trivial financial simplification. It made sense, however, when the woman later explained how this consolidation would have eliminated the bank account that she had established, decades ago, for her now-defunct business. Without a pause, she went on to complain about her diminished ability to walk around the neighborhood without falling and, oh yes, her bitterness about the recent loss of her driving privileges. Each loss was compounded by others. So, no, it was not just about the checking account.

In addition, instability in the larger environment can exacerbate these individual losses. Many of Ben's patients, young and old, have been deeply unsettled by recent environmental, political, and economic instabilities in our world. The restrictions and threats arising from the COVID pandemic caused widespread anxiety and depression. For many, it seemed that the world was spinning out of control. In a recent study of over 5,000 elders in the United Kingdom, there was an increase in the rate of depression from 12 percent of the sample, pre-pandemic, to 28 percent one year into the pandemic[7]. Anxiety, loneliness, and overall quality of life were also measurably worse.

EIR Sub-Task: Competence

Compared with the loss of control, the loss of competence impacts a somewhat different sector of our psychological landscape. Per Erickson's Tasks, a loss of Control threatens Trust and Autonomy. Loss of a loved one, for instance, can engender a global mistrust of the world or of God. Becoming blind or losing the ability to walk can necessitate a dependence on others that engenders Shame. By contrast, the less catastrophic loss of Competence—for example, due to waning strength, partial hearing loss, or arthritic hands—erodes the capacity to engage successfully in the Eriksonian Tasks of Initiative and Industriousness. You just cannot get things done the way you used to, and it can be irritating to constantly have to ask for help. Harking back to childhood developmental milestones, the competence required to ride a bike, make a friend, read a book, calculate numbers, or kick a soccer ball all build self-esteem and are integrated into the evolving sense of Identity. Conversely, in elderhood, the loss of lifelong competencies damages self-esteem and harshly undermines one's Identity. Sometimes we try to deny a decline in competence and end up taking unsafe risks, perhaps resulting in hip, back, or head injuries that actually accelerate our decline.

By late adulthood, elders have mastered many diverse competencies: how to navigate the internet, prepare meals, fix a leaky faucet, host a party, paint a room, lead an organization, repair damaged relationships, pay the bills, take care of grandchildren. A diminution or outright loss of one or more of these competencies is deeply unsettling. Climbing a ladder reminds us of declining balance and dexterity. Picking up a twenty-five-pound bag of mulch becomes less and less feasible. The ability to 'age in place' may be jeopardized. The resulting psychological distress is both internal and interpersonal—we feel bad about falling short of our own expectations *and* we are also concerned about how others may see us. Almost a decade after donning hearing aids, Scott still hesitates and feels a bit of Shame when asking people to repeat themselves in conversation. Of course, if he does not ask, he risks making assumptions about what was said and then might say something inappropriate. He also wonders, did he just miss hearing something because of background noise, or did his brain fail to process the electronic signals accurately, or fast enough? In either case, the limitation is unsettling.

Historically, society has valued elders for their knowledge and experience. Their expertise with agriculture, weather patterns, hunting, fishing, home construction, auto repair, financial investing, cooking, sewing, home remedies, and childrearing made them contributing members of the community. Today, internet resources have largely replaced much of the need for elder wisdom—young adults now go directly to YouTube to find out how long to boil a potato. Elders, having previously enjoyed the sense of being knowledgeable, or even an expert in many spheres of life, today encounter a world of technology, social media, crypto-currencies, unheard of career paths ("What the heck is a 'social influencer'? You can make money doing that?"), and unprecedented political machinations that make them feel confused and lost. The profusion of buttons on a new Smart TV remote control can trigger a panic attack.

Ben played on the football and lacrosse teams during college. He used to be one of the first guys selected for pick-up softball games, but now his macular degeneration has relegated him to catching for both teams, neither batting nor taking the field. And he cannot drive at night anymore. Scott's drives off the tee box used to fly much further down the fairway, so he valiantly tries to make up for it with better chipping and putting. A friend of ours, once a swaggering and confident CEO, now retired, fell backwards off a ladder while trying to store some luggage in the rafters of his garage, and fractured a vertebra. He had dismissed his wife's warning that his recent knee surgery and his faltering balance made ladder climbing a risky endeavor (Oh, those 'I told you so's!'). Like a lot of men, he could not bear to ask for help and now must deal with the consequences of his adolescent-like rebelliousness.

It is a daunting challenge to maintain a sense of being a competent, self-respecting individual as we struggle with confusing online application forms, try to master a new smart phone, adapt to a new residence, or attempt to build a new circle of friends to replace the ones we have lost. Many of us felt reasonably good about ourselves in our old settings, when operating within the parameters of well-defined social and vocational roles. A major change of where-who-when-how in our lifestyle can make us feel like bungling idiots. This is uncomfortable, even Shameful. On the other hand, gaining new competencies, even with something as trivial as figuring out a phone app, can enhance global self-esteem and generate a momentary, but delightful, sense of wellbeing.

EIR Sub-Task: Connection

You have, no doubt, noticed our emphasis on the importance of interpersonal relationships, something we will discuss further in Chapter 8. Human connection can be experienced on several levels: with family and close friends, as part of a larger community, and even with strangers. Connection is a key Task along life's path, and crucial in elderhood.

Intimate relationships include marital partners and immediate family. Vaillant identified having a strong marital partnership as one of the most important factors that protects against serious illness or premature death. Certainly, children and grandchildren also fall within this inner circle. As our kids grow up and move away, and then start families of their own, elders often face difficult decisions. Should they stay in their familiar homes and neighborhoods, or move to be closer to adult children and their families? Should they commit to offering regular childcare, or do they want to preserve the freedom to travel and to take spontaneous trips? Are they willing to take into their home a troubled teenage grandchild who can no longer live peaceably with parents or a stepparent? Sometimes it is a choice between Connection and freedom.

The next category of relatedness includes close friends and extended family. Although some elders have moved around so much that they have friends all over the world, many others have lived long enough in one place to have a circle of close buddies or extended family members who they see frequently. With family, this could have been for ritualized Sunday meals or for birthdays and holidays. With friends, they could routinely meet at church/synagogue/mosque, or get together for longstanding book clubs, weekly breakfasts, or for games of pickle ball. Of course, there is always attrition, with friends and relatives moving away, drifting apart, or dying. And if the elder moves, this entire network of close relationships may be limited to infrequent visits or online contacts.

The next category of relatedness is not with individuals, but rather with groups and organizations. Given the widespread emphasis on radical individualism and non-conformity, today there is a diminished appreciation for the benefits of belonging to a community. There is a powerful psychological impact to feeling that you are an important part of a group, that you have a contributing role, that you are recognized, and that you *belong*. Religious groups, charitable organizations, sports teams, a community choir, or a political action group can generate this sort of important social connection. As the theme song for the *Cheers* TV sitcom reminded us, we do yearn for a place "…where everybody knows your name, and troubles are all the same."

Psychologist Susan Pinker has drawn attention to another generally unappreciated form of relationships in her book, *The Village Effect*. She emphasizes the importance of feeling a connection with the scattered individuals who populate your everyday world. Some you may know by name and talk with regularly. Others you may only recognize by sight, without really knowing anything more about them—like the newsstand guy, a checker at the grocery store, or a familiar barista. These predictable human contacts help us feel comfortable and grounded in a familiar social environment.

In *The Good Life*, Robert Waldinger and Marc Schultz, Vaillant's successors at the Grant Harvard Study of Adult Development, make several recommendations about saying hello to strangers and perhaps even asking their names. These could be servers at a new restaurant, people with whom you share an elevator at work, or someone you encounter as you walk around your neighborhood. It is like karma—random acts of kindness have a way of being reciprocated, or at least it can feel that way. We will offer more on social engagement in Part Two.

EIR Sub-Task: Continuity

One important aspect of our personal Identity is our signature and unique ways of being in the world. This might include our sense of humor, our aesthetic style, or a determination to enliven conversations. These are the behavioral channels by which we communicate, "This is who I am."

The EIR Sub-Task of Continuity brings into sharp focus the question of how much of our past Identity we want to hang onto in elderhood. Do we struggle tenaciously to maintain who we have been, even if the environmental conditions that reinforced that particular adaptive style are no longer relevant? One ninety-five-year-old *Aging Wisely* interviewee proudly told us of her determination to win the (self-conceived) "best smile" designation in her new independent living facility. This would have been a proud reprise of the accomplishment celebrated in her high school yearbook. A retired university professor we interviewed never misses an opportunity to lecture and teach anyone within earshot. (We suspect that this did not win him many friends!) And a poet, after retiring from his career as a high school English teacher, eagerly looked forward to joining the community of writers in Berkeley. However, this was thwarted when his wife was diagnosed with Lou Gehrig's Disease (ALS). Suddenly forced into the role of caretaker, he was initially confused, but then became bitter and resentful. Unlike others in comparable situations, he refused to embrace a revised Identity as someone focused on caring for his wife.

In several of our elder interviews with very bright and successful graduates of Ivy League universities, we noticed a strong tendency to overemphasize the intellectual horsepower that had driven their career success in the past. Unfortunately, many of them had not adequately developed the social networking and relationship building skills that become more essential over time, especially given the increased dependence of elders on others. We should all ask ourselves: Are the strengths and habits that helped me in the past still serving me well? And if not, how can I revise my priorities and mobilize the energy required to change?

Many high-achieving individuals had grown comfortable occupying positions of power and privilege. They were accustomed to people seeking them out and hoping to benefit from their influence. For these people, being stripped of their rank and importance is painfully humbling. Ben had a patient in therapy who, years after his retirement, still angrily mourned the loss of the respect and the status that he had previously enjoyed as a highly regarded physician. Such individuals may be wracked by insecurity when considering just what they really have to offer in everyday person-to-person interactions.

If we are forced to modify our behavior due to changed circumstances, obligations, or priorities, is it with bitterness and regret, digging in our heels to resist change? Or can we muster a good-natured philosophic acceptance and a willingness to try out some new ways of being? For most of us, it makes a huge difference if these situational changes are forced on us abruptly or if we have time to anticipate, and maybe even participate, in the decision-making process. After major changes have taken place, can we continue to feel like our 'old selves' or are we convinced that something essential has been irrevocably lost?

Maybe our 'best days' are behind us, maybe not. Either way, it is critically important that we believe that we still have a Purpose and have something worthwhile to contribute. Even contributing in small ways can be meaningful to friends and family and can bolster our sense of Continuity.

EIR Sub-Task: Consciousness

This EIR sub-task has three elements Self-Consciousness, Cosmic-Transcendental Consciousness, and Existential Consciousness. Together, these elements reinforce the benefits of reflective understanding of ourselves and our environment.

Self-Consciousness. Optimally, individuals should have some awareness of their journeys through the EIR process. This type of Consciousness is 'thinking about thinking' or meta-cognition. Just having this awareness makes one feel a little less out-of-control: indeed, knowledge is power. As previously mentioned, the *Life Review* process during this period is extremely helpful and should include an honest recognition of the highs and the lows. Can you savor the triumphs and gently forgive yourself for your missteps? In forgiving your younger self, it is important to remember that you did not know then what you know now.

After seven decades of life experience, there should be considerable insight into the intricacies of human subjectivity—an acceptance that there is never just a single isolated thought or feeling or motive. Rather, there is always ambivalence and a layered, nuanced complexity to our minds. One may remember important events somewhat differently every time they come to mind. Also, hopefully, one has learned to set wise and realistic goals. A ninety-year-old talked about scaling back his plans for each day so that he could complete his tasks and feel good about himself. Such a sensible adjustment to aging requires a humble and effortful revision of one's self-image.

In his *Garrison Keillor and Friends* column (July 14, 2023), the author describes his conflicts about trying to carry by himself his two bags (one large) and cup of hot coffee (the coffee tipped the scales, he later realized) on his way through a train station.

He was reluctant to ask for help from a baggage handler for fear that it would make him look overly privileged and unmasculine. He ultimately did ask for help, recognizing that "It was a profound moment: a man of eighty accepting his own eighty-ness."

Cosmic-Transcendental Consciousness. This Task, as described by Erikson, involves stepping back from the immediacy of daily activities to contemplate one's relationship with humanity, the natural world, and the infinite cosmos around us. For some, this sort of contemplation generates a feeling of kinship with wise elders of other times and places, and induces the experience of belonging to humankind, writ large. There is also the sobering realization that our span of years represents but a chance coincidence of our one-and-only life cycle with a discrete time and place in human history.

Some people experience a yearning to see themselves as a part of something larger, something more enduring. Much of Mary Oliver's poetry underscores our shared experiences with plants and small creatures in the natural world. As we will read later, neurologist and author Oliver Sachs, as he was dying, had an almost mystical experience gazing up at a night sky teeming with stars—he somehow simultaneously felt tiny to the point of insignificance, but also a part of something infinitely large. Carl Sagan, the late popular astronomer, was quoted famously as saying, "We are [all] made of stardust."

Some individuals focus on their ancestry, their genealogies, and their participation in venerable ethnic groups, and ancient tribal customs. Still others seek deep truths in the study of human history, philosophy or art. Lars Tornstam, a Swedish sociologist, has written extensively about 'Gerotranscendence'—he asserts that this spiritual-cosmic sensibility is a critically important and transformative final stage of human maturity and awareness.

Existential Consciousness. Coping with the deaths of family and friends, along with the anticipation of our own eventual demise, looms larger with each passing decade. The developmental Tasks of Generativity and Guardianship challenge us to remain invested in the future of the world, even though it may not benefit us personally. The jarring acceptance of our own mortality sternly challenges us to keep loving, even though we know that our loved ones will ultimately be taken from us, or us from them. Some seek to soften the threat of mortality by building some sort of legacy that will earn them honorable recognition, both now and after they are gone.

While the prospect of death may be the subject of fervent philosophic contemplation in one's twenties, most younger people subordinate its consideration to their yearnings for adventure, romance, career advancement, and sex. By mid-life, mortality has become far more than academic: it is the ultimate limit, the indifferent boundary to all our opportunities and aspirations. Some awaken in the middle of the night in a cold, heart-pounding sweat—the clock is ticking.

In listening to our elder interviewees, however, we were repeatedly surprised to hear how little fear of death they actually felt. Death was no longer shocking or disturbing; rather, it had become a constant companion. Sometimes there was anguish that they would not be around to see their grandkids grow up, or that they would miss an anticipated milestone event. Sometimes they were reassured that they would not have to live forever with the biting and burning of arthritic pain, or the humiliation of dehumanizing dementia.

Some, looking into the maw of eternal darkness, suddenly feel that all meaning and hope has been drained from life. Why bother? Or maybe they resort to a desperate 'carpe diem' hedonism. There is a radical alternative to this, as suggested by Emily Dickinson: "A Death blow is a Life blow to Some / Who till they died, did not alive become…"

Echoing that same theme, contemporary graphic autobiographer, Alison Bechdel, recently published *The Secret to Superhuman Strength*. When asked directly by National Public Radio's Fresh Air host Terry Gross, "So what IS the secret of superhuman strength?," Bechdel replied, simply, that it is the acceptance of our mortality.

Most authoritative of all, perhaps, is *New York Times* reporter John Leland's book, *Happiness Is a Choice You Make*, which summarizes his experience following six individuals, all over the age of eighty-five, for an entire year. All but one of this group was happy to be alive; in fact, they welcomed each day as a gift. When a new day is not taken for granted, the miracle of existence and human consciousness becomes vividly apparent. Orthodox Jews, upon awakening, thank God for allowing body and soul to come together, one more time. Maya Angelou learned a morning prayer from her grandmother: "Our Father, thank you for letting me see this New Day. Thank you that you didn't allow the bed I lay on last night to be my cooling board, nor my blanket my winding sheet…"

Now that we have provided you with an overview of Generativity, Self-Integrity, and Elder Identity Revision, we return to Frank's and Tony's *Life Stories* and examine how they are coping with the developmental Tasks of elderhood.

Frank's Life Story, Part 2 (91 years old)

Let us pick up Frank's *Life Story* from Chapter 3, starting in mid-adulthood and consider how he has been dealing with the last few decades.

Generativity. Frank retired as an extremely successful and moderately wealthy realtor, had numerous children and grandchildren, and has recently celebrated his seventieth wedding anniversary at an event that included more than forty guests. Currently, Frank and his wife spend much of their time with family, fellow parishioners, and a few neighbors. Their disabled son lives with them and, in fact, the couple moved into their current home many years ago because it was close enough to their son's workplace so that he could walk there, even during inclement weather.

Frank is full of advice and has many opinions to dispense—he is deeply invested in the younger generation and in its future. He is quick to welcome new people into their circumscribed and well-defined neighborhood and has made new friends of some of them. He exudes Generativity and Caring. He has been a pillar of his parish church for twenty-five years and brags that he "double-tithes" (i.e., contributes twice the expected ten percent of his income to the church). He is a tireless and unapologetic ambassador for his religion. Unprompted, he defended the Catholic Church with regard to the pedophile priest scandal, arguing that 300 "bad ones" out of 50,000 total priests "is pretty respectable." (Credible investigations commonly put the number of "bad ones" around 2,000.) Clearly, Frank embodies Guardianship as defined by Vaillant.

Self-Integrity. Frank readily describes the span of his life in the manner of someone who has thought a lot about it. He has put the pieces of this story together carefully in his mind. He is justifiably proud of his accomplishments, his productivity, and his integrity with respect to his values and consistency. Frank sees himself as having been basically the same person throughout his entire life. He is unusually comfortable with the prospect of his own mortality, in large part because he is absolutely convinced that, as a devout Catholic, he will go first to Purgatory for a period of time, and then on to Heaven, where he will be reunited with his parents and, at some point, his wife, children and their progeny. No uncertainty, no need to wonder—it is all laid out in clear and convincing detail according to Catholic doctrine.

EIR—Control. Frank feels confident that he can handle pretty much anything that comes his way. He has been retired for almost thirty years and he and his wife have repeatedly made decisions to keep their lifestyle as stable and unchanging as possible. What they cannot take care of themselves, they readily seek help for from others. One daughter is a nurse practitioner, one son is a financial adviser, and any number of their kids would come over to fix something in the house or yard. The couple can afford a weekly housekeeper, and they are quite comfortable cooking for themselves. They are fully in charge of their daily schedule, finances, and their social life.

Frank does take several medications every day, and he has used a cane for walking for some time now, but he seems to have accepted this accommodation gracefully. It is noteworthy that Frank's religious views give him a heightened sense of control—because of the certainty of his beliefs about both this world and the next. If he continues to play by the well-defined rules of his conservative version of Catholicism, he can claim moral righteousness now and eternal life in the hereafter.

EIR—Competence. Frank and his wife appear to be comfortable with finances, insurance policies, phones, computers (somewhat), and the mechanics of running a household. Frank can still play bridge and is reading some fairly challenging books. They seem to be as busy socially as they want to be. They have been in the same neighborhood, home, and church for more than twenty-five years. Neither Frank nor his wife have challenged themselves by trying to master a new social media platform or phone app, or by investing in cryptocurrency. They have stayed precisely in their lane and the status quo is good for them.

EIR—Connection. Frank has strong connections to his wife, his children, his grandchildren, and to a number of people in his church and neighborhood.

EIR—Continuity. As noted, Frank feels that he has stayed pretty much the same throughout his life. There is a downside to this enviable stability: many of his convictions have rigidified into dogmatic certainties and left him with an intolerance for those whose worldviews differ from his own. Even during this brief interview, he could not seem to contain his urge to proselytize for Catholicism. And his denial of the scope and consequences of the pedophilic priest scandal was disturbing. Even though he evangelized with a twinkle in his eye, at times he came across as pushy, morally superior, and condescending. In general, maybe the healthiest stance with regard to EIR Continuity is somewhere in the middle range between rigid consistency and confused instability.

EIR—Consciousness. Frank demonstrates little awareness of his faults and limitations. His self-image has minimized or excluded anything about which he might have felt remorseful or even doubtful about in the past. Perhaps receiving absolution from the priest in weekly confession meant he no longer needs to recall or even acknowledge his flaws and past injuries to others. Existentially, his religious cosmology unreservedly embraces an acceptance of mortality, with the assurance of an eternal afterlife tacked on for good measure. As for transcendental or universal consciousness, Frank is most cognizant of his family and his fellow Catholics—those outside that circle are to be converted or left to their well-deserved fates. There was little indication of any musings about the natural world, the expansiveness of the universe, distant history, or the future of humanity. Frank appears to be quite forceful and controlling with his family. Perhaps maintaining a narrow view of the world allows him to hold onto an exaggerated sense of control over the circumstances of his life, and his prospects in the hereafter as well.

Tony's Life Story, Part 2 (70 years old)

Returning to Tony's story from Chapter 3, let us consider where he stands relative to the psychosocial Tasks of elderhood.

Generativity. Despite his earlier vocational and financial successes, Tony's life as an elder looks quite impoverished. He is largely alienated from his children and has only a couple of close friends from college. There was no mention of anyone in the next generation that he is close to or really even cares about. Unlike Generative individuals, Tony never developed a 'post-narcissistic love' of humanity, nor has he moved on from a juvenile sense that the world he cares about revolves around him. Similarly, regarding Guardianship, there are no organizations, movements, or cultural institutions that he seems invested in contributing to or preserving.

Self-Integrity. Integrity derives from the fitting together of different aspects of your life and yourself, to construct a coherent autobiographical narrative, and a sense of self that feels cohesive, whole, and worthwhile. Tony had a lucrative and fairly prestigious career that many would have envied. However, he expressed little satisfaction about this, and thinks that he might have been happier as an academic. There was no mention of any individual or organization that significantly benefited from his professional expertise, no pride in a lifetime of work, or any hint that his work had made the world a better place for either individuals or for society.

Erikson writes of healthy individuals having confidence that their life has embodied a "proclivity for order and meaning"—a sense that all of life's pieces fit together, that life is not just random and chaotic.

Self-Integrity is usually accompanied by 'a different love of one's parents,' one softened by forgiveness and an appreciation for the vicissitudes of parenting. Tony never reconciled with his parents and he did not grieve their deaths. Rather than allowing his view of his parents to mature and evolve over time, especially in light of his own experiences as a parent, Tony has kept his adolescent resentments and grievances alive and readily accessible. He can invoke them at will to rationalize his own behavior, or to bolster his claim of having been victimized.

There were similar developmental arrests in the integration of his self-image and self-esteem. Although he had a generous salary for many years, he continues to worry that he still might run out of money. But, in the next breath, he also worries that he has too much: he expressed guilt about his large house and its "carbon footprint," and also about not giving more to charity. This confusing push-pull self-contradiction is sometimes called 'neuroticism,' which suggests a pronounced lack of integration of his ambivalent feelings. Tony's insecurity also was evident in his apparent effort to present himself to us in a curated way. His comments about his carbon footprint, charitable giving, "white privilege," and name dropping the "very popular book" that he was reading all felt like attempts to present himself as more 'woke' and idealistic than he actually is.

Similarly, despite many years of psychotherapy, Tony resists accepting responsibility for his behavior. For instance, he attributed his hot temper to an inherited family trait that he shared with his father and brother. When asked how close he is to being the person he wants to be, he responded, "Reasonably close...but I should give more to charity and live in a smaller house." The first statement appeared to be how he does think about himself, while the second seemed motivated by his awareness that he might have sounded too self-satisfied, so he tempered it with some generic social guilt.

Erikson noted that one indication of Despair, the antithesis of Integration, is an inability to accept the reality of one's one and only life cycle. When asked if he thinks about his own mortality, Tony replied that he is not ready to die; he wants to live to 100, climb Mt. Kilimanjaro, start a romantic relationship, and get his kids "established." And yet he seems immobilized in regard to all these goals. Tony had begun to get involved with some exercise classes and online dating opportunities when the COVID epidemic shut everything down. At the time of the interview, he was feeling quite lonely and isolated. He still lists his former wife as one of the few people he could count on in the event of an emergency.

EIR—Control. Tony does not experience any threats to his Control over his health, his finances, his daily schedule, or his living situation. His Autonomy is similarly unchallenged. On the other hand, his problems with social isolation seem insurmountable. His wife kicked him out of the house, and out of the marriage, his daughters do not want to have much to do with him, and the few casual friends he made at the exercise club are now sequestered. His two close friends from college are preoccupied with their own families and Tony does not seem to have any contact with anyone in his extended family. His social skills have never been a strong suit, and the restrictions and challenges of the pandemic made everything that much harder.

EIR—Competence. Tony enjoys a high level of competence with finances, computer and phone technology, contracts and paperwork, and with keeping his house, car, and yard in good shape. Again, his challenge lies in the social arena. Especially given the unique opportunities and constraints during a pandemic, Tony felt stuck and bewildered. He had initiated an online dating relationship, but then got distracted for a week or two at the outset of the first wave of infections, and the woman unilaterally ended it. He urgently wants another relationship but does not know how to go about meeting someone.

EIR—Connection. As noted, Tony feels most connected to some old college buddies that he has not seen in quite a while, but they are mostly unavailable. Other than these two longstanding relationships, which become more tenuous over time, Tony's life seems desperately barren. Despite his wife's angry rejection of him, Tony holds onto the hope that she would come to his rescue if he needed help. He is a lost and lonely man.

EIR—Continuity. Tony's internal self-representation is like an unfocused and fragmented image. He mostly presents himself as a self-made man, an individual who, after years of struggling, eventually extracted himself from a dysfunctional family and with great effort made himself into a professional and career success. But then, the picture of the successful executive-husband-father was shattered by his wife's intolerance of his temper outbursts, which he still tries to excuse as an inherited trait. He would like to portray himself as a workout warrior and book club intellectual, but his efforts to be persuasive are half-hearted. Similarly, he claims to be concerned about his daughters, but seems to have little idea of who they really are, what they feel or need, and in what directions their lives are headed. His Identity consolidation is as unsettled now as it was during his adolescence and early adulthood.

EIR—Consciousness. Tony has a highly limited self-reflective capacity. Maybe he is more honest with himself in private than he was with us, but we doubt it. His existential awareness is also paltry—he is living as if he has virtually unlimited time. His cosmic-transcendental consciousness is indiscernible. He is so preoccupied with his fundamental relationship deficits and self-esteem hungers that he has precious few resources available for any sort of contemplation of history, eternity, or his place in the world.

Observations and Conclusions

These *Aging Wisely* elders, Frank and Tony, embody dramatically different attachment styles and demonstrate highly discrepant responses to Erikson's developmental Tasks and to the additional challenges of EIR. Their overall life cycle trajectories demonstrate the interplay of inborn constitutional factors with childhood, adolescent, and adult experiences, and the presence or absence of current supportive and sustaining relationships.

We conclude Part One of *The Aging Wisely Project* hoping we have provided you with a useful model that describes the primary challenges and opportunities of human psychosocial development, and how various individuals respond to them. While each of our lives is unique, we hope that you have seen something of yourself in these *Life Stories,* and that the theoretical discussions have stimulated some memories and insights. Looking at one's life through a different set of lenses can be illuminating.

In Part Two, we will describe the primary factors and Healthy Habits™ that can make a substantial difference in our efforts to age wisely.

PART TWO
Minding Your Life Trajectory—GRASP

Introduction

We appreciate your choice to read *The Aging Wisely Project*. Part One described a basic model of psychological development, illustrated with case examples selected from among the fifty-two elders we interviewed. Clearly, some of these individuals present examples of exemplary aging while others are struggling, to one degree or another. A few of them have died since their interviews. We suspect that some of this material may have been challenging for those readers with little or no background in human psychological development—we have tried to be as comprehensible as possible, while still doing justice to the material.

The intellectual progress made over the past 120 years in understanding the workings and complexities of the human mind—how we become who we are, and how our character and Identity are forged—has been nothing short of extraordinary. It is not at all surprising that you may have felt a bit overwhelmed as we delved into the complexity of narrative coherence, detailed Attachment Theory, summarized Erikson's development model, and then introduced Elder Identity Revision (EIR).

Part Two of *The Aging Wisely Project* moves on from the developmental Tasks to the Tools that are critical for aging wisely. But, before we do, we believe it would be helpful to provide a brief overview and to add some context and perspective.

Historical Background

As the U.S. and Europe entered the 20th Century and the rigid moral constraints and confining social roles and structures of the Victorian Age relented, the Western world was primed to embrace a new worldview. Revolutionary thinkers were emerging in numerous fields and disciplines. Charles Darwin's theories about species evolution dismissed the Biblical accounts of *Genesis*, Friedrich Nietzsche declared that God was dead, and then Sigmund Freud's descriptions of the unconscious mind challenged cherished beliefs about our capacities for free will and self-determination.

Trained as a physician and neurologist, Freud originated the theory and the practice of psychoanalysis. He proposed that human beings had much more going on inside their heads than they were aware of at a conscious level. This was a shocking notion at the time—that our unconscious mind could powerfully influence our thoughts, motivations, and behaviors.

Later, after the first generation of psychoanalysts had energetically elaborated the implications of Freud's thinking, another dramatic theoretical shift occurred. John Bowlby and his colleagues began looking more closely, first at adolescents, then at children and even infants, and noticed how early bonding to caregivers (usually parents) established patterns for intimate relationships that would have enduring effects. Thus, Attachment Theory was born. Then along came Erik Erikson.

The Tasks for Aging Wisely

Erikson integrated Freud's internal psychological model with Bowlby's emphasis on attachment relationships, and then added additional insights about culture, as articulated by anthropologists and ethnologists. (Note: although Erikson did not explicitly credit Bowlby, his basic assumptions about the profound importance of intimate relationships, especially during childhood, spring from a psychological worldview that had been heavily influenced by more than a decade of Bowlby's publications.) Erikson's 'psychosocial theory' of development identified eight sequential stages, each of which was primarily organized around a pivotal Task, but which included both an internal psychological dimension and an interpersonal dimension. As a model of progressive development, each stage was built sequentially on the outcomes of prior stages.

Given that our society's current elders, the Baby Boomers, are generally living much longer and healthier lives than were elders when Erikson first devised his theory, we concluded that a ninth developmental Task should be appended to Erikson's original model. Accordingly, we have proposed Elder Identity Revision (EIR) as the final developmental Task.

In some ways, EIR is highly reminiscent of the adolescent stage experienced many decades earlier. Adolescence represented a time when we learned to integrate newfound freedoms and autonomy with emerging strengths and functionalities— physical, cognitive, emotional, social, and sexual. In elderhood, by contrast, we are dealing with the losses of capabilities and people, rather than the gains. The essence of this Task, as one of our elders informed us, is to continually pivot and adapt as internal and external changes present themselves. EIR involves revising and reshaping our Identity so that we can preserve our coherent Self-Integrity as we approach the end of our lives. As described in Chapter 4, EIR encompasses the five-fold Task of responding adaptively and effectively to the challenges of Control, Competence, Connection, Continuity, and Consciousness (the 5 C's).

As we reflected on the inspiring *Life Stories* of our *Aging Wisely* elders, we realized that, while we began to notice patterns and themes, each elder's tale stood on its own as a unique human accomplishment. Each of us moves through Erikson's developmental stages, and our EIR stage, during a particular time and place in human history. We all inherit a unique set of strengths and deficits, and we are shaped and influenced by the specific people and events that we encounter. Hearing from so many dazzlingly varied individuals left us feeling a tremendous amount of respect, even awe, for what each of us has to go through to forge a personal Identity and a meaningful life.

The Tools for Aging Wisely

On the basis of these extremely varied *Life Stories*, and augmented by our own experiences with friends, family, and our own personal development, we intuitively identified five factors that are most influential in predicting how well people age. These are the Tools for aging wisely, and we have labeled them as the Healthy Habits: Gratitude, Resilience, Active Practices, Self-Acceptance, and Purpose (GRASP™).

We knew we needed to subject the intuitive *Aging Wisely* approach to a more objective, scientific scrutiny, so we engaged an outside statistician to conduct a rigorous analysis of our data (see Appendix). From the outset, we were determined to propose a theory, and to make recommendations, based on several lines of evidence. This is why we began with a review of the literature, conducted fifty-two first-person interviews, and then immersed ourselves in the data, striving to notice patterns and trends. We then collaborated in a rigorous statistical analysis, utilizing two sets of independent scores. It was our hope that a significant convergence would emerge from the confluence of these different methodologies.

Warning: Statistics!

As mentioned in Chapter 1, Ben and Scott independently scored thirty variables immediately after each interview. We compared scores and reconciled any scores that were significantly divergent. The items scored for each elder covered a wide range of variables: Erikson's developmental Tasks, EIR, attachment factors, Healthy Habits, and the elders' characteristics during the interview (this included items such as mood, anxiety, openness, and sense of humor). The final item was the *Aging Wisely* score, which represented our global subjective impression about how wisely each interviewee was aging. (See Appendix for a complete list of scored variables and their computed correlations.) Our primary request to the statistician was to determine which of the individual items, or combination of items, best predicted the overall *Aging Wisely* score for each of our elders. We wanted to be confident that we had indeed identified the primary factors driving healthy elderhood before making any recommendations about how to fashion a healthier lifestyle.

We were understandably pleased when the data confirmed that four of the five Healthy Habits correlated very strongly with the overall *Aging Wisely* score: Gratitude, Resilience, Self-Acceptance, and Purpose. (The one outlier, Active Practices, had a fairly high correlation, but one that fell outside the top tier. We will offer our explanation for this later.)

In addition to these four Healthy Habits, two other items correlated very highly: Connection (one of the EIR Sub-Tasks) and Erikson's final developmental Task, Self-Integrity. These top six variables seemed most essential for healthy aging. Statistically, combining any three of these six factors predicted more than 99 percent of the actual variance of the *Aging Wisely* scores. This was robust evidence that these factors are the Tools that will provide you with the leverage to make changes in the trajectory of your elder development.

On to the Tools

As we move into Part Two, we describe each of these six variables in detail and elaborate the rationale for their inclusion as Tools. We include specific strategies for enhancing these attitudes and implementing these practices. We appreciate that the implementation of this 'Toolkit' must be customized for each person, based on individual strengths and weaknesses, and also on one's motivations and resources.

We also acknowledge that translating these insights into actionable goals and new habits is not easy. Unlike most 'self-help' books, *The Aging Wisely Project* does not promise easy answers or quick fixes. We provide a rationale and a pathway for change. In our final chapter, we describe some of the empirically validated strategies for setting and accomplishing goals (Chapter 11).

Our overall intention is quite clear: we want to help you lengthen your life span and invigorate your health span. Read on and consider what changes may help you.

5

Purpose—Meaning Is Essential

As we age, staying active and moving forward can become increasingly difficult, and those with 'grit' have a distinct advantage. Albert Einstein compared life to riding a bicycle, saying "To keep your balance, you must keep moving." Grit powers us to find and to follow a purposeful path despite the challenges we face.

Psychological research has determined that 'grit' is a combination of passion for reaching one's goals, plus the perseverance to keep moving toward them, even when faced with obstacles. With students, for instance, those with more grit earned higher grades and greater scholastic accomplishments. Among our Healthy Habits scores, the highest statistical correlation was between Purpose and Resilience. Those elders with passionate Purpose were Resilient when challenged by stress or adversity, and those with greater Resilience maintained stronger Purpose. We all yearn for the good times but we must also struggle through the tough times to get there.

One challenge during our fifty-two interviews was to discern just what motivated these elders to get out of bed in the morning, to make plans, and to get things done. (How would you score yourself on this item?) Was this motivation weak or strong, and was it consistent from day to day? Did they do what they did with interest and enthusiasm, or with a sense of obligation and burden? Were there people that they were eager to see, and projects that excited them? And were these motivations sustained, even after major losses or life disruptions?

Curiously, research surveys show that most people tend to be preoccupied by goals that offer only fleeting pleasures. In her thoughtful and well-researched book, *The Power of Meaning: Finding Fulfillment in a World Obsessed With Happiness*, Emily Esfahani Smith makes a persuasive case that the things that most people think will make them happy—like a more attractive body, a new car, a larger house, more sex or money or fame—do not actually have a lasting effect. Surprisingly, those who win huge lottery prizes are no happier a year or two later. Emile Durkheim, founder of the field of sociology, made the surprising discovery that individuals who have higher incomes, more education, plenty to eat, and freedom from the restrictions of family or religion also have higher suicide rates than the poor and uneducated. Does having to struggle just to survive somehow give life more meaning?

A recently published investigation involved a phone bank of solicitors who called university alumni for donations, a rather tedious job.[8] A number of these workers were given the opportunity to meet one of the students who had personally benefited from their efforts. These were kids who would not have been able to attend such an elite school without the scholarship money that these solicitors had raised. After meeting with students, these donation solicitors began spending 50 percent *more* time on each call, and they raised almost *twice* as much money as their counterparts who had not met with a student. The staff in the study derived more meaning from their work after getting to know a beneficiary of their effort, which significantly improved their morale and productivity.

The Power of Meaning

Smith's *The Power of Meaning* emphasizes four principles that she called 'pillars of meaning': belonging, Purpose, storytelling, and transcendence. (We have modified these category labels slightly to make them more congruent with the larger body of psychological research and with our own findings.)

Belonging: Relationships

For most of us, our spouses, our children, our families, and our friends provide us with the Purpose to keep going. If we are fortunate, we have someone to notice when we get depressed, someone with whom we can share our happy moments, someone we know we can depend on in a crisis. Reciprocally, there is someone we can care for and support when they need us. Most people do not thrive in isolation.

Viktor Frankl, author of *Man's Search for Meaning*, was an Austrian psychiatrist who spent three years in a Nazi concentration camp. There, he noticed that just wanting to survive the ordeal was not sufficient. The people who survived had someone they wanted to be with, someone to take care of when they got out. During the recent COVID pandemic, many people who were reluctant to get a vaccine to protect themselves were willing to do it to protect their families.

In addition to intimate relationships, we also make significant human connections with communities of people. As already mentioned, psychologist Susan Pinker termed this the 'Village Effect.' Knowing that you belong—that you have a recognized role within the group and feel accepted by that group—can mean a great deal. In a small town or a close-knit urban neighborhood, there may be a favorite coffee shop, a tavern, a group exercise class, or potluck dinners at the church, synagogue, or mosque. In the TV sitcom *Cheers*, the gang at the bar would reliably shout out "Norm!" every time this regular patron came through the door. Who would not want such a warm welcome?

Intimate relationships, by contrast, involve deeper person-to-person engagements and attunements. Optimally, there is a powerful sense of knowing and being known, of being accepted and affirmed, just as you are. It is deeply satisfying, after a long separation from an old friend, to pick up a conversation precisely where you left off years earlier. Two generations of primary investigators with the Harvard Study of Adult Development, George Vaillant and Robert Waldinger, concluded that nothing was more important for healthy elderhood than secure adult attachments. While it is widely held that children need a secure attachment to thrive, our culture has been slow to accept this critically important need *throughout* the human life cycle.

Purpose: Making the World Better

Frankl also detected a second sort of motivation in the Holocaust survivors that he had suffered with: they had a project, a goal, a passion for something that they needed to complete. For one scientist, it was a book he was determined to write. For someone else, it was taking care of fellow camp prisoners. In elders today, it might be a determination to start a safe house for abused women, protecting an endangered species, adopting stray dogs or cats, collaborating on a community garden, becoming a foster parent, or keeping an endangered tribal language alive. The list goes on and on. Like other world religions, Judaism strongly promotes a core value referred to as '*tikkun olam*' in Hebrew (repairing the world)—trying, in ways large and small, to make the world a better place.

Lie detector tests, although not infallible, base their effectiveness on humans having an underlying ethical sensibility. Except for career criminals, and others trained to deceive, lying causes a disturbance in heart rate and variations in breathing or sweating that the machine can detect. Most of us know that lying is not okay. Similarly, humans have a fairly reliable awareness about which activities will help or hurt others. If you make a nice dinner for your family, or help organize a Fourth of July parade, or volunteer at the hospital, you feel good about yourself. Part of the wisdom of growing old is discovering things that you enjoy doing that also help others.

In one research study, individuals were given $20.[9] Half were told to spend it on themselves, and the other half were instructed to spend it on someone else. Later that day, both groups reported feeling happier. However, contacted many days later, only those who had given to others were still feeling happier. Human beings are wired to be social creatures.

As many people get older, they begin to feel irrelevant and fear that no one needs them. This can trigger a crisis of confidence and a loss of Purpose. Maybe the kids are up and out and you are retired from your job. In the movie *About Schmidt*, Jack Nicholson's recently retired character is devastated when he sees that his meticulously prepared office files, accumulated over many years, had been unceremoniously tossed in the dumpster. His work was no longer valued or needed, and neither was he. In the Auschwitz concentration camp, Frankl found that many of his fellow prisoners felt they had nothing more to live for and had lost all hope. He exhorted these men to realize that the future was still expecting something from them, and that they were still needed. This message was amplified by the person of Frankl himself, who continued to function as a therapist, despite his demeaning and inhuman circumstances.

Epidemiological research has found that, compared to elders with a strong sense of Purpose, those with low Purpose die seven years sooner, and they are also at higher risk for early dementia.[10] How could this be? Darwin's theories of survival of the fittest and natural selection focus on the individual's ability to survive and pass on their genes. The field of sociobiology, however, looks at evolutionary theory as it applies to the survival of groups rather than individuals. A sociobiologist would see a connection between purposefulness and longevity by observing that those individuals who no longer contribute constructively to the group actually jeopardize the survival of everyone else. They consume food and utilize resources that could help sustain other more productive members of the tribe.

In the same way that our biologic processes have been shaped by Darwinian forces, they have also been shaped by sociobiological ones. There are lesser-known biological mechanisms such as autophagia (which 'self-eats' neuronal waste products in the brain that cause dementia) and apoptosis (which triggers cell death in unused neurons) that operate by the 'use it or lose it' principle. For those with active, socially engaged minds, these mechanisms keep our brain nimble and efficient by eliminating metabolic waste and unused brain cells. With sedentary, isolated individuals, these destructive processes are turned against the self, resulting in neuronal destruction. Over time, this results in the demise of the individual, but it makes the group stronger. This is the cell biology version of the myth about elderly Eskimos being put on an ice floe when they can no longer contribute. Use it on behalf of the tribe...or lose it.

Although there is widespread ageism in our culture that disparages the vitality and competence of elders, many of our most prominent governmental and business leaders are in their sixties and seventies. In the 2020 U.S. presidential race, Biden (seventy-seven), Trump (seventy-four), Sanders (seventy-eight), and Warren (seventy-one) each vied for the presidency. Although innovations in science and technology tend to be generated by younger brains, elders are rightfully appreciated for their steady, experience-rich knowledge, perspective, and judgment. They are less driven by hormonally fueled aggression or lust, and the wisest of them has moved beyond narrow narcissistic self-aggrandizement. Seniors focus less on immediate gratification and thus are better at taking the 'long view.' This helps explain why corporate governance boards, religious hierarchies, and large charitable organizations tend to be led by Medicare-eligible individuals.

On a more personal level, elders in large families are often important in keeping the clan together and in helping to resolve disputes and petty rivalries. When the matriarch or patriarch dies, often these groups splinter and family members become estranged. The mere presence of elders, the moral example they set, and the stable demeanor they exude, can inspire others to be their 'best selves.' In the animal kingdom, for example, when elephant herd matriarchs are killed, the young males in the herd tend to run berserk and attempt to copulate with every nearby female. Elders help steady the sometimes-erratic moral compasses of the young.

Rabbi Zalman Schachter-Shalomi's insightful book, *From Age-ing to Sage-ing*, is based on the conviction that elders add more value to society than either they or others often realize. Elder sages embody the psychological maturity and ethical foundation that help maintain order and civility in our societies. Schachter-Shalomi emphasizes the importance of embracing and enhancing elders' roles as sages in our communities, a process that requires elders to take themselves seriously. It is curious how many people who fondly remember the influential elders in their own lives consistently overlook their own opportunities to serve in the same role for the next generation. To fully inhabit the Identity as a sage demands a concerted effort in a culture that systemically dismisses, discounts, or degrades elders.

Storytelling: Integrity, Integration, and Identity

Throughout our lives, we put a great deal of effort into creating, for ourselves and others, a personal Identity or, as Smith would put it, our *Life Story*. As noted previously, this Identity powerfully influences who we think we are, how we do things, and how we relate to people. It is the most concise expression of our values and our character. Entering a novel environment where we cannot freely be ourselves jeopardizes our integrity and makes us feel uncomfortable, which engages the EIR Sub-Task of Continuity. This can happen, in a rather concentrated way, when moving from a private home into a communal living facility, or when relocating to a new city.

After such 'dislocations,' finding ways to be ourselves again and to forge new connections can be critically important. There may be opportunities to join an exercise class, an art or gardening club, or a reading group. Even simply initiating a conversation with new people in a communal dining room or at a local coffee shop can reinforce your confidence that you are still appealing to others and that you have maintained effective social skills. Being willing to practice new or old-but-rusty behaviors is essential for this pivoting effort.

Ancient Stoic philosophers underscored the importance of continuing to be your best self, even during times of hardships, exile, or even imminent death. They urged us not to whine or give up. Marcus Aurelius wrote, "Shame on the soul, to falter on the road of life while the body still perseveres." Pull up your socks and keep going! Epictetus added, "Every difficulty in life presents us with an opportunity to turn inward and invoke our own submerged inner resources." It is deeply meaningful to prove to yourself that you can maintain your integrity, no matter what. In a legendary story about a Biblical prophet, a young boy questioned the aged man as to why he continued to rail against injustice and corruption when so many people just mocked him as an old fool. The prophet replied, "I preach not just to change the world, but to keep the world from changing me."

Early one morning in the concentration camp, Frankl was on his way to a dreary work site when he experienced an epiphany. A casual conversation with a fellow prisoner reminded him of his wife Tilly. At that moment, he was cold and hungry, he had not seen his wife for a long time, and he was facing a long day of grueling labor under the watchful eyes of sadistic guards. Nevertheless, the memory of Tilly's smile and her frank and encouraging look lifted his spirits and infused him with hope. This flash of memory led Frankl to two profound insights: first, that human salvation is through love; and secondly, that our last freedom—something that no one can take away from us—is our capacity to choose our own attitude and how we respond to the circumstances of our life. Frankl thought about the few brave souls in the camp who walked through the huts comforting others and giving away their meager rations of bread. These individuals maintained their dignity during the most dehumanizing conditions imaginable.

Scott's father-in-law, Jack Welner, told a story about his time in a labor camp near the Dachau concentration complex. Weak and starving, he was out one day with a work crew that was lifting and moving heavy railroad ties from one location to another. Too tired to continue, he dropped his end of the lumber, bringing on a severe beating from one of the guards. Sixty years later, he did not recall the pain or the extent of his injuries—what he remembered was his silent, angry vow to himself that he would outlive this guard. And Jack did survive. Although he attributed his survival primarily to blind luck, he also would admit that uppermost in his mind had been his goal to survive the camp, find his two sisters and make sure that they were safe—purposeful goals that he achieved.

The magnetic strength in a bar of iron depends on how the iron molecules are aligned. If the positive poles of these molecules all point in one direction, and all the negative ones the opposite way, then the magnetic force will be maximized. However, if a hammer blow forcefully strikes the iron bar, the molecules will be displaced and disoriented, and the magnetic force will be diminished. It is similar with human character: the more consistent we are about our priorities, and the more we align our actions accordingly, the more robust and alive we become. Neurotic anxiety and inhibition, which torment many people and often becomes the focus of psychotherapy, arise from unresolved conflicts, from opposing energies working at cross-purposes. This sort of inner misalignment enfeebles what Epictetus called our 'inner resources,' and what Frankl described as our 'capacity,' in the face of adversity, to control our attitude as well as our actions.

So how can we resolve these internalized conflicts and improve the coherence of our Identity? Deeply entrenched conflicts may require professional psychotherapy. However, a growing body of research suggests that readily accessible activities, such as journaling and meditation, can be hugely impactful.

James Pennebaker, a social psychologist at the University of Texas at Austin, has been a pioneer in the field of expressive writing. Pennebaker took note of research that suggested that when psychological trauma is kept secret, and not shared with anyone, there will be an increased risk of depression, emotional instability, and medical problems such as heart disease and cancer. Over the last forty years, Pennebaker and his collaborators have demonstrated repeatedly that expressing your painful secrets in writing can make a profound difference.[11] Students who wrote about the worst traumas of their lives, for just fifteen minutes a day, for three to four days, subsequently earned better grades. They were less depressed and suffered less from anxiety. They needed fewer doctor visits, had lower blood pressures and slower heart rates, showed improved immune system functioning, and enjoyed an elevated sense of wellbeing. Wow!

Importantly, these benefits were greatest in those who were most earnest in trying to make sense of their trauma: why it might have happened, how they might have avoided it, and how it had affected them over time. Sometimes there were new insights, for instance, that they could have been hurt even worse, or hurt at an earlier age, when they had been even more vulnerable. Some of these students had been gratified by the social support they had received after telling someone. Some realized how surviving the trauma had made them appreciate life more. These are examples of 'benefit finding.'

Pennebaker also noticed that those who gained the most insight were the ones who could 'step back' from their initial strong emotional reactions and look at events from a reflective distance, or maybe consider them from another person's perspective. Those who were able to be more self-reflective in these ways evinced an incremental progression in their narratives, with the later versions becoming smoother, more integrated and coherent. (This converges with our earlier description of narrative coherence and anticipates what we later describe as Self-Integrity.)

Moreover, these insightful individuals appeared to be weaving these previously split-off, unincorporated traumatic memories into their autobiographical narratives, and into their personal Identities. There is an instructive analogy here to what happens when food is digested: experiences that are not reflected upon remain as psychological 'lumps' inside us, causing problems such as post-traumatic flashbacks, unconscious anxieties, and unexplained impulses. By contrast, events and feelings that are imaginatively reflected upon are broken down into their constituent components, associated with related life experiences, and then the useful elements are digested and incorporated into our existing Identity. Such a process makes us stronger.

This sort of thinking converges with the burgeoning literature about 'post-traumatic growth.' Surprisingly, of those exposed to a traumatic event—such as having been close to a September 11 terrorist attack site—only about one-third develop a post-traumatic stress disorder (PTSD). Conversely, almost two-thirds demonstrate some personal growth, such as a strengthening of their resilience or an enhanced gratitude that their life was spared.[12]

By the time someone reaches elderhood, they have inevitably experienced significant losses and probably at least some kind of trauma. With regard to the psychological impact of these adversities, the individual's coping style matters as much as the severity of the trauma. Those who did their best to honestly remember and reflect upon these painful experiences—and the associated anger, guilt, shame, and despair—grew in maturity and became more integrated. This is how strong, coherent Identities are forged and how a powerful sense of meaning develops. As with rebuilding a heavily damaged house, the rebuilding can proceed with more experience and expertise than was available at the time of the original construction.

Alternatively, those who deal with painful or shameful situations by denying, repressing, or escaping into fantasy set themselves up for neurotic conflicts and inhibitions, or worse. Their internal psychological structures evolve to divert, compartmentalize, repress, or override their authentic feelings and deeper thoughts. Inconsistencies, immaturities, and self-contradictions plague their personal narratives and their Identities, as we will see shortly in Daniel's *Life Story*. With a compromised Self-Integrity, they enter elderhood with a fragile and easily disorganized character structure. These psychological difficulties can be further compounded if the individual's attempts at coping lead them in the direction of social isolation, loneliness, and alcohol and drug misuse.

Transcendence: Connection to Something Greater

The final pillar of meaning in Smith's model concerns striving to establish a connection with something greater than oneself, which corresponds to the EIR Sub-Task of Spiritual Consciousness. Some people find substantial meaning in organized religion, some in more individualistic spirituality. As the prospect of death looms ever closer, many yearn to connect themselves with ancestors, with their extended family, and with their progeny. There may be a sudden interest in genealogy, in scrapbooking, family mementos, or in organizing family photos. World history, classical literature, and philosophy may appear to offer important clues. Others turn to a study of the cosmos, to the infinities of time and space. Many begin to notice the small miracles in their gardens, the subtleties of seasonal rhythms, or the personalities and calls of songbirds.

The subject of religion is, of course, one of monumental complexity. The etymology of 'religion' comes from the Latin for *ligate*, a tying to (e.g., to a creed, an organized group, to specific liturgies and rituals), while 'spirituality' derives from the Latin root for breath and respiration. The former is from the outside in, while the latter is from the inside out, although there is considerable overlap. As much as Vaillant's *Aging Well* book impressed us in many ways, some of our findings differed decisively. He concluded that neither spirituality nor religiosity was associated with successful aging, whereas our findings were quite the opposite.

The concept of 'Gerotranscendence' first articulated by Lars Tornstam, a Swedish sociologist, stands in stern opposition to Vaillant's views. Tornstam asserted that spiritual transcendence, examples of which we have mentioned above, represents a critically important and highly desirable final developmental step for everyone. In our own sample, many of our highest-scoring individuals drew great strength from either their religion (see the examples of Omar in this chapter, or Gloria in Chapter 2) or a deep well of spirituality (Ann in Chapter 6).

For Ben and Scott, who are both more secular than religiously observant, this was an unexpected finding in our *Aging Well* interviews. Our more conscientiously religious elders seemed to derive great comfort from the certainties provided by their faith. They did not struggle to the same degree with the existential questions that plague others: Why are we here? How are we supposed to live? What happens after we die? With regard to such matters, religions offer comfort and serenity to many of their adherents. Those of us on the outside, looking in, are left to debate, to ignore, or to continue to seek—which may promote personal growth, if one can tolerate the uncertainty.

We have chosen two *Life Stories* to illustrate how the presence or absence of meaning and Purpose are powerfully influential.

Omar's Life Story (79 years old)

Omar impressed us immediately with his welcoming engagement, his youthful vitality, and his open-hearted candor. This was even more surprising when we learned just how many traumas and tribulations he had endured during his life. For starters, he was the seventeenth of the family's twenty-one children. (He choked up momentarily when acknowledging that he has only four siblings still living.)

When Omar was just seven years old, in 1948, Israel's war of independence with five Arab nations forced him and his family, along with hundreds of thousands of other Palestinians, to flee their ancestral homeland. No matter your politics, this was a significant and traumatic event for many people. Ten of his father's fleet of thirteen taxis were destroyed, and they took the three remaining vehicles with them to Egypt, where the family remained in exile for six years. When they finally returned home to Jerusalem, they found that their house had been stripped bare, with even the window frames torn out of the walls. Omar was thirteen by then and his father told him that he was now a man and needed to find an after-school job. He found one and earned the equivalent of $20 dollars per week, a sum that helped augment the family budget. The family still needed to scrounge for food and stand in line for hours waiting to receive handouts from a United Nations relief program.

During the interview, Omar sobbed briefly when recalling his family's humiliation and hardship. Quickly recovering his composure, he went on to explain how these early experiences motivated him, as an adult, to volunteer time and to donate money to the United Way. "No one should have to be that poor," he said. Omar is a passionate man, quick to feel and express a wide range of emotions, from happiness to sadness to anger, but he rapidly returns to a stable and balanced equilibrium.

His generosity of spirit had obvious roots: Omar described his father as a kind, affectionate man who just loved kids and who went out of his way to care for his neighbors. Omar had fond memories of his father making sweets and teaching him to be kind to others. Omar was even closer to his mother, who told him religious stories and who would sometimes give the family's limited supply of bread to beggars, telling Omar, "Allah will provide for us." And He did. Omar is still impressed that his older brothers took over the taxi business after their father suffered a heart attack at age forty. Omar was proud that one of his brothers learned to speak seven languages, so that he could get work translating and leading tours for a wide variety of international tourists. These siblings spoiled Omar, giving him candy and other treats when they could.

Omar's pride and nostalgia for his childhood family was punctuated by the anger he felt at the British, French, and Jordanian governments, especially King Hussein of Jordan, for mistreating and betraying Palestinians. But Omar was also candid about some of his own missteps, for instance, when a reckless bicycle ride resulted in two broken arms. Being forced to withdraw from school and reduced to being fed by others, Omar felt quite sorry for himself. His philosophic mother responded by commenting that this would make a wonderful story to tell his children someday. Omar's predominant mood, however, was one of gratitude for all the loving care and exemplary moral and religious guidance he received growing up in Cairo and Jerusalem.

Omar's reputation in high school was that of a friendly, popular kid. He is still close to some of his surviving teenage friends and proudly mentioned some of their academic and career accomplishments. He did well in school himself, especially with Arabic studies. As a student Omar enjoyed wide-ranging intellectual interests that included history, art, and culture. He went on to university in Cairo, where he majored in Middle Eastern history. He now regrets having gotten involved in political demonstrations that resulted in him being beaten and jailed. He chuckled when remembering how he and his friends were obsessed with having sex, but they held back because of their religious beliefs and because they could not afford to marry at that point in life.

After college Omar struggled to figure out his career path, but eventually decided that, even though he thought of the U.S. as an enemy of his people, he wanted to join his sister. She had married years earlier and moved to the American Midwest. Because she had already sponsored five of his brothers to come to America, she was reluctant to loan him the money he needed. However, she eventually relented after he threatened (not seriously, he added) to join the Palestine Liberation Organization (PLO) and become a terrorist.

Once in the U.S., Omar immediately got work and repaid the family loan for his plane ticket. He can still remember being paid $2.64 per hour as a stock boy, and then $3.48 hourly at his next job (he was obviously counting his pennies!). His was a classic American success story, working hard at each job he was given, and showing the intelligence, diligence, initiative, and social skills to be promoted quickly to the next level. Ultimately, he rose to the position of vice president of production at a mid-sized manufacturing firm in Cleveland. He married another Palestinian immigrant and together they have raised and supported numerous children and grandchildren.

Omar retired in 2007, giving him and his wife a chance to travel, which they love to do. They have traveled to a half-dozen European countries, Egypt, and Kuwait. He also journeyed on a pilgrimage to Mecca—one of the five pillars of Islam—which gave him forgiveness for his sins.

Omar joked that, after several years of retirement, his wife got sick of him hanging around the house, so he and a friend started a charitable organization that provided free labor for house renovation projects for impoverished seniors. He also helped raise money to build a new neighborhood mosque. Several years ago, during a visit with his daughter and grandchildren in Sacramento, California, he was blindsided when his wife and daughter handed him the keys to his new home! Although he regretted leaving his many friends in the Midwest, the prospect of being close to his daughter and her family was irresistible.

Omar is busy in his new neighborhood. In addition to fundraising to build a new mosque, he goes to the old mosque five times per day (starting at 5 a.m.) and also leads an ongoing elder support group. Predictably, he is developing a diverse circle of friends. Omar is physically and mentally active: walking, cycling, playing pickle ball, reading, and working on puzzles. His wife cooks and he cleans. She lets him do whatever he wants, and eat whatever he wants, and he gives her the same freedoms. He is very happy in his marriage.

Omar has experienced some health problems: he has required five heart stints, has been treated for bladder cancer, and recently came down with a bout of pneumonia. Nevertheless, he feels ten years younger than his actual age. As noted, he does regret exposing himself as a teenager to police violence due to his political protesting. Omar also regrets not having gotten back in time to see his mother on her deathbed when he was detained for twelve hours at the Tel Aviv airport by Israeli security. (Because a brother had been killed by Israeli soldiers years earlier, Omar's name was on a terrorist watch list. His eyes flashed with anger when he talked about having been "treated like an animal" while in detention.) He also regrets having smoked cigarettes for fifty years and he wishes he had been afforded the opportunity for more education.

Throughout the interview, Omar expressed a genuine sense of gratitude for all the blessings in his life, and an absolute devotion to his family, his community, and to Allah. When we complimented him for his sturdy self-confidence, even in the face of setbacks, he replied, "Yes, thank Allah." He has no unfinished business and feels that he has met all the goals that he had set for himself. When there are problems beyond his control, he is content to leave them to Allah.

He concluded by saying that he is doing his best to enjoy life, love others, give to charity, do right, be with people, talk with the birds, and live in the present. Wow, what an impressive guy! In significant ways, Omar reminded Scott of his father-in-law, Jack. Both suffered significant and prolonged traumas in childhood and young adulthood. Despite that, they maintained a common focus in elderhood—family and friends, helping others, gratitude in a tough world, experiencing joy in each day. These are precisely the aging wisely recommendations that we will be making.

Daniel's Life Story (73 years old)

Daniel presented at the interview as an articulate, well-groomed, tall gentleman in a dapper sports coat, which made him the best dressed man of our entire sample. Within the first few minutes, he let us know that he was the only male in his family to live past forty-five, and that he had earned an "advanced degree," which turned out to be a Bachelor's in literature. He repeatedly seemed to be trying to impress us: he said that he started every day by completing the crossword puzzle in *The Wall Street Journal*, which usually took him about fifty minutes. He dropped the names of George Eliot and David Foster Wallace as a few of his favorite authors. He claimed to be walking three hours per day and explained that he had recently gained some weight due to overeating sweets. However, his attempts to present himself in a positive light soon were undermined by the story he told us of his life.

Daniel grew up in a poor family in a small town in Nebraska. He described his father, a truck driver and part-time accountant, as a "happy drunk" who died young. Daniel's mother also struggled off and on with alcohol misuse, but was generally a bright, competent woman. Daniel was the star baseball player at his school, which made him the center of attention in his family, who loved to watch him perform on the field. He was also academically gifted—he earned several advanced placement credits in high school and went on to major in English at the University of Nebraska. Daniel was a bit of a class clown in high school, but mostly stayed out of trouble, especially because he did not want to jeopardize his athletic eligibility. This attitude continued into college, where his overly strict baseball coach threatened to withdraw his scholarship if he joined a fraternity. Daniel's baseball talents even enabled him to play some semi-pro ball after college.

After graduating, Daniel worked a variety of jobs. He had learned accounting from his father, and he helped keep the business going after his dad's death. He also drove a taxi for a time and even dabbled as a stockbroker. Free from the oversight of his college coach, Daniel began to drink, apparently quite heavily. He intentionally let his weight balloon to more than 400 pounds, which earned him a 4F classification (physically unfit to serve) with the Selective Service just as the military draft was ramping up during the Vietnam War. He added that he was not proud of this purposeful act. When we interjected that we were in no position to judge him, he defensively flared up and curtly told us that he had not been "looking for affirmation," but then meekly thanked us.

What really appealed to Daniel was betting on horses at the racetrack—his "life was spent at the track" for the next twenty-five years. He also had "some kind of job" to help support himself during this time but would not specify exactly which job or jobs those were.

Daniel admitted that he had not been close to his dad because he had "just drifted away from him," especially after his dad began wasting away from alcoholism. He did not mention the deaths of his mother or siblings. When asked about who had been the hardest person to lose in his life, he only brought up his buddies from the track and the bars that he had frequented. Daniel did marry his college girlfriend, and they were reportedly happy together for several years until she pressured him to start a family. Once their son was born, marital strife rapidly escalated. Daniel complained that his wife was "no longer the same person." She had changed from a fun-loving girl into someone who sounded more like a mother. She repeatedly nagged him about spending evenings with his drinking buddies.

So, Daniel decided to get out of the marriage. With no further explanation offered, Daniel casually mentioned that his childless sister and her husband later adopted his son. Daniel boasted that he had helped his son by advising him to choose to study something that would help him earn "a certificate" or some sort of professional license. He added that his son initially studied computer science and then went on to law school. Upon further questioning, Daniel reluctantly admitted that he and his son have not had any contact for the past five years. He quickly explained that this was due to his having been admitted to Denver Health hospital five years ago for alcohol-related dementia. He also claimed to have been "over-prescribed" opiates for his chronic back pain. The hospital social worker helped him qualify for Section 8 housing, making him eligible for his current Medicaid-subsidized senior living facility. Daniel claims to have maintained his sobriety since leaving the hospital.

With regard to his current life, Daniel denies being lonely "because I fight it" but admits that most of his drinking buddies and race-track companions have died or lost contact with him. Over the past five years he has not made any new friends from among the 400 residents at his facility. His greatest current pleasures are doing crossword puzzles and watching comedy movies, and he mentioned an obscure film from decades ago (to impress us?). When he is in a "down mood" he thinks about horse races or baseball games from the past. He denies having any regrets, although he thought maybe he should have studied something more practical than literature in college and made fewer losing bets. And, oh yes, maybe he should have stuck with the marriage. But he denies being disappointed because he had never really decided on any life goals to begin with anyway.

Regarding his bucket list of things still to do, he was looking forward to betting on the Kentucky Derby with some of the government pandemic relief money he had recently received. He is frustrated and confused by modern technology, such as computers and smart phones. Daniel said he tries not to think about the possibility of becoming disabled or dying, and just lives one day at a time. He struggled somewhat with suicidal thoughts during high school and college, but then decided that it was easier to just stop trying to make sense of life.

He has never really been religious—"Hell is eternity"—but, he added, Emily Dickinson suggested that we might already be in heaven. He truly never expected to live as long as he has, and he is grateful to be living in such a well-run facility. Spontaneously, he volunteered that his 'daily happiness scores' vary from 3 to 10 out of 10 but could not explain his wide range of moods. He is also grateful that he has now experienced enough in life to understand "the old poems." We did not ask for poem titles as the interview had been exhausting for Daniel and for us.

Case Commentary: Purpose

The contrast between these two elder lives is stark. Viewed from the perspective of Frankl's paradigm, Omar described himself as having felt a powerful sense of Purpose throughout his life. He had assumed that life is all about taking care of his family and friends and being cared for in return. Omar thinks perpetually about how to make the world a better place—building mosques and contributing to charitable organizations. Islam is precious to him and gives him confidence that he has found answers to the fundamental spiritual and existential questions (much like Frank with his staunch Catholicism). He radiates an admirable serenity. All this has not kept him and his wife from enjoying the pleasures of life, including travel, sports, and social time with friends.

Daniel's life, by contrast, appears painfully impoverished. It is not clear if he ever really felt strongly or securely attached to anyone. Despite his high IQ and exceptional athletic ability, he faltered once he left the structured environment of college. Instead of building a career, he slipped into a lifestyle of drinking and gambling for a quarter century. The promising college romance fell apart when he ran from the responsibilities of parenthood, and he has lost contact with his only child. It was bizarre that he would not explain why his son was raised by his sister and her husband. Now, predictably, his drinking buddies are no longer around. And, although living in proximity to hundreds of people for years, he has made no new social connections.

Sadly, Daniel tried hard to present himself to us (as he may with others) as an educated, self-reliant guy who had been victimized by a few bad breaks. He works hard to reflect neither upon his mistakes nor to allow himself to experience a need for human connection. He has a diffuse personal Identity—his *Life Story* felt fragmented, superficial, incomplete, and largely devoid of details about relationships or emotional reactions. Beyond keeping to his daily schedule and maybe winning an occasional bet, he has a scant sense of Purpose. On the other hand, Daniel does seem to have found a peaceful equilibrium, thanks largely to the well-run facility in which he has lived for the last five years. He has seemingly accepted his lot in life, and is content to live out his government-subsidized years with little stress, and with no discernible aspirations.

Insights From Other Aging Wisely Elders

Striving to find late-life Purpose was remarkably persistent in some of our elders. During the COVID pandemic, one of our most kindly and religious women was cut off from her family and quarantined in a small apartment at her independent living facility. She told us that she was ready to die whenever her time came. But when she heard that the recently widowed woman across the corridor was struggling, she felt compelled to help. Positioning her chair at the threshold of her apartment, she listened patiently, across the hall, to this woman's repetitive complaints about her losses and her misery.

Two other *Aging Wisely* elders found significant meaning late in life. One of our Ivy League graduates, Alex, seventy-eight years old, drifted through a modestly successful career in computer technology only to discover, post-retirement, that he had a gift for hand-crafting guitars. (This seemed to be a resurrection of the artistic pursuits that he had enjoyed, but then abandoned, in college.) In fact, he has come up with several original designs that have sparked significant interest among local musicians. Due to a cardiac condition, he no longer can beat his fellow hikers up the mountain trails the way he used to, and he lacks the drive to go into full production mode making guitars. However, he has found it surprisingly gratifying that people line up to buy his creations.

Georgia, also seventy-eight years old, made an agonizing choice in her early twenties to forego her artistic aspirations to marry and start a family. As her husband battled his way through law school, she supported the family with a series of modest jobs while raising their two daughters. She did take on some leadership roles in her children's schools but stepped down each time due to battles with male authority figures. Only after her kids were emancipated did she have the time and the resources to develop her talents fully as a sculptor. Her work earned her much professional acclaim and she made numerous friends within the local art community.

During the interview, Georgia expressed a well-deserved pride of accomplishment. However, she also conveyed a fierce resentment toward her husband and other men, including her two interviewers, whom she saw as having enjoyed gender-based privileges throughout their careers. Her bitterness was absolutely understandable, and well-justified, but the intensity of this righteous indignation seemed to be preventing her from experiencing late-life gratitude, acceptance, and serenity. She is in a desperate race against time to achieve the full measure of artistic recognition and celebrity that she has craved for so long. And it may never be enough to satisfy her.

Observations and Conclusions

Reviewing the *Aging Wisely* interviews in aggregate, it seems clear that many of those with the most enduring sense of Purpose enjoyed the benefit of secure childhood attachments and stable, loving families. For them, there was a deep sense of purposeful connection with family and friends throughout their lives. However, there were others, with varying degrees and types of childhood deprivations, who found deeply meaningful relationships and rewarding activities later in life. (It is noteworthy that both of the brief vignettes above would seem to confirm the assertion of Robert Greene, author of *Mastery,* that people should pay careful attention to their natural interests and talents, and work to build their careers around them.) Still others seemed to have had a promising start to life, only to lose their way. Without exception, however, a strong sense of Purpose was a prerequisite for late-life wellbeing in our elder interviewees.

As a final note, the authors wish to acknowledge that *The Aging Wisely Project* has given our own lives additional meaning and Purpose. The literature review was illuminating and served as a constant point of comparison when listening to *Life Stories*. Interviewing these dozens of *Aging Wisely* elders repeatedly reinforced for us our appreciation for the irreducible individuality of human lives. Some of these individuals became role models whom we yearned to emulate, and some presented us with disturbing cautionary tales.

As investigators, we found that the relational aspect of these interviews was at once challenging and enlivening. This deep dive into human nature, and the developmental arc through elderhood, has been rich with unexpected discoveries. For us, nothing could have been as meaningful as this intensive exploration of other lives lived. This Project has opened up for us new opportunities for writing, teaching, and community engagement. Ben will take what he has learned back to the university and the psychoanalytic institute. Although he is convinced of the powerful efficacy of psychoanalytic treatments, he laments that the expense of this modality severely restricts its availability. Ben hopes that this book, although no substitute for professionally delivered psychotherapy, will nevertheless be therapeutic for some readers. Scott has been appointed to a leadership position on the board of one of the largest low-income senior residential communities in our area. However, we also appreciate that others, with fundamentally different curiosities and passions, might have comparable experiences immersing themselves in art, music, golf, pickle ball, gardening, scuba diving, or a study of the cosmos. Or learning French and traveling there repeatedly to study its art and architecture. Pursuing just one of these options might also lead to social engagements with groups, organizations, or opportunities to contribute as a volunteer.

On a more personal level, *The Aging Wisely Project* has at times stressed, but also deepened our fifty-year friendship, for which we are grateful. Moreover, it has forced us to reconsider and to reimagine our own elder Identities and lifestyles. We thank you and invite you to do the same.

6

Resilience— The Power of Perseverance

Hormesis—the adaptive response of cells and organisms to stress—is a fascinating physiological phenomenon and a great place to begin our discussion of Resilience. We typically assume that stress is bad for our health, and that it diminishes both the quality and the quantity of our life. Let us consider some empirical evidence about hormesis.

Stress and Adaptation

Several years ago, researchers discovered that laboratory rodents that were stressed by receiving only a fraction of their normal daily calories lived longer, rather than shorter lives. Subsequent studies extended this finding by observing how various animals would respond to other adverse stressors, such as extreme heat or cold, and even to the administration of trace amounts of poisons.

One highly regarded theory proposes that certain stressors activate areas of our DNA that would otherwise remain dormant. (Current estimates are that almost half of our chromosomal DNA has no known functionality.) This novel paradigm asserts that optimal levels of 'good stress' can actually be beneficial. Given that establishing healthy new habits is stressful, this paradigm aligns with the 'use it or lose it' mantra. This might also bring to mind Nietzsche's often-cited quote that "what doesn't kill me, makes me stronger," which clearly does not apply to those individuals who develop post-traumatic stress disorder (PTSD) in response to a severe, but non-lethal, psychological or physical trauma. The severity and nature of a trauma must be taken into account when determining whether a stressor is beneficial or damaging.

By the time we reach elderhood, virtually everyone has suffered losses and other sorts of trauma. For the purposes of *The Aging Wisely Project*, and this discussion, we utilize the psychological criterion that 'trauma' is an external stressor whose severity exceeds our capacity to cope with it without suffering some disruption of our functioning and/or our psychic equilibrium.

Resilience, then, represents the physical and psychological capacity to continue to function well, behaviorally and emotionally, in spite of stressful events and circumstances. As we heard the *Life Stories* of our *Aging Wisely* elders, we listened carefully for several important features: what sort of adversity had they suffered? How had they responded? Did the effects of childhood traumas differ from those suffered in adulthood? Had they disclosed their experience with anyone and, if they had, what was the listener's response? (If their listener did not believe them, or did not offer some sort of support, that would have constituted an additional trauma.) Finally, how long had it taken them to reestablish an optimal-functioning equilibrium? (Note: currently, the term 'reorganize' is preferred over 'recovery,' which implies a usually impossible return to a prior status quo.)

As described in Chapter 5, 'post-traumatic growth' has recently been identified, first by Richard Tedeschi and Lawrence Calhoun, and studied further by Barbara Frederickson and Martin Seligman. Empirical evidence has repeatedly demonstrated that the same event that causes PTSD in roughly one-third of the exposed population will lead to 'post-traumatic growth' in the other two-thirds.[13] Clearly, some individuals are more resilient than others. Also, an individual's risk of developing PTSD may be significantly heightened if they had previously experienced an almost-traumatic event that was similar in nature to the current situation.

Sam's Life Story (78 years old)

Sam's energy and engaging smile filled the room as soon as he walked in. One of us already knew Sam, but the other interviewer did not. After a pleasant round of introductions and some small talk about his current independent living facility, we asked to hear the story of his life. Sam was raised in a small farming town in Kansas by a loving, middle-class family. His father owned and operated a small hardware store while his mother stayed home to run the household and to raise the kids. Sam described his hometown as idyllic and his childhood as happy. He seems to have done well in school and in sports, and he was popular with peers.

Although his family did not go to church, Sam tagged along with his friends to the local Lutheran church. When he decided to go through the confirmation process with them, he was shocked to discover the family secret: his parents and grandparents actually were Jewish. His family had left St. Louis to break away from oppressive grandparents, and had taken pains to assimilate into the Protestant culture of their small rural town. His father, for instance, had joined the Masons and the Shriners. This discovery about his heritage caused Sam much anguish and confusion, and triggered in him a protracted struggle to clarify his religious and ethnic Identity. (We were powerfully reminded of Erik Erikson's adolescent Identity crisis, after his family secret had been revealed to him.)

Sam went to college on an ROTC scholarship and later committed to pre-med studies. He initially dated Susan, a girl that he had known since kindergarten, but then they drifted apart. During junior year they reconnected while attending the wedding of some friends and their relationship was rekindled. They were married during their senior years, and their first child arrived during Sam's first year in medical school. This was a tough time for them—Susan struggled to support the family on her meager salary as a special education teacher, and their second child arrived just a couple of years later. Fortunately, Sam's university provided family medical insurance, and their nearby extended families contributed food and other necessities.

Sam first encountered impoverished racial minority families during his third-year clinical rotation, and this experience evoked a strong sense of mission in him. He felt a keen conviction that these were the kids and parents in greatest need. This encounter shaped Sam's entire career. After completing a family medicine residency, he moved his family to Denver, where some of the first Kaiser Permanente family health programs outside of California were being established. In the 1970s, Kaiser Permanente was known for its innovative, holistic model, which included a strong emphasis on preventive medicine. Sam went on to have a spectacular career as a primary care physician and a medical administrator, but he still found time to volunteer as a doctor for after-hours neighborhood clinics and at summer camps.

Since moving to Colorado, Sam and Susan have been staunch members of their local Lutheran church and have participated enthusiastically in its committees and governance boards. Their marriage has been rock-solid, both affectionate and unwavering. And they raised two happy, stable, and successful daughters. The entire family lives within easy driving distance of each other and they get together frequently for family events. During the COVID pandemic, Sam and his wife provided multi-day childcare each week for two of their grandkids.

However, their lives have not been without major challenges. Sam has maintained a healthy lifestyle, exercising routinely, eating healthy food, and refraining from tobacco or excessive alcohol. Nevertheless, twenty-five years ago, Sam was diagnosed with prostate cancer. Despite utilizing every treatment modality available, the cancer metastasized fifteen years later. Eighteen months ago, Sam developed pulmonary metastases that caused such rapid fluid buildup in his lungs that a chest tube had to be inserted to permit daily drainage. He was told to "get your affairs in order" as death was expected within a month or two.

Miraculously, a new chemotherapeutic agent became available, and it dramatically shrank the tumors. Sam and Susan were able to travel again to Hawaii, one of their favorite destinations. They also renewed their season tickets for the theatre and the symphony. But then they noticed that Susan was starting to forget things and frequently became confused. She could no longer follow the complicated recipes she had mastered long ago. She got lost while driving to a nearby store. Their worst fears were realized when Susan was diagnosed with dementia.

After a period of shock and grief, Sam and Susan teamed up to come to grips with these alarming new realities. Sam's cancer, although now in remission, was still a ticking time bomb. Susan's prognosis was bleak. The couple soberly reconsidered their priorities. With only a limited window of time available, they carefully selected the people they most wanted to visit and the trips they most wanted to take. They rewrote their wills and called a family meeting. Amidst tears and sobbing, they gently informed their daughters of the medical realities facing them, and also about their end-of-life plans. Susan and Sam decided to exercise their option for the recently legalized 'physician-assisted death,' and worked diligently to determine which factors would dictate the initiation of that process.

They designated their medical and financial powers-of-attorney, and shared their estate plans, wills, and advanced directives ('living wills') with their daughters. They carefully itemized the contact information for their lawyer, financial advisor, and accountant, and wrote out their banking and investment account numbers. They shared their cell phone and computer passwords and made their daughters co-signatories on various financial accounts to avoid probate complications. They put the title of the house into a family trust. On a brighter note, they also planned some family trips and celebrations to make full use of the time remaining. They even found a way to laugh at some of Sam's misadventures with adult diapers, and found some humor in a few of Susan's more comical memory lapses.

But sometimes you get kicked again when you are down. Sam had co-signed a mortgage loan for one of his daughters several years ago. Tragically, this daughter lost her job, defaulted on the mortgage, and impulsively borrowed money from a predatory payday lender. Daily phone calls and emails from aggressive debt collectors began tormenting the daughter, and also Sam. Catastrophic legal actions were threatened, including a foreclosure on Sam and Susan's home mortgage. Being forced to immediately pay off this entire debt would have wreaked havoc with their once-secure retirement savings. It had always been Sam's responsibility to handle these family financial matters, so he felt personally responsible for this fiasco. He began having panic attacks and had trouble sleeping.

Fortunately, their financial adviser and their lawyer devised a repayment plan that satisfied the lenders. Sam began sleeping soundly again, and their daughter found another job. Sam and Susan were able to resume their social lives, which included going to church, the theatre and the symphony. Sam had to take over more of the household responsibilities, and the couple resumed traveling, although they limited themselves to short day trips with friends. To keep up his spirits, Sam got busy on the internet, sharing humorous jokes and videos, as well as dispensing some of his own personal wisdom on aging wisely to friends and family.

Sam is one of the interviewees that we have followed up with several times. Consistently, we have been amazed at his courage and the integrity with which he has faced his evolving adversities. His generosity of spirit and good-natured manner persist, although not without moments of sober reflection and a grim acceptance of the realities facing him. We were impressed by the candid conversations that he and Susan had held with their children.

More recently, we learned that Susan had fallen repeatedly and had begun to experience difficulties recognizing close friends. This convinced her that the time had come. With the help of hospice staff, a palliative care physician, and a death doula, Susan made the final arrangements to start the VSED (voluntarily stop eating and drinking) program. She recorded a video documenting that this was entirely her decision, that she was not being coerced, was not suicidally depressed, and that she was of sound mind. The immediate family set up a visitation schedule and Sam arranged to eat his meals downstairs so that he would not tempt his wife. Susan experienced some mild discomfort initially, but this was easily managed with low-dose medications. By the end of the week, she was mostly sleeping. She died on the eighth day, surround by family. Sam was exhausted, but at peace—this is what Susan had wanted, and she had been allowed to maintain the dignity of her self-determination until the very end.

Over the course of his long medical career, Sam saw many people die. Susan's dying process was what he had wanted for her, and would want for himself, under similar circumstances. Scott and Ben wondered whether they would be as steady and resolute when their times come. Sam had smoothly transitioned from husband and partner to being Susan's primary caregiver. While he mourned sacrificing much of his freedom and independence, he was resolute in shifting his life's Purpose to caring for her. His Resilience in the face of multiple traumas deeply increased our respect for him, and often left us speechless.

Katrin's Life Story (70 years old)

In contrast to Sam's journey, Katrin's life difficulties were present from the very start. We interviewed her twice and both times she emphasized how hard she and her family had struggled just to survive. Remarkably, despite having experienced numerous traumas and bitter losses, Katrin told her story in an unwavering, smoothly integrated manner. Her parents were among the large number of Germans who were invited by the Russian (Soviet Union) government to move onto farmland in the western part of that country after World War II.

When Katrin was just four years old, however, her parents were forced to move to the extreme eastern part of the country, to remote Siberia. Luckily, Katrin was allowed to stay behind, near Moscow, with her loving and stable grandmother. She described the next three years as the happiest of her childhood. When she was seven, however, her father came to pick her up and take her, along with her mother and a younger brother, to their new home—which was situated in a work camp up near the Arctic Circle. She only got to see her beloved grandmother one more time, and then only for a brief visit.

The winters in their new home were dark and viciously cold, although the government did provide warm clothing and adequate food. The summers were beautiful, but barely three months long. After a couple of years, the family was again ordered to move, this time to a camp in the southern Ural Mountains. This was a much more pleasant place: an outpost where other German refugees had established a well-run community, which included good schools and comfortable housing.

Unfortunately, Katrin's father began abusing alcohol, which led to his leaving the family. Katrin teared up when telling us how their family was so poor that her mother had to beg the neighbors for food. Fortunately, many people took pity on them and provided the family with what they needed. Katrin complained that she was heavily burdened during this time by the responsibilities for cooking and cleaning for her mother and her younger brother. On the other hand, she loved school and her classmates. Katrin joined every available club and even helped to start a theatre group. She also met an inspirational German language teacher who later helped her to prepare for her college entrance exams. With this assistance she was able to get into college, where she earned a degree in German, which later qualified her for a teaching position.

Sadly, the Soviet government decided to build a dam near this community, so everyone was forced to evacuate. The family had to move again. Around this time, Katrin, now twenty-two, married. Two years later she had her first child, daughter Ludmila. When her husband was offered a good job in Africa, he left for a couple of years. Even though her husband turned out to be a poor provider, Katrin stayed married to him for forty-three years. Also, around the time that Ludmila was born, Katrin's mother became so depressed that she could not get out of bed. So, at this point, while teaching full-time, Katrin was taking care of her mother, her daughter, and her younger brother. Then her needy father came back to the family as well. Not surprisingly, by the time she was thirty, Katrin became so depressed that she began to wonder if it was all worth it. She sought out psychotherapy, but never took any psychiatric medications.

Katrin did have a second daughter, Anna, who, as a teenager, traveled to America as an exchange student. While there, she met and married an American, who was Jewish. They are reportedly quite happy together and celebrate both Eastern Orthodox and Jewish holidays. They now have two sons, aged thirteen and nine. Years ago, Anna encouraged Katrin to apply for a green card. She did, and she was granted one which then obligated her to travel to America once every year to renew her status. During this period, Ludmila, at age twenty-four, was killed in a car accident, which made Katrin very depressed. Nevertheless, when Anna had a second son, Katrin mustered the gumption to return to America to help her out. Katrin said that her husband never got over the death of Ludmila, and he died of cancer in 2017. Ludmila left behind an eight-year-old daughter, and Katrin has been trying mightily, but so far unsuccessfully, to bring her to the United States. Katrin is sure that her granddaughter would have much better prospects for a good life in America, so trying to get her here has become a major focus for Katrin.

Currently, Katrin feels more safe and comfortable than she ever has in her life. With all the services provided by her current independent living facility, she has never felt so pampered and secure. Just as she did in high school, she has joined multiple special interest groups and is taking as many classes as she can. Katrin wants to qualify to become a docent at the local zoo. She walks daily, makes new friends, reads detective novels, and cooks. She enjoys television, the internet, and her iPhone. She phones her grandsons, mostly the younger one, almost every day, and she did visit them weekly before the COVID pandemic forced a lockdown of her facility. She is philosophical about not seeing them more, but she is frustrated that she cannot attend their hockey tournaments.

Katrin thinks about her deceased daughter every day—at night, sometimes in the form of nightmares—and also about her granddaughter in Russia. She still mourns for her mother, whose tenacity and selfless love far exceeds anything Katrin thinks she could ever match. Her sister died of cancer sixteen years ago, and her brother, who is still in Russia, has not had contact with the family for years. Katrin says she is somewhat lonely, but she has no interest in a romantic relationship. At this point in her life, she wants to be useful and helpful, and to have a "good life." She is working on thinking less about others and more about herself. She is proud that her difficult life has made her so strong, and she thinks that maybe she will write down her stories someday for her grandkids.

Katrin is quite spiritual and believes that her current good fortune may be attributable to some sort of supernatural intervention, maybe by God, or perhaps some of her ancestors. Although she has some problems with her skin and with chronic back pain, she feels like her spirit is only thirty years old. In closing, we would add that Katrin's English language skills were quite good, given her background. Her multilingual fluency in Russian, German, and English is at least one factor that has helped keep her cognitively sharp. Regarding her interpersonal style, she is friendly and forthcoming, but still maintains a strong interpersonal boundary. This combination allows her to be engaging, but also well-defended.

When we interviewed Katrin a year later (the first interview had been on Zoom, the second was in person), we learned that her daughter and family had moved to Detroit so their boys could improve their hockey skills. Because Katrin had moved to Denver specifically to be close to her family, we would have expected her to be quite upset by this separation, but Katrin denied this, saying that she did not want to interfere in her daughter's life. Besides, she has frequent FaceTime calls with them, and she has plans to visit them soon. Katrin has also arranged to travel to Arizona with some of her new friends, and perhaps might even take a trip to Costa Rica.

Katrin has also changed some of her attitudes: she says that she is now open to a romantic relationship (mentioned with a little twinkle in her eye!). She thinks that she is learning to be more patient, to accept getting older, and to value herself more. She still loves people, although she admits that she gets tired of hearing some of her friends repeatedly complain that they have been victimized by life. Katrin also came across to us as much more religious. Maybe this was because she felt that she could trust us more in this second interview. She talked about praying every day to Orthodox saints, and how several of these saints might well be helping her. She shared a dream involving her deceased daughter—in the dream her daughter was a baby, light and beautiful, and she was happily joining Katrin's mother in heaven. Katrin is confident that she will join them there someday herself.

Case Commentary: Resilience

The *Life Stories* of Sam and Katrin illuminate two strikingly different lives, but with similar capacities for Resilience and robust living. 'Equifinality' is a term used to describe how, in open and complex systems, a specific end state or outcome can be reached by many potential pathways. Sam had a strong, stable, loving family and a near-idyllic childhood. His teenage confusion about his religious and ethnic Identity notwithstanding, Sam's trajectory was steady and upward. In medical school his encounter with underprivileged families struck an enduring and altruistic chord that compelled him to try to make the world more equitable and compassionate. Throughout his life he has been fundamentally sociable and well-meaning in his personal and vocational spheres. Meaning and fulfillment seem inextricably woven into the fabric of his life. When assaulted by prostate cancer, his wife's dementia, his daughter's severe financial problems, and the other expectable losses of aging, he soldiered on, seemingly drawing upon a lifetime of happy memories and self-confidence. He has had a deep reservoir of internal resources and strength to bolster him.

Paradoxically, Sam derived benefit from his adversities. He acknowledged that his lifelong pessimism had given way to optimism after hearing the 'get your affairs in order' speech by his doctor. His attitude became more happy-go-lucky, more focused on living in the moment. As the octogenarians profiled in John Leland's poignant book *Happiness Is a Choice You Make* showed us, they did not take life for granted and they considered each day a gift.

Katrin, by contrast, grew up in a world of chaos, hardship, separation, and loss. After enjoying several of her happiest years with a loving grandmother, she was jerked away to live in one of the harshest environments on the planet, and she only saw her beloved grandmother one more time. Her father became an alcoholic and her parents divorced. While still a child, she was burdened with oppressive and overwhelming household responsibilities. Over time, she saw the weight of endless caretaking obligations reduce her much-admired mother to a state of bedridden depression. She and her family were forced to humiliate themselves by begging for food and clothing. They were perpetually at the mercy of capricious government officials who sent them packing thousands of miles to the east, then to the far north, then back west. Frequent changes of living environments, social milieux, and friends severely disrupted the continuity and stability of her early life, yet she continued to trust in herself, her family, and God.

One of Ben's favorite professors was Louis Sander, one of the first researchers in the field of infant-parent interactions. Sweet Lou, as he was called, was convinced that having at least one loving and committed caregiver was indispensable for a child. Katrin, for all her hardships, had a devoted and self-sacrificing mother, a doting grandmother, and an extremely supportive German teacher in high school. Later, when caring for a multitude of needy family members, she was inspired to try to live up to the idealized image of her martyred mother. Later, when her younger daughter managed to find a more promising life in America, Katrin allowed herself to be swept into this new world. Her devastation at losing her mother and her older daughter had to be set aside so that she could help care for her young grandsons. And, recently, she has found herself in a stable, nurturing senior living facility, which makes her feel almost rich, even though she and her fellow residents are all low-income and Medicaid-qualified.

It was curious that Katrin did not express more sadness or disappointment about her daughter's recent move—but Katrin had learned long ago not to dwell on disappointments or regrets. This sort of emotional compartmentalization is a mixed blessing. From one perspective, it has allowed Katrin to mostly avoid depression and despair. But from another angle, it runs counter to the psychological goals of Integration and Identity consolidation. There are memories and feelings that she must avoid, places in her mind that are dangerously off-limits. Her ongoing nightmares about her deceased daughter, her idealization of her mother (with a reciprocal devaluation of herself), and her inability to let herself react in an authentic way to her daughter's relocation suggest pervasive defenses against grief, disappointment, and anger. This sort of defensiveness engenders an avoidant coping style that prioritizes a sense of security, and which sacrifices emotional honesty and depth. 'Keep it light, keep it easy' may well be her implicit mantra.

Becoming more devoutly religious, and even somewhat mystical, may have been a way of bolstering her positivity. She may console herself with the conviction that the irredeemable elements of her life can be turned over to the divine: 'Let go, let God.' So, yes, Katrin is Resilient and, given the multiple traumas and deprivations of her life, this is little short of heroic. But her Resilience and her forced positive outlook have come with certain compromises and vulnerabilities. (Could she really, for instance, allow herself to fall in love, or even to make anything more than superficial new friendships?)

Does having to work hard just to survive in one's youth give later adulthood more meaning? Does pervasive early adversity prevent one from taking later good fortune for granted? Obviously, childhood traumas crush many people, while others find a way to survive and even thrive. For Katrin, the combination of loving caregivers, high intelligence, and a Resilient temperament seemed to have added up to a winning combination.

What else can we learn from our two resilient *Aging Wisely* elders? First, their stories validate the critical importance of secure childhood attachments. Feeling safe and loved sends a child out into the world with significant self-confidence and optimism. Also, with Trust in relationships, and in the world at large, no matter the adversities or setbacks. Having a nurturing and trustworthy caregiver in childhood fosters an abiding hope for a better future. Both Katrin and Sam had that, although to different degrees.

Katrin had to deal with huge, simultaneous challenges throughout most of her life, but she now finds herself in a snug harbor, although staying in touch with her daughter's family has become more difficult. The arc of her life raises several questions: does having to work hard just to survive in one's youth give later adulthood more meaning (remember Durkheim's higher suicide rates for the comfortably affluent)? Did Katrin's pervasive early-life adversities prevent her from taking her current good fortune for granted? As an adult, she had to endure many hardships and never had much in the way of financial security, but none of this robbed her of her self-confidence and optimism.

Sam, on the other hand, enjoyed loving relationships throughout his life and a rewarding career, one that required much hard work, but which enabled him to give back to others all along the way. But then, on the cusp of elderhood, he faced a long fight with cancer, a spouse with accelerating dementia, and unexpected financial threats. Nevertheless, he faces what time he has left with Purpose and determination. Having lost his wife, he is now committed to sticking around as long as he can for his children and grandchildren. Both these elders are models of Resilience, although their paths were markedly different.

A Personal Note

As a child, Scott fondly remembers listening to the stories of his maternal grandparents, Ruth and Abe Shapiro. They told stories of their lives leading up to their immigration to the U.S. in the early 1920s. They both grew up in an area of the Ukraine called the Pale of Settlement, a region between Poland and Turkey that was established by Catherine the Great in the late 1700s as a ghetto for her Jewish population where they could be corralled and controlled more easily.

Grandma Ruth recalled pogroms when she hid with the village children in root cellars while friends and family were killed in the streets. She was so terrorized by her memories of hiding in small spaces that she resisted riding in elevators for the rest of her life. Grandpa Abe was put on a train when he was thirteen and sent to the town of Kyiv so he could learn a trade as an apprentice to a watchmaker. When the Russian Tsar forced him, at age nineteen, into the army to fight in World War I, he was wounded and sent back to his village to recover. There he fell in love and married his third cousin, Ruth, who was fifteen at the time.

Within a year, they had a child (Scott's Uncle Jack) just as the Russian Revolution began. Rather than go back and fight for the Tsar again, and adamantly refusing to join the Bolshevik opposition, Abe packed up his small family and escaped across the frozen River Prut into Romania. After three years in Bucharest plying his trade as a watchmaker, Abe and his family acquired a precious visa to travel to the U.S. and arrived in Hartford, Connecticut. There, they joined Abe's brother David, who owned a jewelry store. Two more daughters were born, Scott's mom, Sylvia, and his Aunt Beatrice. Years later, after Abe suffered his first of several heart attacks, they sold the store and the family moved to California in 1947.

There is more to the tale, of course, but Scott learned three important lessons from their stories. First, he recognized the danger and hardship that his grandparents had endured to journey to this country. Arriving penniless, and unable to speak English, it had required tremendous grit, determination, and Purpose for them just to survive. Although not unique, their immigrant story made an indelible impression on Scott, one which he would later draw upon when faced with his own challenges in life. Second, their story helped him realize just how easy his life had been, and still is, in many ways. He feels fortunate and humbled by the sacrifices made by his ancestors. And finally, their story instilled in him a deep appreciation for the loving and supportive caregiving that he received from grandparents, parents, and extended family. For all their shortcomings and idiosyncrasies, they enabled him to establish the secure attachments that gave him a great start in life.

Enhancing Resilience

As she described it in her powerful 2019 TEDx Talk, *The Three Secrets of Resilient People*, Psychologist Lucy Hone was just returning home after finishing her graduate program when she faced one of the pivotal junctures in her life. First, she found herself in the midst of the horrific carnage caused by the earthquakes that devastated Christchurch, New Zealand, in 2014. The death toll ultimately reached 185. Second, and soon after, her twelve-year-old daughter was killed by a reckless driver. Hone had just earned a degree in Positive Psychology—the earthquake and the sudden loss of her daughter were severe tests of whether she could use her knowledge and her therapeutic skills to get through this two-fold trauma. She was emotionally devastated, of course, as anyone would have been. Ultimately, she was able to claw her way out of her depression and despair and, in doing so, she came to realize that there were three principal strategies that had helped her.

Strategy #1—Accept That Tragedy Strikes Everyone

Hone begins her TEDx Talk by asking people in the audience to stand up if they had lost a close family member, or had been through a divorce, or had lost a job. If she had more time, she could have asked about having your house burned down, being afflicted with a chronic or terminal illness, or any number of other tragedies or setbacks. In response to her questions, almost all the audience had stood up. She was making the point that tragedy is ubiquitous, it strikes all of us at some point.

Appreciating this can help you shake off any notion that the Universe is picking on you personally. Sitting around feeling sorry for yourself gets you nowhere.

Human beings have a deeply ingrained tendency to create scripts and narratives to make sense of the world. Some of these interpretive narratives can be quite self-defeating. For instance: 'I'm a loser' or 'Bad things always happen to me.' Rabbi Harold Kushner's classic book, *When Bad Things Happen to Good People*, offers an alternative narrative. Kushner describes how the devastating loss of his young son forced him to reconsider his attitude toward God and, subsequently, compelled him to elevate his faith to a more sophisticated and nuanced level. How do we sustain our faith—in God or in life—after suffering such a personal tragedy?

Holocaust survivor Viktor Frankl emphasized the importance of 'tragic optimism,' which is the ability to maintain hope and find meaning in life despite its inescapable pain, loss, and suffering. Scott's father-in-law Jack thrived after the war, despite struggles as a new immigrant, losing his young wife to leukemia, and facing challenges of a single parent with three young children. His 'tragic optimism' came not by finding God, but rather by reinforcing his Connections with family and friends as the pillars that anchored and sustained him.

Strategy #2—Clarify What You Can Control

Many individuals with alcohol abuse disorders use intoxication to deal with feelings or circumstances that overwhelm them. Alcoholics Anonymous (AA) has helped many such individuals find support, understanding, and guidance about how to develop greater resilience and maintain their sobriety. Many AA meetings involve the recitation of the Serenity Prayer, which underscores the importance of trying your best to control what you can, and accepting with serenity those things you cannot control. Lucy Hone's story about her approach to tragedy echoes this message.

Joan Didion's bestseller, *The Year of Magical Thinking*, honestly confesses the author's recurring denial of her husband's death. She admitted that she could not bear to get rid of his shoes, for fear that he might someday need them. Yes, this sounds absolutely crazy, but extreme trauma can make us all somewhat crazy.

As obvious as it may sound, we must start by accepting cruel reality, over and over again: the one we love has died, the terrorist attacks cannot be undone, the earthquake did destroy most of our town, our home did burn down, our company did go bankrupt, our spouse did leave us, the diagnosis is malignant cancer. We must be patient with ourselves and others; it takes a while for the shock and sense of unreality to wear off (it took Didion more than a year). Next, once the fog in our brains has lifted, we must survey the wreckage. Where do we want to go from here? What resources do we still have to work with, and how can they be mobilized? All the inevitable losses and changes of aging can feel traumatic, and they force us to grapple with the Tasks of EIR. When Alice in Wonderland asks the Cheshire Cat which way to proceed, the Cat replies, "That depends a good deal on where you wish to go." Where indeed?

Many of Ben's psychiatric patients and Scott's executive coaching clients found themselves stuck in a passive mindset. They felt victimized by circumstances that they felt were responsible for their feeling helpless and hopeless. This is the passive position. The first essential step toward health is to help these individuals find within themselves a more active and adaptive mindset. In virtually all situations, there are choices to be made. These may not be the choices one most wants ("I just want my husband back"), but there are important choices nevertheless ("As a widow now, do you want to stay in your house, or move closer to your daughter?"). Just considering realistic options can move us from a passive 'victim' mindset to an active 'survivor' stance.

Martin Seligman, before becoming the father of the Positive Psychology movement, studied the phenomenon of 'learned helplessness.' Dogs (poor dogs!) imprisoned in a metal cage were subjected to random shocks.[14] After trying every way to escape, they came to the realization that they could not get away from the shocks or even predict when the next one would occur. This is the essence of 'learned helplessness.' Not surprisingly, these dogs became depressed.

Many people experience such learned helplessness. Seligman identified the three assumptions underlying this pernicious mental state: the individual feels that they have no control, that the situation ruins everything, and that they are somehow responsible for it. But we have the option to look at this same situation differently. The healthy alternative is noticing that you have some choices, even in a bad situation; that there are aspects of your life that are not ruined; and finally, that this bad event does not have to be taken personally. It could have happened to someone else, and probably has happened to many others.

As noted in Chapter 5, Frankl reminds us that freedom of thought cannot be taken from us. We can choose our attitude about a situation, what aspect we focus on, and how we think about it. Our minds are powerful tools. Astronaut Scott Kelly—trapped and isolated in a tiny orbiting space capsule for a year—learned to get through difficult moments by thinking in a granular, detailed way about pleasant memories of the past, or by imagining the future joyful reunion he would have with his family. Similarly, psychologist Mihaly Csikszentmihalyi has described how immersing oneself in an enjoyable and absorbing activity can put you into a 'flow state' that mentally removes you from your immediate circumstances, at least for a while.

Mindfulness exercises, as described by Jon Kabat-Zinn, teach how narrowly focusing one's attention on breathing, listening, or sensing the tactile sensations in your neck or feet can bring about a temporary escape from the here-and-now chatter of our minds. In related research, recent clinical trials have found that losing yourself in an engaging game on a virtual reality headset can distract chronic pain patients so much that they forget to ask for their next scheduled dose of medication.[15] Utilizing one or more of these maneuvers gives us options, both in external reality, and inside our own heads. This realization is empowering and, once again, it moves us from passivity to activity. Some trial-and-error experimentation is likely necessary to determine which of these alternatives might work best for you.

Strategy #3—Monitor What Is Helping

Dr. Hone and her husband were tempted to attend the trial of the reckless driver who killed their daughter, but they asked themselves if that would help them or not—and then decided not to go. Determining what is helping depends upon monitoring how you are doing, which requires the final element of EIR: Self-Consciousness. It can help just to take stock of what sort of adversity or trauma reaction you are up against. Knowledge is indeed power.

Trauma falls into three categories, each of which is associated with a particular pattern of normal and pathological reactions:

1. **Acute Trauma.** This is what most people think of as causing post-traumatic stress disorder, PTSD. Acute trauma is caused by sudden, unexpected, shocking experiences, such as a car accident or being victimized by random violence. Symptoms of PTSD include high levels of anxiety, nightmares, sleep disturbances, flashbacks of the traumatic event, an inability to concentrate, restlessness, irritability, mistrust, fear of trauma repetition, and extreme avoidance of triggering situations or places. Depression, physical symptoms, and substance abuse are also common. If these symptoms are severe or persistent, professional help should be sought. Psychotherapy involves helping an individual regain a sense of safety and security and

gradually exposing them to the triggering memories or stimuli. The goal is to incrementally dampen the 'fight or flight' response that is causing their symptoms. This must be done gradually and sensitively to avoid retraumatizing the patient.

2. **Strain Trauma.** This trauma results from the cumulative effects of long-term adversities. Strain trauma occurs when prolonged stress becomes unbearable over time; for example, a child being exposed to frequent family violence, or an adult quarantined for an extended period during the COVID pandemic. Another common situation might be caring, for many months or even years, for someone with dementia or extreme physical disabilities.

    Some fixes are quick: if current politics or environmental disasters are upsetting you, put yourself on a 'media diet' and turn off your radio, TV, smart phone, and computer. If there is a toxic relationship in your life, you might have some tough choices to make—and you might start by considering your own contribution to the problem. Other dilemmas, such as how to deal with long-term caregiving responsibilities, can be oppressive and difficult to manage. (See the *Care Giving Navigator* by Ronald E. Roel listed in the Appendix Suggested Reading List.)

    For caregiver burnout, it is important to start with a searching psychological self-reflection. Be honest with yourself about your frustration, your rage, your guilt, your despair and confusion, if that is what you are feeling. (Although many of us might aspire to being selfless saints who would never harbor such dark feelings, most of us are more human than that.) Have you reached out to others for help? Sometimes just having someone to listen to your woes can offer relief. Also, there are many caregiver assistance programs and other community resources to identify and explore. Making the commitment to take care of yourself is an important first step.

3. **Loss and Grief.** Ben and his wife Carol have participated in a peer-led support group for grieving parents and siblings, The Compassionate Friends, since their twenty-two-year-old daughter Hiliary died ten years ago. The path of grieving—for Ben and Carol and for their fellow group members—differs radically from person to person. As insightfully described in Mark Epstein's *The Trauma of Everyday Life*, beating yourself up because you feel that you are not grieving 'the right way' just adds insult to injury. Many people misunderstand Elizabeth Kubler-Ross's stages of grief, which apply

to the dying patient, *not* to the grieving family. Kubler-Ross also cautioned that most individuals do not march through these stages rigidly in order—they bounce back and forth and sometimes skip or combine stages. Also, for nearly everyone, it is best to not suffer through this kind of grief alone. Those in a bereavement group, for instance, draw strength from being with other grieving individuals. They are not alone. And they are hearing that others are depressed, feeling bad, and doing some of the same 'crazy' things (remember Didion and her husband's shoes?) that they are feeling and doing. Getting to hear how others are grieving reinforces the understanding that each person must find their own grief pathway.

Most importantly, virtually everyone experiences a significant cathartic benefit from just telling their story to other caring people. Losing a child, spouse, sibling, or parent is so powerful that it can be difficult to separate normal reactions from an excessive one. A broad array of feelings and behaviors are normally associated with grieving: protest, denial, self-blame, anger, avoidance, social withdrawal, depression, and an impaired ability to function at work or in one's personal life. These sorts of reactions typically come and go, often quite unpredictably. However, if one particular emotion or behavior becomes too extreme or persistent, the individual may develop a pathological condition. Frequently, for instance, bereaved individuals return to a sentimental place that may evoke fond memories and temporarily reconnect them with their loved one. For others, however, a consuming obsession with objects associated with the lost person may develop into a full-blown hoarding disorder.

Recently, the diagnosis of Persistent Complex Bereavement Disorder has been added to the psychiatric diagnostic manual (DSM-V-TR). Anyone meeting these criteria may well need professional help. And because the capacity for self-reflection is often one of the first psychological deficits to develop after a major loss, the bereaved person may be unable to make this determination for themselves. Under such circumstances, someone who knows them well, and cares, may need to intervene, which, unfortunately, may not be initially well received.

We have included this description of the different forms of traumatic reactions so that you can more carefully consider how you are dealing with the traumas in your life. Hone's third strategy for enhancing Resilience begins with the question: *Is what you are doing helping?* If your Resilience is lagging, perhaps it is time to try something different. Maybe take a trip, change some of your behavioral routines, choose a different way home, or call up an old friend. Most importantly, do not be too proud to ask for help—as Scott's wise Jewish grandmother was fond of saying, "It couldn't hurt!"

When addressing trauma (and many other situations) it is essential to be as self-reflective as possible. Can you identify the external and internal forces and situations that are tormenting you, or holding you back? Keep in mind the 'Rumpelstiltskin Principle' from the classic fairy tale: if you can name it, you can begin to control it. And, as noted, writing things down or telling them to another person is significantly more potent than just thinking about them. (Writing and speaking mobilize more regions of your brain.)

Recalling Pennebaker's research (Chapter 5), finding a way to step back from the immediacy of your feelings to reflect upon yourself can be transformative. Is there a future threat looming that you have avoided thinking about? Are you so numbed or stricken by a loss that you just cannot think straight? Have things gotten so bad that it has begun to affect your sense of your Identity, your self-esteem, your self-confidence? How do you see yourself responding to these stressors? Can you learn something from looking back to how you have responded to difficult situations in the past? Are there particular coping strategies that have served you well in the past? Is there something that keeps you from being your best self in the current situation?

Observations and Conclusions

Optimistically, there is a growing literature about 'resilience competence,' based on the hypothesis that elders have dealt with so many past crises that they are better able to manage the current ones. They have more confidence that 'this too shall pass.' As Frankl reminded us, we do have a choice about how we see things and how we respond.

Laura Carstensen, whose work was described in our Introduction, conducted a study examining how almost 1,000 subjects, aged eighteen to seventy-six, responded to the COVID pandemic.[16] Despite the fact that elders were at the greatest risk of hospitalization or death, they reported significantly fewer negative emotions, and more positive emotions, compared with their younger peers. Carstensen's Socioemotional Selectivity Theory would explain this as one of many examples of elders having learned how to cope with threatening situations and how to maintain their focus on critical priorities, on meaningful goals, and on close relationships.

Carstensen concluded that the many frailties and losses of aging are offset by superior emotional wisdom—which is manifested as enhanced Resilience and a more tenacious focus on Purpose.

Resilience is fundamental for the healing of our psychological wounds. It helps provide the propulsive determination to keep us moving forward. Knowing how to maintain and strengthen our Resilience is a critical aspect of aging wisely. With that in mind, we turn to the Healthy Habit of Self-Acceptance.

7

Self-Acceptance—
Knowing and Embracing the Self

S elf-Acceptance is critically important for aging wisely—statistically, it predicts more than three-quarters of the global *Aging Wisely* score of our fifty-two elders. Although we considered alternative concepts such as 'self-esteem' or 'self-regard,' we settled on 'Self-Acceptance' because it pairs naturally with the all-important factor of Self-Integration. Two dimensions to Self-Acceptance span the lifetime trajectory of human development: externally, how you compare yourself with others; and, internally, how your current self-image matches your wished-for ideal self.

Dimensions of Self-Acceptance

Growing up, we compare ourselves to siblings, cousins, and playmates. Once we get to school, we compare our grades, our athletic skills, our artwork, and our social success with same-aged peers. This external comparative process continues throughout life. In elderhood, we are aware of how our families and careers, our net worth and our social status, our physical capacities and intelligence, and our attractiveness all compare with that of our contemporaries. We also tend to compare ourselves with cultural icons such as celebrity performers, fashion models, prominent politicians, and corporate moguls. Comparisons with our peers risk leaving us feeling either inferior or superior, neither of which is beneficial. For elders, this tendency to compare is probably most pronounced when moving into a new communal residence, or joining a new special interest group. This dynamic adds significantly to the stress of such transitions.

The other dimension of Self-Acceptance is inwardly directed. Whether we realize it or not, we carry around within us an internal image of ourselves, our 'actual self.' Intertwined with this, we have another image: the person we would like to be, our 'ideal self.' The discrepancy between these two representations largely determines our self-esteem. If our actual self is reasonably close to our ideal self, we probably feel pretty good about ourselves. If the two are quite far apart, we have a problem. Self-Acceptance is a frequent focus in psychotherapy—helping patients to become more insightful about their actual and ideal selves, how these internal constructs come about, and how they influence our feelings and behaviors. In elderhood, Self-Acceptance globally reflects how well an individual feels they are doing with the developmental Tasks of this life stage.

Many people make themselves miserable by clinging to an unrealistic and unachievable ideal self, perhaps based on an idolized parent or a famous celebrity. On the other hand, they may be tormented by a distorted and despised image of their actual self, as if they are seeing themselves in a fun-house trick mirror. Either sort of problem can burden people for years, or even a lifetime. When you are young, it is easy to believe that you will inevitably become more and more the person that you have always wanted to be. For us elders, however, time is running out: they may begin to dread that this goal is beyond their reach.

The identification of EIR as the final developmental Task highlights several dimensions—the 5 C's—that affect elder Self-Acceptance. As elders increasingly feel that they are losing Control and Competence, their positive self-regard is shaken. As they begin to lose family and friends through residential moves, conflicts, or deaths, the image of themselves as having Connections, as a loving person who is also loved, can slip away. Similarly, the sense of Continuity, of being the person that others have always known them to be (energetic, funny, knowledgeable, or stylish) can become increasingly difficult to sustain. Finally, their Consciousness, with regard to self-awareness, mortality, and spirituality, is challenged by menacing threats, diminished cognitive capacities, and pervasive self-doubt.

Jimmy's Life Story (82 years old)

Jimmy walked into the room, bent forward at the waist. A lifetime of labor as a fisherman had wreaked havoc with his spine. Nevertheless, his manner was warm and welcoming, and he thanked us for taking an interest in his life. A born storyteller, he quickly launched into his history. Jimmy was the son of an eminent Boston lawyer and a prominent philanthropist mother. Growing up in such circumstances was double-edged: there were many privileges, but also very high expectations of him. He was sent to an elite college preparatory school.

Unfortunately, Jimmy probably suffered from undiagnosed dyslexia and he reported that he just could not absorb what was being taught in the classroom. Also, to further complicate matters, his older brother was a star athlete who was heavily recruited by several colleges. Although Jimmy strove to distinguish himself athletically, he was undersized and not particularly gifted physically. In addition, as a teenager, he had been hit by a car while on his motorcycle, which had severely damaged one foot and required the amputation of several toes.

Characteristically, Jimmy was quick to declare forgiveness of the driver who hit him—apparently just an "old guy" who had not even seen him on his motorcycle. Instead of feeling the expected bitterness or anger for his injury, Jimmy conveyed genuine compassion for how devastated this guy must have been after the collision. Jimmy's voice then softened as he remembered how his mother had lifted him out of the roadside ditch and cradled him lovingly in her arms. His rehabilitation from this injury was slow and arduous, and his athletic career was put on hold for many months. Fortunately, his coach reassured him that he would be just fine and reinforced this point by sharing that he himself had lost some toes while incarcerated in a World War II prison camp. Jimmy's gratitude was palpable: "He was a great guy." His tendency to credit others, and his ability to see the good in people, even during difficult situations, was pervasive throughout the interview.

Years later, the military initially rejected Jimmy's application to enlist because of his injured foot, but he was determined to serve. His father asked a favor of a retired general who he knew, and Jimmy got his waiver to enlist. While stationed in the Philippines, Jimmy befriended a soldier who eventually asked him to be the best man at his wedding. With sadness, Jimmy told us this man was later killed in Vietnam, leaving behind a wife and three young children. Clearly, Jimmy had been deeply affected by this death, as he also had been by the deaths of several friends during his adolescence. In fact, he named his first-born son after a deceased boyhood buddy. A sudden insight occurred to Jimmy at this point in the interview: perhaps he had developed a drinking problem in adulthood to keep himself from thinking about these tragic early deaths. "I didn't know that we were going to get into this [in the interview]," he said.

After mustering out of the Army, Jimmy went to live in the seacoast town where his family had summered for several generations. He had always admired one of the wise old fishermen there, and he had exchanged some letters with this man's daughter while stationed in the Philippines. Sure enough, they began dating and soon were married. The couple decided to settle in that same town and, ultimately, they had four children of their own, two of whom still live quite close to them. Jimmy's older son followed him into the fishing business.

Raising four kids was not easy—one had recurrent asthma attacks and another was diagnosed with clinical depression as an adolescent. When we asked about his own back problems, Jimmy replied, "You can't cry about it; you pick your path, you pay the price." Of greater concern to him was his wife's serious heart problems, especially because both of her parents had died from heart attacks. Jimmy also shared that he had had considerable trouble controlling his temper in the past, especially after a couple of beers. Eventually, after one particularly angry episode, he swore off alcohol for good, and he has never touched another drop. Now, to cope with disturbing situations, he has learned to just "let things go."

Jimmy also has come to realize that many people have it worse than he does, for instance, the disabled veteran who became the minister at his local church. As mentioned, Jimmy is an engaging raconteur, and one tale seamlessly flowed into the next, each ending with some sort of an appreciation for the kindness, or wisdom, or determination of one person or another. He has developed quite a reputation locally for calling people up, quickly thanking them for something they have done, and then abruptly saying goodbye.

Jimmy repeatedly told us how blessed he feels: a sixty-year marriage, children, grandchildren, and steady employment. For many decades, he and his wife were very involved with church and town work groups and governance committees, but no more. They have now turned these responsibilities over to the next generation. Jimmy fondly recalled some of the admirable men and women of the previous generation who contributed so much to the town. For him, these people were like giants but, sadly, few people today even recognize their names. He accepts that, similarly, his many efforts will someday be forgotten as well, but that is okay with him. This is how it works, and he is just happy to have been a part of it.

We asked our routine questions about whether there had been someone who had hurt him that he just could not forgive, or whether he had any unfinished business; he responded, no and no. Jimmy now gets daily inspirations from a book of Christian readings, but he is quick to admit that he has not read the entire Bible. Speaking like an elder sage, he advised us to try to help the younger generation and added that we should do this more with our actions than our words because the younger generation has its own way of doing things. Regarding thoughts about mortality, Jimmy feels that he has had a full life. He has had a good run, and he is ready to go whenever it happens.

It is noteworthy that Jimmy could have been frustrated by not achieving the lifestyle of his wealthy and accomplished parents. He could have been bitter about his lack of success in school and athletics. The decades of hard manual work, and the permanent damage to his body, could have left him resentful and aggrieved. His children and his wife have suffered from various afflictions that have not only hurt them, but also may shorten their lives. He has given much to his small town, but he anticipates that his legacy will be fleeting.

Despite all these challenges and disappointments, Jimmy is deeply and genuinely satisfied with his progeny, his contributions to his church and his town, and with his consequential decision to give up drinking. He is convinced that his life has been rich and meaningful, filled as it has been with family and close, loyal friends. He seems to have made his peace, spiritually and existentially, with the good and the bad, the lucky and the unlucky. He accepts himself in his characteristically humble and uncomplaining way. As he recounted his *Life Story*, Jimmy exuded gratitude at every turn. Clearly, he has been committed to cultivating this attitude, which again reminded us of John Leland's book *Happiness Is a Choice You Make*.

Susan's Life Story (78 years old)

Susan recalled many happy childhood memories while growing up on a farm in Virginia. She talked of the wide-open spaces, the horses they owned, the nearby friends she played with—it all sounded quite idyllic. However, as her story continued, serious problems complicated the picture. As her father's agricultural supply business grew, he began spending more time away from home, and he started to cheat, repeatedly, on his wife. Deeply hurt by this, Susan's mother became irritable and withdrawn. As her parents became increasingly preoccupied with their own problems, one of the farmhands physically abused Susan. Previously a top student, it became harder and harder for her to focus on her schoolwork. She was sent off to boarding school, and later bounced from one college to another, before ultimately dropping out. She married young, had two kids, and began drinking heavily every day.

Over the next couple of decades, Susan blew through three marriages, and repeatedly failed in her attempts to stop drinking. She acknowledged that she just did not know how to be in a relationship. During this tough time, she became increasingly alienated from her children, who were raised primarily by her first husband. Finally, after years in and out of Alcoholics Anonymous (AA), Susan made a sustained commitment to the program, and sobered up in her early forties. Around this same time, she met Bill, a rancher who was also recovering from alcoholism. Although he was still prone to significant mood swings, she and Bill were determined to make this relationship work, and they did. After an increasingly stable twenty-year partnership, Bill died a few years ago from pancreatic cancer. Happily, during these last couple of decades, Susan has reconciled with her two children. She is now confident that they love her, she loves them, and that they have forgiven her for her past shortcomings as their mother.

Of all the fifty-two elders we interviewed, no one demonstrated as much candor and humble self-reflection as Susan. Her lengthy struggle with alcoholism forced her to think about the losses, the traumas, and the shameful chapters of her life—all of which had contributed significantly to her addiction. But she has now learned to forgive and be forgiven, to not dwell on the negative, and to not worry about things she cannot control. She has learned to focus on the 'here and now,' to take one step, and one day, at a time, and has accepted that she will always be a "work in progress." Despite all the factors working against her, Susan has friends, in and outside of AA, and she has discovered activities that are meaningful and that challenge her, mentally and physically. Susan is a sterling example of how overcoming weaknesses and bad habits can make someone even stronger, and certainly wiser, than a person who's had an easier go of it in life.

Given the pervasive dysfunction of her childhood family, the abuse she suffered, her interrupted education, her multiple failed marriages, and her chronic alcoholism, Susan in mid-life seemed destined for an unhappy and foreshortened life. Remarkably, she radically changed the arc of her life, largely due to her persistent engagement with AA and her healthy relationship with Bill. (Susan seems to have figured out what a healthy lifestyle looked like many years earlier, but she just needed to connect with the right people to actualize it for herself.) Because Bill had been through multiple failed marriages as well, Susan knew that the two of them needed to learn together how to build a strong and successful relationship. At the time of his death, they had been committed to each other for twenty-three years.

At our first interview, Susan had decided to move to South Carolina full time, largely to avoid the harsh New England winters. We noticed, and she acknowledged, some uneasy ambivalence about this decision. Indeed, when we met with her again two years later, she had changed her mind, and had moved back permanently to her small New England town. It was the close relationships in this town that had drawn her back. It also helped that she had gotten more comfortable with asking for help, especially during the frequent blizzards and periodic power outages in wintertime. Susan thanked us for listening to her in such a patient and supportive way. She talked as if these interviews had been therapeutic. She did know about psychotherapy, had actually been in it several times in the past, and was open to returning to it again, if necessary. She now believes that talking about her problems to a trustworthy person "cuts them in half."

Susan and Jimmy offer shining examples of people who have learned to overcome the powerful human tendency to avoid thinking about difficult feelings and situations. This has allowed them to keep difficulties and shameful mistakes in mind, to process and integrate and learn from them. This process culminated for them in the emergence of a high degree of Self-Acceptance, which has allowed the diverse elements of their lives to come together, and to fit together, in a coherent way. This is the essence of Self-Integrity, the crown jewel of human development.

As we will describe in a later chapter, this achievement of wholeness and self-actualization is a complex and multi-faceted challenge. Their long struggles to find themselves have made Susan and Jimmy stronger as individuals, but also taught them to ask for help when they need it, and to hold their family and friends close. They have given generously to others and do not feel entitled to much in return. They both exuded Gratitude for the benefits and bounties of their lives.

Class Reunion

Ben and Scott were recently part of a fiftieth-class reunion event at their alma mater, Yale University. Members of our class, with a median age of seventy-two, were sent a questionnaire in advance of the reunion. They were asked how they wanted to spend the rest of their lives, which statistically, would average about fifteen years. Channeling the spirit of Peter Pan, several admitted to wanting to stay young forever. Half were still working, either full-time or part-time. Whether in a paid position or as volunteers, many of our classmates were working for idealistic causes, such as strengthening democratic processes at home and abroad, or protecting the environment, or fighting for equity and social justice. Others were mostly at home, taking care of grandchildren, disabled children, or spouses. Most were simply enjoying the prerogatives and the heady freedom of retirement.

Many classmate responses emphasized the theme of acceptance—accepting their lives as they had lived them, accepting that some goals were now not feasible, and accepting that they and their loved ones were, and would be, burdened by affliction and loss in the years ahead. For those who could most whole-heartedly embrace Self-Acceptance, their thoughtful responses resounded with serenity and Gratitude. Here is one example, leavened with charming, self-deprecating humor:

> "Well, jinx. I assume the algorithm already exists that throws cold water on my fantasies of travel, writing the major motion picture screenplay, breaking seventy [for a round of golf], and playing in the NBA. The data isn't there...when you figure in atrial fib and a melanoma, the 'over' on fifteen [years of additional life] looks like a poor bet...and I am completely cursed with the vision of what retirement should look like: it is a man wearing khaki shirt and pants, sitting on a compact tractor, a John Deere to be specific, disking up a small garden plot for spring planting. So, I will enact that scene for sure. But really, if I can peacefully find a way to accept the world, to extend love and kindness to all, but especially my family, to give up struggle and to accept each moment and each breath as a magnificent gift, complete of itself, I will be very satisfied."

As Shakespeare noted, "Many a truth is said in jest." Quite a few of these classmates joked about wanting to magically reverse climate change, eliminate political partisanship, or bring about world peace. Behind these fantasies are, no doubt, remnants of youthful idealism, now seen through the lens of experience and realism. For the most part, there seemed to be an acceptance that their contributions, large and small, to making the world a better place—was enough. ("Enough"—such a powerful self-affirmation!) There is, in this, the clear implication that the baton was being passed to the next generation, as it had been passed to them, decades ago, by those who had gone before.

Here is another reunion comment:

> "I plan to use the time not complaining, not regretting, not fearing...in other words, doing my level best not to turn into a *kvetching*, reactionary grump. Yeah, I can't ride my motorcycle anymore, can't ski the rocks and chutes with the college kids, and I have cancer. I also have perspective, judgment, appreciation, experiential knowledge...all the gifts of age. Like everybody, I've made some dumb decisions and wasted more time than I should have. Yet I would not re-live one moment of my life. I am the happiest I have ever been and intend to stay that way."

In this comment we hear self-forgiveness for mistakes made and for time wasted. It would be unfair to expect that our younger selves should have known and understood everything that we do now, but many people engage in this form of self-flagellation. This fellow accepts his medical condition and his diminished physical capacities with grace, and he wisely reminds himself of the compensatory benefits of age-related wisdom. Here is one last quote, this one from a female classmate:

> "I want to help my husband have some good experiences, in spite of his cognitive decline. I want to help my daughter enjoy life. I want to get back to Massachusetts in order to spend time with my son and his wife, and with my sisters. Hopefully, I can develop and maintain an exercise routine. I really need to paint (oils, watercolors). I long to visit the Cape often, to walk the beaches and swim. It would be nice to visit cousins and friends, see the horses of Chincoteague, revisit favorite art museums, and maybe even visit another country."

Her statement is imbued with an impressive equanimity, and much generosity of spirit. She is taking care of family members, but also keeping alive her hopes for future freedoms and opportunities. It demonstrates a lovely balance between caring for others and self-care. And there is neither resentment, nor impatience, nor surrender to despair or defeat.

These notions about Self-Acceptance converge with some of the mindfulness practices of Jon Kabat-Zinn, mentioned earlier. Both shift the emphasis from *doing and judging* to just *being and accepting*. Although many mindfulness exercises focus on body-based experiences, they share with Self-Acceptance an appreciation for self-awareness and serene self-affirmation. Self-Acceptance focuses on a keen awareness of the nuances and layered complexities of both your *Life Story* and your bio-psycho-social Identity.

Observations and Conclusions

Inevitably, there is a mature appreciation that self-judgment is arbitrary and unreliable; what seems 'good' or 'bad' at any one point may change over time, as you process new experiences and gain additional perspective. Hopefully, such a philosophic insight would promote a more Zen-like acceptance of the totality of yourself, and how you have lived your life. Such an appreciation would discourage the inclination to judge, censor, edit, condemn, or defend. Surely, you have made mistakes, as we all have, and perhaps in those same circumstances you could do better now. But, at the time, maybe you did as well as you could have at that particular moment. Welcome to the human race.

Concluding with a few final thoughts, we recognize the extensive intersection of Self-Acceptance with the other Healthy Habits and with the elder developmental Tasks 5 C's of EIR. Those with a strong sense of Purpose find it easier to forgive themselves. Those with Resilience have confidence that setbacks and mistakes will not defeat them. And, as evident from the inspirational *Life Stories* of Susan and Jimmy, those with Self-Acceptance deeply appreciate what they have, and the people they love. They are imbued with Gratitude and a high degree of Generativity and Self-Integrity. With Self-Acceptance at the helm, we are well-equipped to navigate the shoals and treacherous currents of elderhood with relative grace and confidence.

Connection and Active Practices— Keep Moving!

B ecause they have much in common, we have chosen to describe two important variables together: Connection, which is a component of EIR, and Active Practices (AP), which is one of our five Healthy Habits. Connection focuses narrowly on social engagement and the quantity and quality of our relationships, while AP broadly encompasses medical self-care and activities in the social, intellectual, and physical realms.

Warning: Statistics!

As noted previously, we use the global *Aging Wisely* score (AW#), to summarize our overarching assessment of how successfully each of our elders had aged. Connection, for example, was responsible (as determined by the variance calculation) for 86 percent of AW#, while AP determined 46 percent, which is still fairly high. (The two together add up to more than 100 percent because the overlap between them is counted twice.) Although these are both high variance scores, the magnitude of the Connection score highlights the preeminent importance of interpersonal relationships.

In trying to understand why the AP contribution to AW# was only moderately high, we dug a little deeper into our elder cases. We found that there were a number of individuals who were struggling socially, but who appeared to be trying to make up for it with increased physical and intellectual activities. This compensatory effort was only partially effective—it lifted their AP scores, but their overall AW# was only mid-range. Our conclusion, once again, is that *there is no adequate substitute for social engagement.*

Connection: What Makes a Good Life?

There is nothing more important than relationships in aging wisely. This is also what George Vaillant concluded after more than three decades sifting through the massive data files of the now eighty-five-year-old longitudinal Harvard Study of Adult Development. His successors at the Harvard Study, Robert Waldinger and Marc Schulz, in their recent best-selling book, *The Good Life*, heartily concur. And, as you will read, plentiful research from around the world supports this confident assertion.

In Waldinger's TED Talk, *What makes a good life? Lessons from the longest study on happiness,* he asks a roomful of mostly young people what they are seeking in life.[17] When he mentions choices such as finding a good job, earning a high salary, or achieving important things in a career, many hands go up. Surprisingly, however, all these common aspirations turn out to be of only secondary importance. Waldinger goes on to share the findings of the Harvard study, which resoundingly singles out the unique importance of relationships.

Psychologists use the term 'affective forecasting' to describe the accuracy of our attempts to predict how we will feel in an imagined future situation. Often, humans are fairly lousy at this—winners of mega-lotteries, for example, drift back to their habitual levels of happiness after a year or so. In recent decades, there has sprung up an academic discipline committed to studying the science of happiness. Much of our baseline level of individual happiness appears to be genetic. Martin Seligman, founder of the field of Positive Psychology and author of *Authentic Happiness*, admits that he was born with a below-average level of happiness. Clearly this contributed to his motivation to figure out how people can improve their life-satisfaction scores.

Good news: Seligman's colleague, Sonja Lyubormirsky, after years of exhaustive study, concluded that fully 40 percent of our happiness is based on the lifestyle choices that we make.[18] This means that you could be born into the lower half of the happiness curve but, by dint of wise and disciplined intentionality, you could lift yourself into the top quartile of happy people. And this starts, in large part, with the social aspect of your life.

Waldinger and Schulz describe the various categories of relationships as if they were concentric circles. The inner circle, of course, includes your spouse or partner (or partners, for the unconventional). Adults, not unlike infants, need to feel the safety and security of knowing that there is someone who can be depended upon should a crisis arise. This is a fundamental property of a 'secure attachment.' Vaillant's longitudinal research identified seven controllable factors that were protective against physical and psychological afflictions: having a stable, loving late-life partnership is one of them.[19] The other protective factors, which we discuss below, may or may not surprise you: not smoking, not drinking excessively, not being obese, exercising regularly, completing more schooling, and using mature coping strategies.

Optimally, an inner-circle partner is perceived to be someone who is available, sensitive, and responsive. Having such a comforting relationship has profound effects on body and mind. In one experiment, for example, subjects (who were being monitored with brain scans) were told that a painful shock was forthcoming.[20] Half the group was allowed to hold the hand of a loved one, while the other half were unaccompanied. The result is not surprising: the neurological activity in the brain regions associated with fear and pain were significantly less activated in those who were holding hands with a supportive companion. In daily living, having reliable companionship can help us manage our anxieties more effectively, endure our hardships with aplomb, and cope more wisely with unexpected challenges. Needless to say, this reduces the long-term wear and tear on our physical and mental capacities. And, oh yes, relationships also help us celebrate and enjoy our happy times with higher levels of satisfaction. A party of one is like the sound of one hand clapping.

As we elaborated earlier in our remarks about childhood attachment, there is a clear correlation between one's early family experiences and later adult partnerships. Emmy Werner set out to demonstrate the long reach of childhood experiences by following each of the 690 children born in 1955 on the Hawaiian island of Kauai.[21] When she evaluated those individuals at age thirty, the adversities of their childhood, many of them family related, were associated strongly with a variety of psychological and medical problems. (This finding has been unequivocally confirmed by the recent flood of research on adverse childhood experiences, or ACEs.) However, encouragingly, one-third of Werner's subjects, who had suffered a typical amount of adversity, were able to grow up to become attentive, kind, and emotionally well-adjusted adults. The factor that rescued these survivors was the presence of at least one adult who was concerned, available, and emotionally invested in them. These individuals, years later, were primed to choose loving partners who would provide that same sort of support for them in adulthood.

One of the critically important skills in an intimate relationship is the ability to resolve the inevitable interpersonal conflicts that arise. There is an age-old debate about whether it is better to deal directly with personal problems, or whether one should just move on, and not dwell on them. The Harvard Study's longitudinal data speaks rather decisively to this matter: middle-aged individuals who routinely avoided thinking and talking about their difficulties suffered, thirty years later, from more early dementia and less life-satisfaction.

The healthiest adult partnerships, the ones that promote health and happiness, are the ones in which partners openly and honestly share their feelings, especially if they can do so in a respectful and affectionate way. This often requires making oneself vulnerable, admitting to mistakes, and asking for help at times. Such couples strive to understand each other empathetically, and try to look at the situation through their partner's eyes. Curiously, empathetic accuracy—accurately perceiving how your partner feels—has less impact than *being perceived by your partner as making an effort* to be empathetic. Effortful empathy conveys caring and commitment. This is especially important for a male partner to demonstrate. By contrast, an insecure partnership attachment engenders hostility, withdrawal, secret keeping, and 'keeping score' of wins and losses in the relationship.

Partnerships with intense recurring problems may require professional help. For others, however, the WISER model has been empirically validated as an emotional-assistance tool:

Watch—noticing carefully what is going on, and how you are responding to it
Interpret—deciding which narrative best explains the motives and feelings of each person
Select—after considering your options, choosing the best response
Engage—implementing your response in a caring, sensitive way
Reflect—evaluating how well your response has worked out, adjusting if necessary

The WISER model helps people step back from a repetitive dysfunctional interaction and reflect more deeply about possible feelings and motives in themselves and others. It is easy to assume that we already know a partner so well that we do not really need to listen carefully to what they are saying, or to consider unexpected meanings or motives. That is a mistake. Ben, in his psychoanalytic practice, was constantly being surprised by the thoughts, emotional reactions, and behaviors of patients with whom he worked intensively for years. Human beings are complicated, and they continue to change over time. Making assumptions can be a risky strategy when managing conflict in an important relationship.

The complexity of human psychology has led Buddhist practitioners to recommend the 'beginner mind,' embodied by the phrase "I don't know, please explain." Refraining from knee-jerk reactions requires self-control and the humility to admit that maybe there are aspects of the situation that you have not yet considered. Slowing the process down in your mind, and refraining from responding immediately, can allow for the emergence of new insights. There is an iconic joke that is routinely told to psychoanalytic trainees: "Don't just do something, sit there."

In addition to dyadic partnerships, relationships with immediate family and close friends are also considered to be 'strong ties.' There is a familiar movie trope that depicts a Thanksgiving dinner turned disastrous by wildly eccentric or obnoxious relatives. Although we may be sorely tempted to just expel such difficult people from our lives, this might come at a steep price. Families can be split apart, sometimes permanently, by short-lived conflicts or temper outbursts, especially if the family culture leaves little room for apologies or reconciliations. An additional consequence of banishment arises if there are children involved— these kids would potentially grow up without the enriching, loving contact with aunts, uncles, and cousins.

Impulse control and the practice of self-reflection can prevent many of these family meltdowns. It is helpful to start by trying to identify exactly what is quite so provocative about these individuals. (If you were to portray them theatrically, how would you play the part?) Do they monopolize the conversation, or brag about themselves endlessly, or rant angrily about one subject after another? Do others also find their behavior intolerable, or is it just you? Any ideas about what in their life might have made them the person they became? (We love the Maya Angelou quote, "Most people, if they could do better, they would.") Could you humanize them by noticing attractive things about them that do not fit their caricatured reputation? Could you tolerate at least a brief but cordial conversation with them, and then find an excuse to step away? All of these internal reconsiderations require psychological work—it is tempting to just avoid them, rudely if necessary. But you should be wary of sawing too many limbs off the family tree.

For families living close to each other, sitting down regularly for meals can nurture and sustain familial bonds. Each member at the table may have something different to contribute—this can broaden everyone's worldview. The kids may have some hot news about emerging technology or popular culture. The elders can put current events into an historical perspective or recall some important family history. Later, as the kids move out or parents relocate, geographic distances can make maintaining family ties more challenging. Routine visits, such as during holidays, birthdays, or religious events, can help sustain family cohesion. During the COVID pandemic, Scott's wife, Bev, was successful in organizing group video calls with a cousins' group. This global group continues to meet periodically, and an additional group for younger cousins is also coming together. Also, welcoming in person a new baby (life begins) or attending memorial services (life ends) reminds everyone of deep family bonds. Although new technologies can be off-putting, or even scary, for elders, they are increasingly essential for sustaining family connections.

Beyond family, close friendships are part of the psychological life-blood that sustains us. A twelve-year study with more than 1,100 seniors found that the most social among them, compared with their least social peers, had 70 percent less cognitive decline.[22] Social interactions challenge us to try to understand another person's point-of-view, which in turn builds up brain regions such as the frontal lobes and the amygdala.[23] A large longitudinal study in Australia found that, for people over the age of seventy, the risk of dying over a ten-year period decreased by almost one-quarter for those with the most vigorous social lives.[24] One researcher tried to estimate the maximum number of social contacts that were beneficial, and the conclusion was 150![25] How many of us can claim a personal social network of 150 individuals that we keep up with on a regular basis?

In an investigation involving more than 2,800 nurses stricken with breast cancer, those with ten or more friends were four times more likely to survive than those with none.[26] For these nurses, there was nothing that improved their recovery more than having an active social network and confidence that they would be supported by others. This was often someone outside of the family who would go with her to appointments, take her to chemotherapy, stay with her during the infusion, and then get her home, fed, and tucked into bed. (So as to not overburden any one individual, it is best to have a team of people that can take turns.) This is what secure attachments in adulthood can look like.

In animal studies, half of a sample of female rats were assigned randomly to a condition of social isolation.[27] About 50 percent of those in isolation developed breast tumors, compared to only 15 percent of those living in a normal social environment. In rodents and humans, friendly interaction with peers lowers stress hormones such as cortisol and adrenaline, and energizes the immune system, which attacks both disease-causing microbes as well as pre-cancerous tumor cells.

Friendship, for American men especially, can be conflictual. Acknowledging a need for friendship can feel shameful, as if this is a weakness, proof that they are not as independent or manly as they should be. Men can be reluctant to call a friend or even set up a social lunch appointment. Those in the Harvard Study, and their wives, were sent a questionnaire when they turned seventy.[28] They were asked if they were satisfied with the number and the closeness of their friendships—30 percent of the men were dissatisfied, but only 6 percent of women. One of the male participants said, "I've never really had a close friend." Close friendships buffer us from some of worst aspects of trauma and loss. For example, those men who saw combat in either World War II or the Korean War were less likely to develop PTSD if they had served in a military unit that was cohesive and connected.[29] Many of these fortunate individuals continued to call, write, or visit their fellow soldiers for the rest of their lives.

These sorts of long-term relationships are vitally important. Especially during mid-life, when one is besieged by the unrelenting demands of family and work, it is easy to lose touch with significant people in our lives. As these demands later ease up (for most of us) in elderhood, there is an opportunity to reach out to old friends, or to make new ones. Making the first move might require pushing past some awkwardness and the possibility of rejection. Maybe with certain old friends, there might have been an unresolved conflict that came between the two of you, years ago. If so, could you humble yourself enough to acknowledge the problem, and to apologize for your part in it? Could you convey that you wish to resume the friendship?

Lillian Rubin and others have attempted to characterize the difference between male and female friendships. They describe men as preferring 'side-by-side' friendships organized around activities and structured settings. Women, by contrast, have more informal 'face-to-face' friendships, with unscheduled exchanges of intimate thoughts and feelings. Subsequent research, however, has suggested that these are, at best, half-truths: male and female friendships have much in common.

Our discussion thus far has focused on what the psychological literature calls 'strong ties'—people you can depend upon for companionship or for help in a crisis. But many of these psychological advantages can also accrue from relationships that are categorized as 'weak ties.' As described previously, psychologist Susan Pinker's *The Village Effect* describes the benefits of feeling that you are connected to a wide circle of people around you. Pinker studied the one place in the world where men live as long as women: on the island of Sardinia, off the western coast of Italy.

Per capita, there are ten times as many centenarians in Sardinia as in the U.S. Some of this may be genetic, some attributable to a healthy diet, but much of this difference seems related to their social lives. The neighborhoods in Sardinia are a maze of narrow streets, alleys, and cottages with small back yards. Everyone is on a first-name basis and, if something significant is going on, everyone seems to know about it. (Again, we are reminded of the TV sitcom *Cheers'* theme song: "…where everybody knows your name, and troubles are all the same.") Elders are not shunted aside as irrelevant—they remain a part of the fabric of the community. No one is left out. Although introverts may shudder at the prospect of such unrelenting engagement, the longevity data are hard to dismiss.

So, what might the Sardinia evidence mean for the rest of us? In your walks around your neighborhood, do you strike up conversations with the people you bump into? Maybe there is a grocer, a postal carrier, or a security guard who you have seen multiple times—do you ask them their name or inquire about how their day is going? In one coffee shop study, half the group of customers were coached to be quick and efficient, while the other half were instructed to smile at the barista, make eye contact, and engage them in social conversation.[30] The latter group came away feeling better, and with a stronger sense of belonging. Cumulatively, these 'weak ties' add up to something quite substantial, both for us and for those with whom we interact.

The Good Life encourages us to reconsider the time we spend at work. As noted, Scott and Ben found that half of their fiftieth college reunion classmates are still working in their early to mid-seventies, either full- or part-time. The work-life balance is a crucial factor when deciding whether, and when, to retire—this decision brings one's priorities into sharp focus. In a study in the United Kingdom, for instance, it was calculated that the average eighty-year-old had spent, over their lifetime, about 8,800 hours with friends, 9,500 hours with intimate partners, and…112,000 hours at work![31] Some fortunate individuals absolutely love their work. Scott often asked his coaching clients, "Do you live to work, or work to live?" The answer largely determines one's career path, lifestyle tradeoffs, and retirement timetable. It is worth noting that vocational work is good exercise for your brain. But, if you truly accept that you do not have unlimited time, it is worth asking yourself just how you want to spend what time remains. Any of us could be on the receiving end of a terminal diagnosis at any time. If this happened to you next week, would you have regrets about how you have prioritized your time allocation so far?

If you do continue to work, are you making the most of your social opportunities there? Commonly, work is seen as a silo, separate and distinct from 'real life.' Many workplace cultures are all about 'the numbers': sales closed, customers served, revenue generated. However, even in settings such as these, small acts of kindness can go a long way. Noticing a co-worker's unusual coffee mug or asking about their weekend while riding together on the elevator—perhaps these and other overlooked moments could build Connections. Some particularly sociable individuals come to think of fellow workers as a second family. Following the COVID pandemic, many people now work primarily or even exclusively from home. Although convenient, this does make workplace socializing considerably more difficult, and can increase social isolation.

Civic and Community Engagement

Robert Putnam, in his *Bowling Alone* books and lectures, highlights the rapid decline of civic engagement and communal memberships in America. Although the book title was inspired by the attrition in bowling league participation, membership in religious practice groups (churches, synagogues, and mosques), Rotary clubs, sports leagues, and parent-teacher associations have all been hollowed out in recent decades. Putnam has identified the erosion of 'social capital'—trust and reciprocity—as the fundamental cause of these societal changes. This sea change in social cohesion has significant implications for individuals and for our society at large.

There is a causal link between the decline in social capital and the generalized mistrust of government, news media, and medical and economic 'experts.' This also helps explain lower voter registration, fewer community volunteers, lower levels of charitable contribution, greater pessimism about the future, fewer friends and confidants, more TV watching, decreased happiness, and a lower perceived quality of life. Putnam claims that belonging to one group will lower your per-year mortality rate 50 percent and belonging to two lowers it by 70 percent. Do not bowl alone!

Vivek Murthy, the U.S. Surgeon General (Senate confirmations in 2014 and 2021) declared that loneliness in America is a public health epidemic. While that is a strong statement, he arrived at this conclusion based on several lines of evidence. First, he learned from his own patients, like the one who had won a large lottery payoff. This man had been quite content for many years, socially engaged at work and with neighbors. Like many lottery winners, he immediately quit his job and bought a nicer house in an upscale neighborhood. But, ironically, he came to believe that winning all this money was the worst thing that ever happened to him. By quitting his job, he promptly lost his work friends, many of whom were probably jealous of his newfound wealth. And, by moving out of his neighborhood, he began to lose touch with his other friends. It was not long before he developed high blood pressure and diabetes. He was miserable.

This segues to the second body of evidence for Dr. Murthy. Julianna Holt-Lunsted and others, reviewing more than 140 international studies involving more than 300,000 individuals, decisively documented the medical and psychological risks of loneliness.[32] Specifically, loneliness increases the likelihood of heart disease and strokes by about 30 percent, and ratchets up the risk of dementia by 50 percent. It also impairs the immune system. In short, loneliness *doubles* the risk of premature death—it is as bad for you as smoking and worse than significant obesity. Those with the fewest social ties, compared with those with the most, were more than twice as likely to die at any age. So, for those of you keeping score at home, a sociable eighty-year-old has a 6.5-percent risk of dying sometime during that year, while a lonely peer has a doubled, 13-percent risk.

On any given day, about half of America feels lonely, and it is even worse for elders. There is a powerful downward spiral for older adults: difficulties with hearing, vision, walking or driving all increase social isolation. Being isolated predisposes people to poor hygiene, vanishing social skills, cognitive decline, and a preoccupation with body pain—all of which makes them even less sociable, and less attractive to others. Also, in elderhood, loneliness is the single greatest risk factor for depression. Compared to the rest of the world, elder Americans are considerably less involved with their families. According to Pew Research data (2010-2018), only 6 percent of U.S. adults over the age of sixty live with extended family, while the average across the globe is 38 percent![33] And 27 percent of U.S. seniors live alone, versus 16 percent worldwide. The number of single-person U.S. households has doubled in the last sixty years. Connection builds, loneliness kills.

The final piece of evidence that convinced the Surgeon General about loneliness was his own personal experience. Murthy had enjoyed extraordinary successes in his life—with his career, his marriage, his kids, and his extended family. But, upon finishing his first tour of duty as Surgeon General, he found himself feeling lonely and depressed. He was separated from all his work colleagues, the people he had spent so many long days with over many years. He had also come to realize that, because of his absolute commitment to his work, he had let his relationships with family and friends languish. In retrospect, Murphy now appreciated that, even when he had been with the people he loved, he had often been distracted, and eager to get back to his emails and work obligations. When he thought about trying to reconnect with old friends, he felt embarrassed and was afraid of rejection. Most disturbingly, he was having an Identity crisis—he was just not sure who he was anymore.

To weather this dire personal crisis, Murthy had the profound good fortune to have the unwavering support of his wife and children, as well as daily calls from his mother, father, and sister. All told, it took a year for him to feel like himself again. Happily, his old companions welcomed him back, which lifted his spirits. This harrowing personal experience forcefully impressed upon Murthy the cost of becoming separated from one's social milieu. He now can use his position as leader of our nation's public health program to prioritize the importance of social Connections.

Because actions speak louder than words, Murthy has made several concrete recommendations, some of which are quite relevant to elders. He encourages all of us to take fifteen minutes every day to reach out, especially to people we have lost touch with. We should say hello to neighbors and notice when someone is struggling. Also, we should look for opportunities to help. Nothing relieves loneliness as quickly as helping others and feeling that you are needed. (Some groups of elders living alone have set up phone trees, so that everyone gets a call every morning to make sure that they are alright, and are starting their day on a positive note.)

We agree wholeheartedly with Dr. Murthy and these other experts. Our interview data are quite convergent with this data and the explanatory theories proposed. Ella (Chapter 1), Gloria (Chapter 2), Frank (Chapters 3 and 4), Omar (Chapter 5), Sam and Katrin (Chapter 6), and Jimmy (Chapter 7) would all readily agree that relationships are the heartbeat of their lives. Each of them is also involved actively in their religious practices and they are emphatic about the importance of their religious communities.

Our other high-scoring elders, Susan (Chapter 7) and Ann and Skip (Chapter 9), are more spiritual than religious, but all are active in community groups, including churches. Each of these exemplary individuals has a strong partnership, except Susan, who lost her soulmate a few years ago (and who has substituted for this loss with remarkable creativity). None of our low-scoring elders—Natasha (Chapter 2), Tony (Chapters 3 and 4), Daniel (Chapter 5), Don (Chapter 9), and Mike (Chapter 10)—has significant friendships or religious or community affiliations. And, of these, only Natasha has a successful late-life partnership. Taken together, these case studies offer additional supportive evidence regarding the strong linkage between Connection and aging wisely.

The power of human relationships appears everywhere. *The Good Life* book was made possible because of the long and fruitful collaboration of its co-authors, but also by the loyalty that many of the study participants felt towards a remarkably engaging social worker, Lewise Gregory Davies. She was given much of the credit for the Harvard Study's extraordinary 84-percent lifelong retention rate—many of the men admitted that they had not dropped out because they did not want to disappoint Lewise.

Similarly, Scott and Ben's now fifty-five-year friendship provided the relationship safety net that allowed *The Aging Wisely Project* to survive the potentially disastrous self-doubts, mood swings, narcissistic injuries, and conflicting writing styles that sternly challenged us over the six-year project timeline. And, just as we were beginning to resolve our initial conflicts over semi-colons and the use of statistics, suddenly we had to figure out how to conduct our interviews virtually during the COVID pandemic. (Really, a *pandemic*? *Now*?)

Neither one of us could have completed this project on his own. Starting with our initial bonding as anxious eighteen-year-old college freshmen, together we faced the expectable vicissitudes of female rejections, nitpicking professors, and nagging parents. Later, early in our careers, we met for bi-weekly lunches. We supported each other through early job insecurities, parenting challenges, and failed first marriages. We celebrated the first forty years of our relationship with a scuba diving trip to the Florida Keys. When Ben's youngest daughter died, Scott's kind, steady voice greatly comforted him. When those close to Scott struggled with mental health challenges, Ben offered pertinent psychiatric insights and valuable perspective. Now, on the verge of our retirements, we have again thrown in together to make sense of this next and final stage of life. We have indeed grown up, and old, together, and it has been sublime. All this would not have been possible without the companionship, trust, and mutual support shared between us.

Active Practices

There is a lot of 'tired' in 'retired.' Historically, retirement has conjured up images of La-Z-Boy recliners, rocking chairs on the porch, and a steady diet of TV game shows. These are the first steps down a slippery slope, a downward spiral towards senescence and decrepitude. Happily, many media portrayals today depict elders being active and engaged. Becca Levy, a Yale psychologist mentioned earlier, has proposed and validated her stereotype embodiment theory (SET), which links the stereotypes that we have about aging with the kinds of elders that we actually become. A self-fulfilling prophecy.

When endocrinologist Hans Selye popularized the notion of psychosomatic stress in 1956, he tried to make the point that 'stress' was anything that pushes people to change and adapt. He distinguished 'bad stress' (distress) from 'good stress' (eustress), but somehow most people still came away with the impression that all stress is bad for you. As already discussed, the concept of hormesis turns this thinking on its head: you may recall those underfed rodents who lived 50 percent longer. Underfed humans have reduced inflammatory elements in their blood.[34] How can this be?

University of Washington scientist Daniel Promislow, a biogerontologist, is one of several researchers studying the difference between genetics and epigenetics. Epigenetics ('upon the genes') refers to the processes by which the genes in our DNA are turned on and off. The genes themselves are fixed, but their degree of activation is dependent on a wide variety of organismic and environmental factors. This is how 'nurture' interfaces with 'nature' and is one more way that our species has evolved to adapt to changing conditions. Simply put, certain stressors in the mild-to-moderate range turn on health-promoting genes that would otherwise remain dormant and inactive. This is one of the keys to healthy aging.

For more specific lifestyle recommendations, we can turn to another University of Washington faculty member, John Medina, a self-declared 'developmental molecular biologist.' His *Brain Rules for Aging Well* is a humorous and reader-friendly summary of the scientific literature (up through 2017) about optimal Active Practices for aging. We will also augment his material with more recent scientific findings. It is a good thing that Medina has an endearing sense of humor, because, as he admits, his recommendations can come across like a combination of your mother and your doctor: incessant scolding and nettlesome rules.

Social

Because you have just read about the biopsychosocial importance of relationships, we begin there, but only briefly. It is worth adding that social interaction is terrific for your brain—as long as it is not associated with a 'toxic relationship.' Bad partners, bosses from hell, and toxic friendships can *literally* cause brain damage. Conversely, engaging in complex, intimate, positive relationships keeps you mentally on your toes. It is easy to overlook just how busy your brain is when you are looking into someone's eyes, noticing their facial expressions and body movements, and monitoring the semantic and musical elements of their speech. You are simultaneously hearing their vocabulary, processing their sentence structure, resonating with their metaphors, and tracking the narrative they are spinning. And, on a deeper level, you are trying to discern their feelings, their motives, and their attitude toward you. Naturally, you are wondering what they are going to say next, and trying to extrapolate where the conversation is going. Perhaps you are also thinking about how their communication relates to you, your thoughts, your life. Quite a cognitive workout!

As noted, even when Ben has worked multiple times a week, for several years, with a psychoanalytic patient, he constantly hears things that he did not anticipate. Scott, in his corporate and executive coaching roles, has worked hard to differentiate between what people are saying, compared with what they really mean. For example, an employee complaining bitterly about their low salary may really be unhappy with the quality of their relationship with a supervisor, or an unsatisfying work environment. And, of course, our spouses and children constantly surprise us, just as we surprise them.

Clearly, our minds get vigorous exercise when we engage interpersonally. And, extra brain stimulation points will be awarded for interacting with children, or people from different backgrounds, or those with different political persuasions. Simply sitting around, shooting the breeze in a superficial way with people much like yourself does not get your brain out of its BarcaLounger. Again, the goal is mid-level stress that keeps you on your toes, and that challenges you to engage and to understand.

Cognitive

When Ben was in medical school, it was widely accepted that Alzheimer's disease, the most common form of dementia, was caused by an accumulation of amyloid plaques and neurofibrillary tangles in brain neurons. There was no known intervention to prevent or to treat Alzheimer's. One of the first major studies to cast doubt on these assumptions was the so-called Nun Study, which involved 680 nuns from the School Sisters of Notre Dame convent, located just outside Minneapolis.[35] Beginning in the mid-1980s, these nuns generously allowed David Snowdon and his team to evaluate their cognitive functioning during their lives, and then post-mortem, to study their brain tissue under the microscope. It was expected that there would be a strong causal relationship between the degree of neuronal abnormalities found in their brains, and the measurable cognitive decline that had been evident during the last years of their lives.

One of the most dynamic of these nuns, Sister Mary, had taught middle school for seven decades and, even after her retirement from teaching, had been a force to be reckoned with in convent life. She ultimately died, still active, at the age of 101. When pathologists examined her brain, it turned out to be a complete mess—the quantity of plaques and tangles would have led one to assume that she would have been bedridden and incoherent for years. The converse also was true—there were a number of her sister nuns who were totally demented and debilitated, but whose brains looked relatively normal.

These findings sent shock waves through the medical community. Still, there was one more very curious discovery. As part of the admissions process for those seeking to join this order of nuns, each of these young women had been obliged to write a brief autobiography. Decades later, when these writing samples were analyzed, a remarkable pattern was detected. Of the nuns who had written linguistically complex and thoughtful autobiographies, only 10 percent went on to develop dementia. This contrasted starkly with those who had written rather simple and superficial autobiographies, 80 percent of whom later became demented. The conclusion was rather obvious: the more these women had developed the habit of energetically using their brains, from an early age, the less likely they were to develop dementia many decades later.

This intuitively appealing notion—that the more you use your brain, the less likely you are to lose it—is borne out by large-scale epidemiological studies. These findings have lent credence to the notion of 'cognitive reserve.' Three major lifestyle factors seem to provide protection from developing dementia: the number of years of formal education, working at a cognitively demanding job, and having a life that is bustling with intellectual, social, and physical challenges. At a neurological level, these lifestyle factors increase the thickness of the cerebral cortex and strengthen the connectivity between brain regions—more neurons, more branches on each neuron, and more fibers between neurons. On the flip side, there are three factors that appear to increase the risk of dementia: chronic psychological distress, chronic sleep deprivation, and a monotonous lifestyle that is devoid of novelty or enlivening stimulation.

Denise Park and her team at the University of Texas recruited a group of more than 200 elders, aged sixty to ninety, and randomly assigned them to different activities, fifteen hours per week for three months.[36] One group was tasked to learn a new skill—such as digital photography, quilting, or both—which required active engagement and tapped into working memory, long-term memory, and other high-level cognitive processes. A second group listened to classical music or played word games and puzzles, while a third group engaged in social events, such as group field trips. At the end of three months, only the first group—who had experienced persistent intellectual challenges—showed improvements in memory. Only continuous and prolonged mental challenge stimulates cognitive function improvement.

In a particularly ambitious study by Shirley Leanos and colleagues, elders were challenged to learn three new skills simultaneously: Spanish, drawing, and musical composition.[37] After three months, their measured scores for working memory, cognitive control, and episodic memory were equivalent to that of individuals *thirty years younger*! Subsequent investigations have confirmed these findings.

Although reading light fiction does not do much for your brain, reading demanding text, with difficult vocabulary and novel ideas, does improve brain function, especially if you stick with it for four hours per day. Learning a new language, or a new (or long-neglected) musical instrument gives your brain a good workout. Those who are fluent in two languages have less dementia, and those with three even less than that. (Medina joked that everyone should take their first Social Security check and immediately invest in a foreign language course.)

You do your brain a big favor by becoming a lifelong learner—even better if you have the opportunity to teach others. Conclusion: *to improve your brain, you need to exercise it regularly and to push yourself routinely beyond your comfort zone*. And the more that different parts of your brain are being activated and engaged, the better. What is critically important is to establish healthy routines and habits.

For more than four decades, scientists and medical professionals commonly believed that elders were losing thousands of brain cells every day. This notion justified significant pessimism about the aging brain—it is true that the overall size of a brain does shrink in elderhood.[38] However, recent research by Harvard's Bradley Hyman and colleagues has found that the brains of fifty-seven-year-olds have roughly the same number of neurons as those of ninety-year-olds.[39] The overall shrinkage in brain volume is primarily due to the loss of myelin, the sheath that insulates the neurons—which is comparable to the plastic insulation surrounding electrical wires. Changes in the brain, such as myelin degradation, as well as lower levels of neurotransmitter chemicals, and fewer receptor sites, do diminish neuronal efficiency, but this is much less consequential than an actual loss of neurons would have been. Also, remarkably, when there is significant age-related deterioration in one area of the brain, neurons from other, functionally unrelated regions can be recruited to maintain cognitive capabilities. (And this is most pronounced in those with high levels of 'cognitive reserve.') This rewiring process is most obvious after a stroke or other major brain injuries.[40] Ah, the adaptive virtuosity of our bodies!

(Another, albeit unrelated, example: although red blood cells are normally produced by our bone marrow, if the marrow is too damaged, there are cells in both the spleen and the liver that can be repurposed to produce red cells. Such amazing built-in redundancy in our bodies!)

There has been extensive research conducted on the neurological effects of cognitive training with elders. Some researchers are convinced that certain forms of mental exercise actually change the anatomy of the brain. This involves increasing the number of neurons (neurogenesis) and/or by adding new branches and synapses to existing neurons (synaptogenesis). Myelin is also added, further adding to the benefits of the exercise.

Other scientists were convinced that, rather than building new structures, cognitive exercises were beneficial primarily because they modified the way in which the brain used its existing anatomy. It has been established that mental stimulation does elevate blood flow and cerebral metabolism in the brain areas being activated. Over time, these brain regions show more efficient functioning; in some studies, these anti-aging effects endure for prolonged periods (up to five years). In many other investigations, however, the benefits of a brain stimulation program fade quickly. This is the sobering aspect of 'use it or lose it'—you have to *keep using it*. Also, sadly, nearly all the functional improvements are limited to the specific skills and tasks being practiced. Improving your crossword puzzle vocabulary, for example, does not improve your processing speed. Therefore, the exaggerated claims of various for-profit brain stimulating computer and phone app programs should be considered with a good deal of skepticism. Look for those programs validated by solid research.

For most people, the best strategy is to find mentally challenging activities that you really enjoy, those that can become a routine and regular habit. In the best of all possible worlds, these activities would also entail a strong social dimension, such as tutoring a student, reading to young children, or engaging in group learning or problem-solving.

Psychological

Depression, severe anxiety, post-traumatic stress disorder, substance abuse, severe personality disorders, prolonged grief, and psychotic illnesses such as schizophrenia are all associated with disability and a shorter life span. About 20 percent of the U.S. population each year are afflicted by one or more of these conditions—if you are one of them, you should seek professional help. A recent scientific publication evaluating more than 1.4 million individuals from Denmark found that a diagnosis of depression, at any time after the age of eighteen, more than doubled the risk of dementia in elderhood.[41] (Note: this study did not distinguish those who received treatment, and those who had gone untreated.) Anxiety in elderhood increases the risk of Alzheimer's by 45 percent. Either anxiety or depression also increases the risk of cardiovascular disease, autoimmune disorders, and premature mortality. Some of the Healthy Habits described here can help individuals with mild versions of these psychological conditions, however moderate to severe disorders usually require specialty care.

The modern world is highly distressing, sometimes by design. Online and print media intentionally elicit fear, shock, and anger to capture more attention and to sell more products. Automated online and phone-based customer service can be maddeningly frustrating. Some corporations and managers attempt to maximize productivity by keeping workers fearful and insecure. Politicians provoke fear, mistrust, and rage to elevate their poll numbers, and to advance their careers. Those oppressed by structural agism, racism, sexism, homophobia, transphobia, or other forms of prejudice are at high risk of psychosomatic disorders. Low income, blue-collar, and service workers without a college degree age about ten years faster than their professional peers.[42] We saw the effects of these systemic forces in our *Aging Wisely* interviews: individuals of color, and those living close to or at the poverty line, looked and acted a decade older than their more affluent, white counterparts. They were also suffering with significantly more autoimmune disorders (e.g., arthritis), impaired mobility, and memory problems.

With regard to intimate family relationships, those with chronically high levels of family conflict, stress, and even violence are more likely to be diagnosed with anxiety, depression, and stress-related medical illnesses. A perpetually unhappy marriage can slow wound healing by as much as 40 percent.[43] Serving as a long-term caregiver for a disabled child or a demented partner is known to shorten the telomeres on your chromosomes, a strong indicator of accelerated physical aging.

Biologically, we are built to deal with short-term threats. Our 'fight or flight' (or 'freeze') reactions allowed our ancestors to outrun predators and to fight off or hide from dangerous adversaries. The activation of our sympathetic nervous system pumps up both heart rate and blood pressure to maximize our physical capabilities. It also triggers the release of hormones such as adrenaline (epinephrine) and cortisol into our blood stream. Unfortunately, overuse of these emergency measures is damaging. John Medina is even more emphatic—he points out that chronic stress, with a persistent elevation of these fight-or-flight hormones, causes the very same changes in blood pressure, blood clotting (risking strokes and heart attacks), pre-diabetic symptoms, and brain damage that are seen in typical aging.[44]

Put simply, chronically high stress accelerates the aging of our bodies. Therefore, it is particularly important for elders to avoid unnecessary stress because, once the fight or flight activation is triggered, it takes much longer for the bodies and minds of elders to turn off these emergency measures. Ben and Scott used to routinely wait until the last minute to complete important tasks, knowing that a deadline would kick in powerful motivations. Now, they find that the escalation of performance anxiety not only feels quite disagreeable, it also lowers their productivity. So, belatedly, they have learned the advantages of completing work well in advance. We encourage our readers to consider whether, over time, you have changed your response to deadlines.

The opposite of fight or flight is deep relaxation. Medina is a strong proponent of Jon Kabat-Zinn's mindfulness exercises, whose efficacy has strong empirical support. Habitual mindfulness practitioners enjoy a wide variety of mental, emotional, and physical benefits. These include improvements in attention, memory, mental flexibility, verbal fluency, immune system functioning, and sleep. They also have measurably less brain shrinkage, depression, anxiety, and loneliness. There are also published reports of other effective relaxation exercises: listening to classical music or to bird songs or engaging in deep 'forest bathing.'

There is also a burgeoning literature about 'flow states' as first described by Mihaly Csikszentmihalyi. A flow state involves immersing yourself so completely in a pleasurable activity that you relax, forget your problems, lose track of time, and sometimes even begin to feel that you are a part of something greater than yourself. A similar deep absorption can be achieved with virtual reality helmets. Scott achieves this flow state when reading a good book or when immersing himself in an evening of Israeli folk dancing with wife Bev. He can also get there when playing golf with good friends—if he can forget about the poor shots quickly and savor the good ones.

In 1981, Harvard psychologist Ellen Langer conducted a remarkable study.[45] She gathered a group of seventy-year-old men and sequestered them for five days in a remote location. The environment was carefully designed to create the illusion that they were back in the world that they had inhabited in their late forties. From the music, the magazines on the coffee table, and even the vintage NFL playoff game on the TV—the setting recreated 1959. As expected, this environment lifted their mood. But these participants also experienced measurable improvements in grip strength, manual dexterity, posture, visual acuity, hearing, and cognitive functioning. On the final day, one of the rejuvenated elders cast aside his cane and joined in an impromptu game of touch football! This paradigm-shifting investigation came to be known as 'The Counter-Clockwise Study.'

These findings, replicated by subsequent research, led Langer to conclude, "[W]e feel there is enough evidence to suggest that the 'inevitable' decay of the aging human body may, in fact, be reversed through psychological interventions." Medina was so impressed by this extreme form of stress relief that he recommends to his readers that they create a 'reminiscence room' that provides a multi-sensory immersion back in the world of their late teens and early twenties. During this period of development, most people lay down vivid 'permastore' (permanent storage) memories that are most potent in evoking pleasurable Dopamine-fueled nostalgia. He recommends spending a little time in such a space every day: your own personal 'Fountain of Youth.' For us Boomers, listening to the popular music of the 1960s and 1970s, looking at old family photo albums, or reminiscing with long-time friends and classmates can evoke the same positive effects.

Physical Activity

Almost weekly, new studies are being announced about the importance of physical exercise. The Fact Sheet put out by the World Health Organization (WHO) in October 2022 summarized the many benefits of exercise.[46] These include weight loss, improved strength and stamina, and diminished risk of a wide variety of afflictions: heart disease, stroke, high blood pressure, diabetes, dementia, infectious disease, and cancer. Surprisingly, vigorous exercise also helps to induce new brain cell formation (from dormant stem cells) in the hippocampus, which enhances memory. Many elders enjoy improved sleep quality after exercise.

The WHO recommends 150 to 300 minutes per week of moderate exercise, optimally spread out across three or more days ('moderate' is defined as exercise that would make it difficult to carry on a conversation). Alternatively, you could opt for 75 to 150 minutes of weekly vigorous exercise (activities that cause panting respiration). To diminish the risk of falling, WHO also encourages "varied multi-component physical activity that emphasizes functional balance and strength training at moderate or greater intensity." Yoga, exercise classes, or stretching activities help keep joints limber and diverse muscle groups working together. Weight-bearing exercise, even just using your own body weight, improves bone density: push-ups, planks, and all those calisthenic exercises that we grumbled about in gym class.

Standing on one leg strengthens balance, particularly if you use specially designed balance pads. (Many elders tie this to brushing their teeth—shift legs as you move from lower teeth to upper.)

Elders who fall are at risk of concussions and hip fractures, and hip fractures are associated with a high mortality rate. In Australia, falls by the elderly account for 5 percent of that nation's annual medical expenses.[47] Medina is particularly bullish about the benefits of dancing and other forms of ritualized movement, such as tai chi and martial arts. Scott's wife, Bev, is an expert practitioner of Israeli dancing, and Scott has danced alongside her for more than twenty years. Going to national and international dance workshops has helped them get to know participants from all over the world, some of whom they have visited when traveling. That is quite the trifecta—enhancing balance, improving coordination, and strengthening social connections!

Medical Self-Care

In *The Longevity Project*, Friedman and Martin combed through the massive longitudinal files of Stanford's Terman Study to try to answer a simple question: what single factor best predicts longevity? Intelligence? Being a hyper-social extrovert? Big-city residence, or living in the fresh-air countryside? The answer was much more pedestrian: it was *conscientiousness*.[48] This involves not driving drunk, not playing with guns, not walking through sketchy neighborhoods at night, and not undertaking reckless mountain climbing. This enlightened path also requires going to the doctor and dentist, taking your medicines as prescribed, keeping up with your vaccinations, and getting that colonoscopy, mammogram, or prostate exam on schedule. No fun, right?

It is important to remember that, until the past hundred years of human history, most people did not live past their fifties. Our bodies did not need to hold up that long because disease, famine, violent accidents, predators, or battling with a rival tribe tended to do our ancestors in by middle age. Now, we expect our bodies to carry on for at least twice that long. And, if we have reasonably good genes and are lucky, they can, but only if we take good care of ourselves. The advances in preventive medicine, early diagnosis, and advanced treatments give us huge advantages that were not available until recent decades. We also know about healthy diets; the Mediterranean diet and the MIND diet, among others, help prevent dementia and extend lives.

Those struggling with obesity can avail themselves of new emerging interventions. Vitamin D and C supplementation and daily calcium all prevent common dietary deficiencies. Dental hygiene—brushing, flossing, and the use of an electric toothbrush—not only helps preserve teeth and gums, but also prevents chronic low-level inflammation that can, over time, tax the immune system. And, of course, there are many more specific health recommendations, based on your specific medical history, family genetic history, individual risk factors, and current environmental exposures.

Sleep

Over the last several decades, there has been a growing appreciation for the importance of healthy sleep habits. It is during sleep that information encoded during the day into short-term memory is transferred to long-term memory storage (although this process may be less important for elders). It is also a time for the nervous, digestive, and immune systems to reset themselves. While we sleep, the waste products of cellular metabolism in the brain are washed out by the glymphatic system, particularly during Stage 4, slow-wave sleep (SWS).

Unfortunately, there is an age-related incremental dysfunction in the regulation of our daily circadian rhythms. This curtails the amount of SWS in elders, which diminishes the efficiency of this waste-removal process. This may be one reason why, as noted earlier, chronic sleep deprivation reduces cognitive reserve. (Healthy sleep habits in middle age are a strong protective factor against late-life cognitive decline.) Habitually inadequate sleep in elderhood is causally associated with neurodegenerative disorders such as Parkinson's, Huntington's, and Alzheimer's Diseases. There is also a correlation with depression and anxiety disorders, although the direction of causality is unclear.

Building upon the pioneering work of Peter Hauri, and further elaborated by CBTi (cognitive-behavioral therapy for insomnia) researchers, the basic parameters for healthy 'sleep hygiene' have been established:

1. Exercise, physically and socially, early in the day.
2. Avoid caffeine, tobacco, and alcohol six hours before bedtime.
3. Avoid bright lights (especially screens with blue wavelength light) prior to bedtime. Expose yourself to bright lights early in the morning (unfiltered sunlight is best), and subdued light in the evening.
4. Although there is much variation between individuals regarding the average duration of sleep, six to nine hours is recommended. Try to go to bed at the same time each evening, but not before you are sleepy.

5. Never remain in bed more than thirty minutes if you cannot get to sleep or cannot go back to sleep. Get out of bed and read (literature not on electronic screens) until you are sleepy.
6. Set your alarm to wake up at the same time, even if you have slept poorly—this is important for resetting the circadian clock in your brain.
7. Keep your bedroom reserved for sleeping and sex: No eating, working, or TV. Also, keep your night-time bedroom temperature cool, around 65 degrees Fahrenheit, if possible.

This program has proved successful with a majority of sleep-disordered patients. If it does not work for you, a referral to a sleep specialist may be in order. Beware of medications for sleep; elders in particular are susceptible to side effects that may cause confusion or falling. If necessary, you could try low-dose Melatonin, 0.3 to 1 milligram, and gradually increase the dose if needed. Consult with your physician before trying prescription sleep medications.

Religion and Spirituality

Another underutilized resource for many people today is in the domain of religion and spirituality. A Pew Research Center report from 2021 found that almost 30 percent of Americans were religiously unaffiliated.[49] And, between 2011-2021 the number of people affiliated with Christianity dropped from 75 to 63 percent. True, there are many well-documented problems with organized religion, from priest pedophilia to religious leaders cozying up to flagrantly deplorable politicians. Nevertheless, there are still many admirable individuals and organizations that offer theological wisdom and the opportunity for belonging to a supportive community of fellow believers.

Given our culture's skepticism toward orthodoxy and unquestioning obedience to ancient traditions, it is understandable that many find themselves religiously disaffected. There are, however, radical alternatives to mainstream beliefs and practices. Moving beyond the concrete notion that 'faith' is a set of rigid orthodox beliefs, German theologian Paul Tillich defined faith as "the state of ultimate concern," a determination to grapple with fundamental questions about life and death, about meaning and relationships. As a military chaplain during World War II, he had ample opportunity to appreciate the unhelpfulness of smug religious dogma. Tillich went on to develop a version of Christianity that is deeply steeped in existential philosophy and real-world angst. He has been described by a peer as the theologian whose words comfort when you awaken at midnight in a cold sweat. Many of us need that, at times. Other contemporary religious thinkers such as Henri Nouwen, Martin Buber, Barbara Brown Taylor, and Thich Nhat Hanh offer spiritual wisdom that speaks powerfully to contemporary readers.

Regarding spirituality, sociologist Lars Tornstam, mentioned earlier, has asserted that developing a 'Gerotranscendent' sensibility towards nature, time, and the cosmos was a particularly ennobling elder developmental achievement. University of California Berkeley professor Dacher Keltner makes a similar case for the importance of transcendent experiences in his book, *Awe*. Keltner defines 'awe' as follows: "Being in the presence of something vast and mysterious that transcends your current understanding of the world."

Keltner and a colleague shared this definition with diverse groups of people in twenty-six different countries and then asked them to describe such an experience. They collected 2,600 stories and found that 95 percent of them could be categorized as one of the "Eight Wonders of Life."[50] These transformative wonders run the gamut: examples of human courage and integrity; accounts of beauty found in nature, music, or visual design; poignant stories of a religious, spiritual, or existential nature; and the experience of a conceptual epiphany. Awe gives rise to wonder, openness, curiosity, and the appreciation of mystery. Isaac Newton and Rene Descartes were so inspired by rainbows that they devoted themselves to the study of mathematics, physics, and human perception. Awe is not unique to *homo sapiens*: Jane Goodall reports that chimpanzees do the 'waterfall dance' when they see water splashing down from above or notice a torrential surge in a river.

Neuroscientists have identified the brain's Default Mode Network (DMN) as the likely source of our self-centered attitudes: we are all separate individuals, we need to be in control, and we must compete with others. Experimentally, the DMN can be activated or deactivated. When individuals stand on a lofty perch, and see a vast landscape beneath them, or if they view an awe-inspiring video montage of the BBC's *Planet Earth*, this default network is deactivated. In this alternative state of mind, people experience themselves as being personally small, but also a part of something greater. (This is similar to what orbiting astronauts felt when looking back at the Earth, or what some of the scientists in the Human Genome Project experienced as they were unraveling the mysteries of our DNA.) At such moments, people are willing to donate more money to charity and are also more inclined to commit time to volunteer organizations. They feel themselves to be a part of a larger human ecosystem, so that helping others also helps themselves.

The sense of community with others is beneficial on multiple levels, and many find this in religious organizations. Among our fifty-two interviewed elders, the highest-scoring individuals had a strong religious or spiritual life. This engagement seemed to help solidify their personal Identities, provided a clear set of ethical guidelines, strengthened their sense of gratitude and Purpose, and satisfied the desire to belong to a community. At times of need or adversity, this fellowship could offer them safety and support. There are also, of course, pitfalls for people of strong faith: dogmatism, arrogance, and intolerance for other religions and for people outside their group. Nevertheless, a resolute religious faith clearly made some of our *Aging Wisely* elders stronger as individuals and facilitated a deeper Connection to fellow believers.

Observations and Conclusions

The research findings and associated recommendations highlighted in this chapter illuminate a potential path forward. Virtually all the lifestyle changes discussed here are available to everyone. The determining factors are not financial or proximity to a world-class gym. They are primarily intentionality and perseverance on an individual level. Of course, you will need to choose the best and most appealing options for yourself, and customize your improvement protocol to meet your individual needs.

Connection and Active Practices—from physical exercise, to learning new information and skills, to deepening one's spiritual life—are critical for building stronger minds and bodies, which fortify us as we age. High-quality information can prompt a change in attitude, which may motivate the development of new health-promoting habits. Such changes can make a substantial difference, and we will offer more on this as *The Aging Wisely Project* journey continues with another Healthy Habit, Gratitude.

9

Gratitude—
Choosing the Half-Full Glass

T he current widespread recognition of gratitude often comes across as trite and overused. *Lower-case* 'gratitude' suffices for a square of Belgian choco-late, a good cup of coffee, or a victory by a favorite sports team. By contrast, we have identified *upper-case* 'Gratitude' as one of our foundational Healthy Habits.

Attitude of Gratitude

Gratitude constitutes a basic attitude, a fundamental posture or outlook on life. The *Oxford English Dictionary* describes it as "a warm sense of kindness received, involving a feeling of goodwill toward the benefactor, and a desire to do something in return, gratefulness." This captures the sense of appreciation, with humility, hap-piness, and a wish to reciprocate. Gratitude is not transactional—what has been received has not been earned, and there is no entitlement. Robert Emmons, one of the seminal researchers of Gratitude, has defined it as "the felt sense of wonder, thankfulness, and appreciation for life."

For elders in particular, adversity and losses sternly challenge the feeling of Gratitude. At seventy, eighty, or ninety, is the glass still more than half-full? The tug-of-war between optimists and pessimists is ubiquitous. According to William Butler Yeats, "An aged man is but a paltry thing, a tattered coat upon a stick..." but then he adds a counterpoint, "unless soul clap its hands and sing, and louder sing for every tatter in its mortal dress." Gratitude, we would suggest, is an integral part of that soul-clapping. Bette Davis's pillow was inscribed, "Old Age Ain't No Place for

Sissies." And then the obverse, from Joan Chittister, in *The Gift of Years*: "A blessing of these years is to realize, early, that this stage of life is full of possibilities, full of the desire to go on living, to seize the independence, to create new activities and networks of interesting new people."

We interviewed two men, one just over ninety and the other approaching ninety. One would have agreed with Chittister and the other with Davis. Both men were raised in families with strong work ethics and both went on to become quite successful as senior-level corporate executives. Both had been retired for more than twenty years when interviewed, and both had lost their wives during the previous decade. They were comfortable financially, but each had children with psychological challenges and financial difficulties.

Skip's Life Story (91 years old)

Skip was a friendly, easygoing guy who welcomed us into his cheery, simply furnished home. Although he presented himself as an "open book," he maintained a certain reserve and he declined to discuss several personal matters, which we accepted without challenge. He was raised in rural Iowa by a loving family. When he got involved in a couple incidents of minor adolescent vandalism, his family sent him to military school for a few years. Skip said that he had to learn to shut up and listen, to obey orders and rules, and to 'fit in' with a highly disciplined group of students and faculty. He apparently learned these lessons well, because he subsequently fit in quite successfully in the Navy, then in college, and later in several large corporations. Skip had a very good career, with multiple promotions and job changes along a sales and marketing career track. He had a happy marriage, and he and his wife raised three healthy children.

When he retired at age sixty, Skip felt somewhat at a loss, but he was quickly invited to join the leadership teams at his church and his country club. These commitments got him socially involved with new groups of people, and they provided venues to continue utilizing his organizational and financial expertise. He also began volunteering at a local hospital. Skip and his wife remained busy with golfing, travel, and busy social lives for the next couple of decades. But then their happy marriage of sixty years came to an abrupt end when his wife was diagnosed with an aggressive malignancy, and quickly succumbed. Skip was devastated and really missed the closeness and the partnership he had enjoyed with her.

After several years struggling with loneliness, he asked the golf pro at his club if there were any unattached women that he might be interested in meeting. He was introduced to a woman fifteen years his junior, and they hit it off immediately. Skip said that he had waited to find a woman he could respect, someone who had done something with her life, and who was at least somewhat religious. They have been close friends ever since. They have a good time together playing golf, traveling, and engaging socially with friends.

Skip does worry about his children and their families. One son has a severely disabled child. Skip looks for opportunities to help them out financially, but he does not want to make them feel like a "charity case." Skip maintained his jocular manner throughout the interview, and he claimed that he does not let himself dwell on negative thoughts. At this point in his life, he "shrugs off politics." Skip chuckled that both his wife and his girlfriend have beaten him at golf and regularly bossed him around. With a twinkle in his eye, he claimed that he never wants to grow up, that he is ornery, and that he wants to make it to ninety-five. He does worry about his health. He had a cardiac pacemaker and defibrillator installed several years ago and, early on, it mistakenly discharged several times, knocking him off his feet. He has learned to be somewhat less trusting of, and more discriminating about, his physicians and his treatments.

When Skip looks in the mirror, he is surprised to see how much hair is missing, and he feels his age in a number of ways. He cannot lift a propane tank anymore, and is increasingly short of breath, even on short walks. He stays active mentally by reading such things as the New Testament book of Corinthians. When one of us showed interest in the detective novels scattered about the living room, Skip readily offered to give us the one he had just finished. When asked what advice he might give others, he said that sometimes you just have to "suck it up and keep going" but that, mostly, you should just try to have a good time and not take yourself too seriously.

When we re-interviewed Skip a couple of years later, he was still jovial and welcoming, but a little less animated. He told us that he was just recovering from an episode of COVID, despite having been fully vaccinated and boosted. The illness did not require hospitalization, but he has not been able to play a complete round of golf since then. Also, he had recently fallen down a flight of stairs. Although he had not broken any bones, the treatment of his badly skinned legs had required specialty care at a wound clinic.

When prompted, Skip scored himself five out of five on Gratitude, and described himself as having had "a fine and varied life." Starting out as a "farm boy," he had thought of himself as "low man on the totem pole" so he was pleasantly surprised by all the opportunities and accomplishments during his life. He had survived hurricanes, floods, and economic depressions. Although the U.S. Naval Academy had turned him down, he had attended a good college, done well in business, and been able to live and work successfully in New York City.

He had a wonderful marriage, children, and grandchildren, and now even a couple of great-grandchildren, who are teaching him some new slang. He does regret some of his past mistakes, but not excessively. Skip feels that he has been engaged in an ongoing process of self-reflection and learning. At age eighty, he put himself through a *Life Review*. At one point, he decided to stop drinking alcohol. At another juncture, he realized that he was cursing too much. Over time, Skip came to appreciate that he had been holding onto a grudge against his overbearing older sister. He decided to just forgive and forget—this has helped both the relationship and his internal equanimity considerably. His sense of humor has helped him not take things too seriously, especially himself. And no, he does not think much about death or worry about its approach.

Don's Life Story (89 years old)

The interview with Don differed quite significantly. His home was nicely furnished with fine furniture, but the interview had to be conducted from across the room because the chair next to his was reserved for his small dog. Don's manner was stiff and reserved, almost standoffish, although he warmed up some as the interview proceeded. His delivery was flat, matter-of-fact, and consistently devoid of humor or fond reminiscences.

Don was raised in suburban Philadelphia by a civil servant father and schoolteacher mother. He described his father and his grandfather as never showing him any affection, and after he left home there was scant contact with them. Don grew up with an older sister and a stepbrother, and he was quick to dismiss both of them as careless with their money, unfocused, and not willing to work hard. Don had suffered from asthma as a child, so he had not liked sports much, but he had developed an interest in stagecraft and music. He used to play the French horn, including at his church, but he stopped performing many years ago and has not touched the instrument since. He liked the songs of the 1950s and 1960s but is quite put off by contemporary music. With regard to giving up music, he remembers being frustrated as a kid that his mother would not ride horses with him—but he now understands why older people quit doing things that they had previously enjoyed.

These memories somehow prompted Don to mention the cardiac rehab program he had recently completed for his arrhythmia. The program staff had counseled him about changing his diet, but he still likes his two drinks each evening for relaxation. Don met his future wife in college where they were both studying the sciences—she, chemistry, and he, geology. He went on to work for a major petroleum company, and ultimately helped to broker international oil and gas contracts. He was paid quite well but grew to hate having to socialize with important clients. After retirement, he refused to eat in a restaurant for many years.

He and his wife were married for sixty-one years, and he has been quite lonely since her death. They used to "talk about things." He misses her, "subtly." "It's just part of life," he explained, "you have to cope…[or] you could stay in bed all day and drink." He does have a couple of friends with whom he talks, mostly on the phone. One of these friends is so critical of his kids and grandkids that he has driven them away, and Don reminds himself that he is better off than this guy. But then he thinks about his disappointment with his own kids. His eldest, a son, moved across the country and is completely alienated from the entire family. His middle child, a daughter, has a college education but insists on working, for just above minimum wage, as a pre-school teacher. She has three kids of her own and she lets them eat junk food and skip school whenever they want. His youngest, a son, seems to be suffering from a chronic mental illness, perhaps schizophrenia or bipolar disorder. None of his kids know how to manage their money.

His own health is not great; he had an abdominal blockage in the past that required surgery and his enlarged prostate causes him a great deal of difficulty every day. In addition to the recent arrhythmia, his appetite is poor, and his energy is so depleted that he has to push himself to walk a mile each day. He struggles to manage his anxiety at times and sometimes needs to resort to taking psychiatric medications. It bothers him that he cannot be himself around family. He is not comfortable with smart phones and computers, so he often has to ask for help from his grandkids. He denies having any unfinished business. He does not think much about death, but he does not want a long, drawn-out dying process. With regard to God, he thinks that there is something out there, but he is pretty sure that there is no reunion with family members in an afterlife.

Case Commentary #1: Gratitude

When Don was asked about his level of Gratitude, he thought that it was pretty high. He added that he did not envy anyone and that he felt quite fortunate. Our best guess is that he was referring primarily to his career and his financial status, because he certainly had a profusion of complaints about his health, his father, grandfather, children, and grandchildren. He was disdainful of contemporary music, smart phones, and computers. Over the course of our first few elder interviews, we realized that most people want to think of themselves as grateful, and this is also how they want to be seen by others as well. So, we stopped asking about Gratitude directly and, instead, paid attention to the ratio of blessings versus complaints mentioned spontaneously. In Don's interview, his complaints far exceeded his expressions of Gratitude.

By contrast, Skip had modest expectations for himself and for his life, and so was pleasantly surprised by how well things turned out. Clearly, he was and is, a 'people person.' He developed a delightful sense of humor and he has tried not to let things get him down. In dealing both with his retirement and, decades later, the death of his wife, he struggled for a while, but then found a way to re-engage with people and with meaningful activities. Don, by contrast, seems to have avoided emotional and interpersonal intimacy throughout his life, except perhaps with his wife. He repeatedly focused on money and hard work, as though these were the sole touchstones of a good life. After the death of his wife, he became increasingly isolated, bitter, and aggrieved. Unlike Skip, he did not describe any instances of self-reflection or psychological course correction during this elder phase of life. Don died a year after this initial interview, so we were unable to conduct a follow-up meeting with him.

Five of the six elders featured in John Leland's *Happiness Is a Choice You Make* were pleased to wake up every morning with another day to enjoy life. His title summarizes his overarching conclusion and reminds us that we *choose* the attitude with which we approach life. Certainly, each of these oldest-old individuals had their share of aches and pains, were dealing with physical and psychological limitations, and all had suffered major losses. But they no longer took life for granted—being alive for one more day was experienced as a gift. As George Burns, in his late nineties, said at the opening of one of his shows, "I'm happy to be in Toledo tonight...I'm happy to be anywhere tonight."

Although she was not one of our fifty-two interviewed elders, Rebecca, aged seventy-four, had a story to tell about Gratitude. It began when she was in an Al-Anon meeting thirty-five years ago, on the Tuesday before Thanksgiving. Attendees were invited to come up to the lectern to share what they were grateful for, and Rebecca was distressed to realize that she had nothing to say. She rationalized that you could only honestly express Gratitude if you were happy with your life, which she definitely was not, at that time. However, this experience made her realize that she needed to make some changes. Now, when she wakes up in the morning, if she is not feeling happy to be alive, she forces herself to notice things for which she is grateful. She will look out the window and think, "Thank you leaves, thank you twisted branch, thank you chickadee, thank you sun, thank you streak of cloud in the sky." Sometimes she needs to keep going: "Thank you blankets, thank you quilt hanging on the wall..." and so on. Once she gets up and moving, she can launch herself into her morning rituals, and things start to flow, at which point the day feels full and active. If she hits a low point later on, she gives herself a 'pep talk' by employing the 'thank you' ritual again. Rebecca claims that this works very well for her. This is an explicit example of a Gratitude Practice, and an echo of Leland's *Happiness Is a Choice You Make*.

Ann's Life Story (72 years old)

Ann welcomed us into her brightly lit, artfully furnished home in a gracious manner. Classical music played softly, and the sunlight streaming through the large windows splashed across the polished floor tiles and colorful rugs. She offered us tea and motioned us towards several closely spaced cushioned chairs. We felt immediately at ease, and so did she. When prompted, she began telling us the story of her life in a coherent and candid manner. Ann grew up in a moderately-sized Catholic family in a suburb of Baltimore, not far from the Chesapeake Bay. She spontaneously mentioned how growing up at land's end with views of endless water was a strong and calming counterbalance in contrast to the highly-charged world at home. She was born into a second-generation Eastern European family that had immigrated to New York City and then subsequently moved to the outskirts of Baltimore, where her father became a very successful building contractor.

As the oldest of four girls, Ann had many responsibilities, helping her mother attend to the needs of the family. Her mother was highly competent in the role of homemaker, but was quite emotionally constrained. Curiously, if there was a problem with one of Ann's sisters, her mother would call Ann in to deal with it.

Later in life, Ann realized that her mother had been conflicted in the roles that had been thrust upon her. If born at a different time, it is likely that she would have gone to college and pursued a business career. Many people remarked that she would have made a very impressive CEO. Her father's behavior was "mercurial." One minute he was a gregarious charmer, the next he would fly into a rage. Ann and her sisters never knew what to expect. Oriented towards peace and harmony, Ann quickly cast herself in the role of family peacemaker. Despite their shortcomings, Ann gave credit to both parents. She feels that she got her sense of fun, spontaneity, and charisma from her dad, and her love of school, her helpful spirit, and strong will from her mom.

Ann has clearly thought a great deal about her life, and said that it had not turned out as she had expected. Ann ended up "reinventing" herself a number of times, the first when she was just eight years old. In the midst of one of her father's angry explosions, she remembers saying to herself, "I have to find a way to get away from here." Ann saw education as the way to do this, and from that age onward she devoted herself to learning through schoolwork, working with teachers, and in a wide variety of extracurricular activities. The activities ranged from speech and debate, to track and field, to singing in a folk group, to starting an interracial social club in high school. Throughout her life, Ann has been committed to equal rights, having grown up in a rather biased and uneducated extended family.

In addition to school connections, Ann began developing deep friendships with a small circle of women at school. Those steady, dependable relationships were treasured, especially given her uncertainty and unpredictable home environment. As we talked about her fierce independence, Ann suddenly exclaimed: "This is an 'Ah-Ha' moment for me." Her openness to new realizations and experiences was evident, even during this two-hour interview. Ben has frequently seen psychotherapy patients react this way when they had a sudden flash of insight. Surprisingly, this sometimes happens when the content of the conversation seems quite innocuous and unexceptional.

After college, Ann got married but she never stopped taking care of her family. At this point in the interview, she looped back to her teenage years, as if she had realized that there were narrative gaps to fill. At age thirteen, with a dying grandmother at home and her mother in the hospital giving birth, Ann had to become a "little mother," cooking meals and taking care of her younger siblings. Her grandmother soon died and, after that, Ann's mother had a "mental breakdown," becoming a "ghost" to the rest of the family. This harsh reality forced Ann to become the primary caregiver, particularly for her youngest sister. She had to start cutting short her after-school socializing to get home to take care of the family.

After her recovery, Ann's mother treated her as a peer, treating her as a confidant; at one point, her Mom even asked Ann if she should leave her marriage. Ann was smart enough to know that this was not a decision for her to make. When her father started raging, Ann was the only one in the family who could stand up to him. "But I was only a child," she remembered, and then started sobbing quietly.

Her family caretaker role continued, even when she was attending college. Married at the age of twenty-five, Ann considered several career options. She worked as a caseworker for abused and neglected children, and as a job counselor for teenagers. Although initially drawn to social work, Ann realized, by virtue of those two jobs, that she did not want a career that would feel like a repetition of the emotionally charged role that had been forced on her in her family. Ann chose a related path, going to graduate school to earn a Master's degree in psychological counseling. That enabled her to get a position at a national laboratory in the training and development department. She quickly realized that this was an ideal use of her skills.

While all this was going on, Ann and her husband were struggling to get pregnant. Years of experimental medical treatment, along with three surgical procedures, did not correct the infertility problem and her husband did not want to adopt. Ann was crushed because having children had been a passionate desire for as long as she could remember. She then found out that her husband was having an affair. She promptly left him and moved in with a close girlfriend. When she was offered a highly desirable position with a Chicago consulting firm, she agonized briefly, but then decided it was time to make a significant break, leaving behind her ex-husband and her still-needy family. This was Ann's second reinvention of herself.

Ann thrived in Chicago. She went on to have a stellar career and became one of the pioneers in new, more psychologically based methods for leadership training and executive coaching. Ann and a colleague started a firm that garnered sizable contracts with major organizations in the U.S., Canada, and South Africa. Ann learned that she was particularly gifted in using her intuitive powers to build relationships with resistant executives and facilitate their coming to important insights, which led to significant growth and personal change.

She shared a story of working with one unhappy middle manager at a major bank in Toronto. As she listened at length to this woman, Ann tuned into the woman's desire to leave the corporate world to "do her own thing." Boldly, Ann suggested, "Sounds like you want to go join the circus." After a few moments of stunned silence, the woman mumbled: "Yes, I want to ring-lead my own organization!" Several months later Ann received a Thank You note on the stationery of the woman's new communications consulting firm.

In mid-life Ann sustained another major loss: she met Robert, her soul mate, twenty years ago, and they had a passionate, deep connection before he died suddenly and unexpectedly a decade ago. Now Ann offers comfort to other single, widowed, or divorced older women in her community. She has started several support groups and meditation classes for them.

Ann is now retired and living in a small town in New Hampshire. She has organized a support program for older people in her community, worked with local heritage organizations to develop cultural and historical tours of the area, and until sidelined by an ankle injury, was an enthusiastic participant in The Older Women Dance Project. Ann loves her time in nature, taking daily walks and hikes in the mountains around her town.

Ann is deeply spiritual. Somewhat hesitantly, she shared with us that she has been guided by an inner voice since childhood. That, and the strong connection she feels to ancestors, and to those who have recently died, enables her to never really feel alone. She is still close to her sisters, and her connection with her niece and nephews is such that they choose to come visit often. Ann has no unfinished business, no pressing bucket list, and there is no one she cannot forgive. She has thought a lot about mortality and has made her peace with it. She now feels that death is a benign companion. She is truly a WOW, a wise old woman.

Case Commentary #2: Gratitude

A solid body of empirical evidence has substantiated the benefits of learning and practicing Gratitude. Martin Seligman, a psychologist at the University of Pennsylvania, is one of the founders of Positive Psychology. As he describes in a dynamic TED Talk, he spent the first half of his career trying to lift depressed and anxious people up to the normal range of functioning and happiness. Then, he began to ask himself if this was good enough. As someone who is himself on the lower end of the genetic happiness curve, Seligman knew that even average happiness was not so great. He committed himself to studying happiness, Purpose, and Gratitude. He wondered if Gratitude might be a learnable skill that could, over time, become a habit. This is, in fact, what he and his colleagues have demonstrated in several decades of rigorous research.

Although the earliest academic psychological studies of Gratitude go back to the mid-1980s, Robert Emmons and Michael McCulloch brought the subject into the mainstream with their landmark 2003 study entitled *Counting Blessings Versus Burdens*.[51] After reviewing the psychological and religious-philosophical literature, they conducted three of their own studies, with two different subject populations, and three different timeframes. The basic intervention was the same: to heighten the experimental subjects' "grateful outlook" by having them journal about five recent things for which they were grateful or thankful. One study involved journaling once weekly for ten weeks, and two studies examined the effects of daily journaling (one for thirteen days and the other for twenty-one days). The cumulative conclusions were impressive: there was a significant increase in positive feelings, fewer negative feelings, improved life satisfaction, and more optimism about the near-term future. People also became more helpful towards others, and they felt more connected. Some, but not all of the studies, found that Gratitude journalers began exercising more, slept better, and had fewer physical complaints. (The control groups journaled about adverse events, or random events, or made social comparisons between themselves and others.) Also, daily gratitude journaling had a larger effect than once-weekly journaling.

A 2012 study entitled "To Have and to Hold" focused on the effect Gratitude journaling has on intimate relationships.[52] The outcome was impressive: people felt more appreciated by their partner and appreciated their partner more. They were also more attentive to their partner's needs, felt more committed to the relationship, and they were more likely to stay in the relationship.

In an article published in Berkeley's *Greater Good* magazine, there was a focus on how Gratitude training might actually change brain functioning.[53] The experimental subjects were asked to write a series of letters expressing Gratitude to someone who had helped them in the past; and they did not even need to mail the letters. The results suggested that writing about Gratitude unshackled them from 'toxic emotions,' although the results were not immediate. While there was no measurable benefit at one week, significant benefit surfaced at four weeks and even greater changes arose at eight weeks. Their conclusion was that this shift in attitude was robust, but that it took time to fully develop. Also, the changes seem to last. Three months after the original experiment, using sophisticated MRI (magnetic resonance imaging) technology, the subjects' brains were imaged as they engaged in a 'pay it forward' generosity task. After being handed some money, they could decide how much to keep for themselves, and how much to donate to a charity of their choice.

You guessed it: the Gratitude letter-writers donated more money, and the brain scan strongly suggested that they were using their rational thinking medial pre-frontal cortex, and not their guilt-driven subcortical brain regions.

In addition to the research on Gratitude journaling, psychologist Judith Moskowitz of Northwestern University has elaborated an entire program to enhance Gratitude:

1. Notice when you are enjoying something; stop and savor it.
2. Later on, remember these experiences and tell someone about them.
3. Recall people that you are grateful for and imagine drafting a 'thank you' letter.
4. Actually visit one of these people and read them your letter.
5. Identify your personal strengths and notice when you use them.
6. Set an achievable goal and track your progress.
7. Reappraise hassles and disappointments; find some benefit in them.
8. Practice random acts of kindness; put a smile on someone's face.
9. Meditate ten minutes per day (e.g., mindfulness or loving-kindness meditation).

Oliver Sacks, the renowned neurologist and author, exemplified someone who exuded Gratitude. In fact, *Gratitude* was the name he selected for a posthumous collection of four essays that he wrote in the last few years of his life. Sacks described himself as an individual of violent enthusiasms and extreme immoderation in all his passions. He was fascinated by chemistry, the Periodic Table of elements, botany, marine biology, the lives of scientists, mathematics, poetry, autism, Alzheimer's, migraine headaches, 19th Century medical case studies, music, primates, weightlifting, and high-performance motorcycles, among other various and sundry matters. If life is indeed experienced as a gift, someone like Sacks eagerly tore off the wrapping and played with it in every way imaginable.

Given Sacks' loving and financially secure parents, his world-class education, and his success as an author and physician, it is easy to dismiss his love affair with the world as a natural consequence of his favorable circumstances. But the full story is much more complicated and illuminating. During the Nazi bombing of London at the start of World War II, Sacks, along with more than 800,000 other children, was evacuated to the safer countryside for four years, beginning when he was just age six. Tragically, he was left in the care of a sadistic headmaster who subjected his students to frequent beatings, meager rations, and repeated emotional abuse. The secure childhood attachments he had formed with his parents were significantly eroded by this prolonged separation and mistreatment—a secure attachment is largely based on the Trust that one's caregivers will protect you, no matter what.

When, at age ten, he returned home from this ordeal, Sacks struggled with extreme social withdrawal. He later described himself as suffering from "the 3 B's": inabilities to *Bond* interpersonally, to *Belong* to any group, and to *Believe* in God, religion, or any authority figures. (He later compared notes with others who had been similarly evacuated from London as children and found that these same disabling deficits were shared with many of them.) An additional obstacle was his lifelong 'facial blindness' (prosopagnosia), which made it difficult for him to recognize the faces of even close friends in social situations. This made him much more reclusive. Sacks was to experience a subsequent trauma as well, as you will learn shortly.

Sacks grew up surrounded by a large, extended Orthodox Jewish family. In loving detail, he wrote about the elaborate preparation for the celebration of the weekly Sabbath—these were deeply meaningful times of family cohesion and togetherness. However, as a late adolescent, Sacks was asked about his sexual preference by his father. Sacks acknowledged that he preferred boys, but quickly added that he had not actually acted upon these impulses. He asked his father not to mention this to his mother, but his father did anyway. The next morning, with a look of horror on her face, his mother shrieked her accusation that he was "an abomination" and wished that he had never been born! It was not lost on Sacks that his mother had used the precise term 'abomination'—found in the book of Leviticus, which commands that homosexuals should be put to death. These harsh words made Sacks hate religion thereafter for its bigotry and cruelty. In one fell swoop he had (mostly) lost his family, his community, and his religious faith. Upon his completion of medical school in the U.K., he moved permanently to America, where he underwent specialty training in neurology.

During early adulthood, Sacks' personal life was egregiously and dangerously unstable. He drove more than 100,000 miles on his BMW motorcycle, repeatedly streaking overnight from Los Angeles to the Grand Canyon for the weekend, and back again, often driving at 100 miles per hour. He developed a serious amphetamine addiction. Later on, he recklessly solo-climbed a treacherous mountain trail and almost fell to his death. Due to the harsh homophobia of the time, Sacks was not able to establish a stable, intimate partnership until the last few years of his life. Starting in mid-life, he was celibate for almost forty years. For decades he lived a rather obsessive, almost monastic existence, with a rigid daily schedule and a highly restricted, ritualistic diet. In short, he had numerous experiences that could have made him bitter, regretful, and despairing. Nevertheless, when he fell off that mountain and his life flashed before his eyes—he thought he was about to die—his predominant reaction was one of Gratitude.

By the time he wrote the second essay of the *Gratitude* series, Sacks discovered that he had metastatic cancer. Although still vigorous enough to swim a mile each day, he knew that his luck had run out. Such devastating news could have driven him to denial, depression, or despair. Not so for him. He honestly admitted to some regrets and fears. But, once again, he was unequivocal that his predominant reaction was one of Gratitude. Reflecting upon his life, he concluded that he had loved, been loved, given to, and given back. He had "read and traveled and thought and written...above all, [he had] been a sentient being, a thinking animal, on this beautiful planet, and that in itself has been an enormous privilege and adventure."

It is worth contrasting this with some of the states of mind that negate Gratitude: entitlement, arrogance, envy, harboring grievances, and taking one's blessings for granted. Regarding being alive on our beautiful planet, as a scientist Sacks realized that even minor alterations in the laws of physics or chemistry could have made our planet unlivable and made the presence of biological, self-replicating life impossible. The universe could have been a cold, vast, lifeless void. Also, as a physician who had dealt with so many individuals afflicted with dementia, stroke, or severe cognitive impairment, he knew first-hand that being sentient, and having the capacities to think lucidly, and learn, and imagine, should not be taken for granted. These realizations made him much more appreciative for what he had, for who he was, and for what a gift his life had been.

Even with all the adversities and limitations he had endured, Sacks found much in life to love. And these passions had deepened, rather than diminished, over time. They had even survived the prospect of his impending death. This is the fundamental challenge for all of us: how to find something, and someone, to love—and to keep loving, even while facing the inevitability of loss and death.

An Irresistible Addendum

Although there is academic literature on such topics as 'awe' and 'savoring' that we could insert here, we choose instead to add a (lightly edited) conversation about Joy, an integral part of Gratitude, engaged in by two of our 'wise old women,' Ann and Rebecca:

Joy is an attitude or feeling that originates from within. It is more than just the absence of depression or despair.

Learning to experience joy is a process of discovery—sometimes it surprises us. You have to be open to experience. It often begins with our starting to notice those times when we feel good about something, when we experience a sense of pleasure.

I sometimes will catch myself whistling or humming and I'll stop and notice how I feel just then in order to register this deeper feeling of lightness and ease.

In the beginning, we need to consciously notice when we catch glimpses of pleasure—after a while the noticing becomes more natural.

Pausing to feel the pleasure is a 'stepping stone' to being able to register similar moments. It's as if you are taking note of examples of your joy for future reference. It may be helpful to write it down, to specifically and sensually describe your experience.

Often it is when we slow down (from doing) and give ourselves a peaceful space in which we can cultivate joy (and just be).

Often people feel a strong sense of joy when their experience lines up with who they are and what they value. Who are you when you feel most like yourself?

When I realize that I am not looking forward to something, I consciously shift the neutral or negative sense to light-filled anticipation. As in, what is available for me to contribute positively? In this opportunity to be present, to show up alert and awake, how do I want to present myself? What will I learn?

Enlivening, grounded, connected, expansive, irradiating, non-defensive.

Let go of depletion and baggage.

Sometimes you feel child-like,

Sometimes it feels sacred.

Could you allow yourself to be awed by beauty, or to be thrilled by a random act of kindness?

Observations and Conclusions

Simply stated, the capacity for gratitude and joy influences many aspects of personality and life. Gratitude contributes to Self-Acceptance by diminishing the emphasis on social comparisons—you are less likely to be envious of others and less inclined to judge your own success in comparison to the success of others.

A focus on Gratitude is a choice to shift your perspective toward abundance and leave scarcity behind, to look for what is right in the world and express optimism for the future, and to demonstrate appreciation for what you have. Whether reflecting on the past, engaging with the present, or envisioning the future, our happiest *Aging Wisely* elders habitually did this. And choosing Gratitude enhanced their social, cognitive, emotional, spiritual, and physical wellbeing.

By strengthening wellbeing, your Purpose is deepened. By elevating hopefulness, Resilience is enhanced. In the statistical analyses of our interview data, Self-Acceptance, Purpose, and Resilience were all highly correlated with Gratitude, and all four factors were highly predictive of Self-Integrity, which we discuss in the next chapter.

10

Self-Integrity— Fitting the Pieces Together

Although we all carry within us a vague sense of who we are and how we got to be this way, our *Life Story*, our autobiographical narrative, takes on particular relevance in elderhood. Who have we become? Can we discern some Continuity across the various chapters of our life? Does our life as a whole make sense? If we can fit the pieces of our life together in some sort of meaningful way, we will feel more complete, more whole. The disturbing alternative is to experience ourselves as incomplete and unfinished, and to see our life as having been, to some degree, chaotic and random.

As previously described, we scored twenty-nine variables for each of our fifty-two elders. The final score, the *Aging Wisely* score (AW#), represents a global assessment of how well each elder had aged—how much health, happiness, and wellbeing we observed at the time of their interview. Naturally, we wanted to find out which of the other factors was most responsible for determining the AW#, because this would indicate what to focus on, should we want to make changes. Of all twenty-nine factors, success with the Task of Self-Integrity had the highest correlation with AW#. This is somewhat surprising because Erikson's description of Self (Ego) Integrity is intuitively powerful, but also imprecise and quite multi-faceted—characteristics that tend to lower statistical correlations.

Self-Integrity and Despair

Erikson describes Self-Integrity as encompassing caring for things and people, adapting oneself to triumphs and disappointments, and generating progeny or

173

products or ideas. That covers a lot of ground. He adds that Integrity is a "state of mind" that consistently seeks order and meaning, and is one in which self-centered narcissism has been supplanted by an investment in others and in the world at large. This sort of Integrity entails a mature acceptance of one's one-and-only life cycle. It is also strongly associated with a revised appreciation for one's parents and a sense of shared comradeship with wise elders of other times and places. Despite all of the limitations and missteps, there is an overarching affirmation of the singular life that each one of us has led. Such a highly desirable outcome is most likely when a child has been able to Trust their caregivers, who themselves had Integrity.

The polar opposite of Self-Integrity is Despair, which is fraught with anguish that there is not enough time to realize one's goals, or to complete the elder developmental Tasks of EIR. Despair often presents as a pervasive disgust, with an externalization of blame—with the implication that the reasons for failure lie outside the self (for example, with parents, bosses, or perhaps just bad luck). In a Despairing state of mind, the prospect of death is especially terrifying. We are fond of Erikson's closing words on the subject: "Healthy children will not fear life if their elders have integrity enough not to fear death."

We have previously mentioned numerous of our *Aging Wisely* interviewees who exemplify Self-Integrity: Ella (Chapter 1), Gloria (Chapter 2), Frank (Chapters 3 and 4), and Jimmy and Ann (Chapter 9). Each of their *Life Stories* shared certain common elements. Focusing on Ann's story in particular, her autobiographical narrative felt genuine, authentic, and very personal. It candidly included some events that put her in a favorable light, and others that could be seen as eccentric or even embarrassing. It was evident that her capacity to organize her story so clearly and coherently was the result of persistent self-reflection and soul-searching. She has come to terms with the traumas of her childhood and the tragedies of her adulthood. She has graciously forgiven her parents for their limitations, and generously thanked them for the value they had given her. This diligent integration of her narrative has allowed her to hold in mind, simultaneously, the story she wanted to tell, *and* the task of telling it in a coherent, chronologically organized fashion. Although this sounds simple enough, it is not easy at all, as the disorganized and fractured *Life Stories* of others has vividly demonstrated.

Unlike Natasha (Chapter 2) or Mike (presented below), sudden eruptions of raw feeling or unresolved issues did not ambush and derail Ann's story. (The German philosopher Ludwig Wittgenstein asserted that true understanding permits explanations that are simple and concise. The Jewish sage Hillel claimed that he could summarize the entire Torah while standing on one foot: "That which is hateful to you, do not do unto your neighbor; the rest is commentary, now go and learn."

Ann came across as transparent; she had little to hide, so she had no need to be defensive. She seems to be the same person on the inside as on the outside. People like Ann draw you in. You want to be with them, and you want to be more like them. Ann is a leader, a community builder, someone who has a keen understanding of what others need and want. She is confident enough in herself to not need to constantly seek approval. This frees her up to focus on connecting with others and working to make the world a better place.

Narrative coherence pertains to the content of the story as well as the story's form, structure, and the manner in which it is told. We previously invoked the metaphor of the magnet and how the internal alignment of the iron molecules strengthens the force of attraction. Conversely, narrative coherence is weakened when pervasive ambivalence ('neuroticism') and conflicting story lines pull in opposing directions. For the listener, this incoherence is like witnessing a tug-of-war, with different motives and intentions competing to explain the same autobiographical events. As interviewers, when we saw and felt this conflict coming from an elder, we knew that they were struggling mightily to stitch together contradictory elements of their narrative.

Extensive research regarding the Adult Attachment Interview (AAI) correlates narrative coherence with attachment security in adulthood. Not surprisingly, the AAI covers much the same ground as our *Aging Wisely* interviews—any comprehensive treatment of human relationships must delve into the dynamics of attachments, both secure and insecure. The rigorous scoring system that was developed for the AAI takes into consideration both the content of what is said, and the linguistic form in which it is articulated.

There are four dimensions to this linguistic analysis:

1. **Truthfulness, Consistency**: Do the details of the anecdotes contradict the generalities? (e.g., "My mother was a saint...who would slap us upside the head when she got mad.")
2. **Quantity**: Is there either too much or too little detail?
3. **Relevance**: Is there a steady progression of the narrative, or are there lengthy digressions, tangents, or disjointed fragments?
4. **Structural Orderliness**: Is there a logical order, for instance, a chronological progression to the story? Are there complete sentences, subject-verb agreements, correct pronouns, and avoidance of vagueness, repetitions, or odd jargon?

These might sound like the nit-picking concerns of your high school English teacher, but substantial research has demonstrated that parents who have high levels of narrative coherence tend to raise children who are securely attached. How is this possible? Parents who can talk about their own relationships (in both childhood and adulthood) simply, honestly, and consistently convey an authenticity to their children that engenders trust and intimacy. Although it is certainly preferable to have experienced a happy, stable, and non-traumatic childhood, it is even more important to be honest with yourself, and others, about what actually did happen to you. This starts with allowing yourself to remember and process all the experiences of your life—the good and the painful, the happy and the shameful. (This describes much of the work of a successful psychoanalysis.)

As previously noted, a lie detector test can pick up subtle changes in heart rate, breathing, or sweating in most people (except for career criminals and anti-social personalities) when they are lying. Lying creates an internal conflict between saying what makes you look good, versus honoring your inherent preference for saying what is honestly in your mind. This psychological conflict generates measurable physiological distress. These same dynamics are in play when telling your *Life Story*. Any attempt to deviate from your truthful memories disrupts the straightforward coherent structure of the narrative. Individuals who have done a lot of self-reflection, and have worked to resolve internal conflicts, are the ones most likely to have made their peace with how they have lived their lives. This allows them, as country folk say, "to tell it straight."

Natasha (Chapter 2) is an example of someone with a long history of insecure attachments and unresolved psychological conflicts, although she was making a valiant effort to turn things around in elderhood. Her *Life Story* was strikingly devoid of any heartfelt examples of her emotional reactions, or any insightful descriptions of intimate relationships. For instance, she offered no real explanation for why she had left her first husband, beyond the vague complaint that he had become lazy. Also, she waited until the last few minutes of the interview to tell us that she had had no contact with two of her children for more than ten years. In addition, there were several sudden intrusions that disrupted the flow of her narrative: at the beginning of the interview, Natasha blurted out twice that her parents had lacked any parenting skills. These forceful utterances had an unplanned quality to them—it was as if her unconscious feelings had urgently insisted on being heard, even though out of context. As you can tell from this comparison of Ann and Natasha's interviews, narrative coherence was an essential element to be considered in scoring these interviews.

Mike's Life Story (80 years old)

Even more striking was the case of Mike, an eighty-year-old living in an independent living senior community. Mike seemed anxious and insecure as we began, and he complained about "too much technology" after the staff at his facility had set up the conference room video call (which was necessary because of the COVID lockdown). Given this focus on narrative coherence, we will diligently try to convey the flow of his thinking.

When asked to tell us his *Life Story*, Mike responded by telling us the acreage and location of the family farm in South Dakota, and then followed this by adding that going to school had been "a rude awakening" for him. (Of all the people we interviewed, no one had so completely skipped over their early family life. This was the first of many unusual discontinuities in his discourse.) He went on to describe the brick schoolhouse, built in 1917, where he attended class. His teacher made the class climb the fire escape during a fire drill. While climbing, he had "frozen in fear." But she had forced him to continue to the top of the ladder, apparently causing him much embarrassment and shame. He never forgave her for this insult. (As we just described with Natasha, people with unresolved psychological conflicts, or needs, feel a powerful unconscious pressure to express these issues, in one form or another, whether in psychotherapy or even in casual conversation. Neither Natasha nor Mike seemed to have any awareness about how odd these *non sequitur* intrusions sounded to others.)

Mike then told us that the family attended a Methodist church, although his father had only gone once. He interjected at this point that he thought his current "mental process" was beginning to fade, and that he was having more trouble recently with finding the right words. (This raised the question of whether Mike was suffering from some evolving cognitive impairment, but this seemed unlikely to us, given that his speech production was brisk, with an above-average vocabulary, and with quick recall of names, dates, and places. Also, he later told us that he had been reading T.S. Elliot and *The Rubaiyat of Omar Khayyam*, not easy-reading literature.) He then mentioned having a sister four years his junior and gave the date of her birth. Mike jumped further ahead to tell us about his eventual career as an undertaker, and how he had made this choice impulsively in high school after hearing that undertakers got to work in a suit and tie (classier than how farmers dressed?). After a year in mortuary school, he got a job working at a local mortuary, which made him quickly realize that he needed to own his own business.

Mike then looped back to describe his childhood family, which had been impoverished on several levels. They lived in a poorly maintained, century-old house. His mother was a teacher but was forced out of her job because of the regulation at that time against teaching while pregnant. His father preferred hunting and fishing to farming, so there was chronic financial distress. Mike was bullied constantly in school. He thinks this was because he was gay (although, a few minutes later in the interview, he described himself as bisexual). When he was in the ninth grade, his mother went back to teaching and Mike felt "lost." His father came down with severe pneumonia, barely survived, and was "not good for much after that." Mike resented that his father made him get up early to milk the cows.

Mike followed this with the abrupt disclosure that he now has Parkinson's Disease (perhaps to explain why he could no longer milk the cows?). He rode around with the man who drove the local milk delivery truck, and also spent a good deal of time with an Army veteran neighbor—he wishes now that he had listened more carefully to what these men had told him. (Mike seems to have had a powerful 'father hunger.') He was thrilled when these men treated him like an adult. He had two uncles, but neither one made any attempt to get to know him. Mike complained that his high school principal allowed him to be bullied (another inadequate father figure). Throughout his early-life challenges, his mother gave him the advice to just grit his teeth and bear it.

When Mike finished his last day of high school, he went home and climbed to the top of the woodpile and shouted. (There was no mention of any graduation celebration.) After graduation, he spent a year in a mortuary training program and then got his first job. The mortuary owner became a "surrogate father" to him, so much so that Mike almost converted to Judaism. Working the overnight shift at the funeral home, he got depressed at times, and his ability to function effectively fluctuated. At this point in the interview, he digressed by adding that, twenty years later, he was diagnosed with bipolar mood disorder, and he was prescribed lithium, which worked for a while, but then he stopped taking it. During his mortuary training he began drinking heavily, always by himself, and sometimes he would get "vertigo." Again, he departed from his narrative to tell us that he had fallen three times at his current facility during the previous week, and that firemen had been called to help him. (Was this an exaggeration?)

He admitted to stealing some silver plates when on a home visit for the mortuary, but he later lost track of them during one of his moves. He admitted to losing a lot of things like that over the years. He moved from one mortuary to another, multiple times—one was mostly for Catholics, another overworked him. Mike was in the National Guard sometime during this period. He dated a number of women, including the daughter of one of the mortuary owners, but "when it got too close to love" he would insult them, and they would break up with him. By age twenty-two he was feeling burnt out, so when his father died, he quit his job and went home "and caught up on my sleep." Later he went back to work, got his girlfriend pregnant, married her, bought a funeral home, and then went on to purchase an even bigger one in a nearby town. By this time, he was twenty-nine and he became depressed again. He engaged in mutual masturbation with a seventeen-year-old boy, so he decided that he had to move out of town. He became even more depressed, made a suicide attempt, and was hospitalized. His wife got a job in Denver, so the family moved there.

Mike then worked for one of the big funeral homes in Denver, but he claimed that his boss was "a martinet." He messed up a funeral for a high-profile client, and one of his co-workers sabotaged him. Then he asked for a raise, and was turned down, so he quit, and began driving a taxi. Mike inserted at this point in the interview that he now has COPD (chronic obstructive pulmonary disease), a serious respiratory condition. Returning to his story, he began drinking heavily again, and his wife divorced him. He then jumped more than a decade ahead in his story to say that his fourteen-year-old daughter killed herself. Mike had visitation rights with their three children after the divorce. One night, when his daughter was sleeping over at his house, he had gone to the bathroom, but then, while naked, he lingered by her bedside. She woke up, saw him, and began screaming. She killed herself a year later, and his wife blamed him for this death. Mike also blames himself, but he added, as an alternative explanation, that his daughter might have been raped at some point.

After he finished his free-form narrative, we began asking our standard follow-up questions. Mike admitted that he spends a lot of time thinking about the past. He has many regrets, such as selling his mortuary business and losing his wife because of his drinking. He has now been sober for the past thirty-seven years. He has a son and a daughter, both of whom are stably employed. He has weekly phone calls with his son, but is estranged from his surviving daughter, because, like his ex-wife, she blames him for her sister's suicide. She also is appalled that he got caught sending photos of nude women through the mail. Mike has been in his current Medicaid- subsidized independent living facility for ten years and has no real friendships. He complains about the food that they serve but likes it that "no one messes with me." He watches a lot of TV because his glaucoma has made it hard for him to read. He is back on Lithium for his bipolar disorder and he also takes a strong tranquilizer for anxiety.

His most recent crisis involved a teenager that he played chess with for a couple of years. When this boy talked about having had his first sexual experience, Mike brought up masturbation and then mentioned that he had engaged in gay sex. The boy became alarmed and left, never to return. Mike lamented to us, "I blew a lot of things in my life." Mike does not think he will live much longer because of his COPD and does not feel he can pursue anything on his 'bucket list' at this time. He mostly just tries to keep up with his doctors' appointments. His only real connections these days are with his psychologist and his psychiatrist.

Mike is still enraged at a former gay partner, whom he labeled "a sociopath" because this man reportedly stole all his possessions while Mike was in the hospital having gall bladder surgery. Mike says that this man currently runs a foster home, where he allegedly abuses some of the children. Mike says that he believes in God, but distrusts religion because some ministers are hypocritical, for example Jim Jones (who was responsible for the mass suicide in Jonestown, Guyana). Mike feels more like he is sixty than his actual age, and he is pretty close to being the person that he wants to be, thanks to the help he received from Alcoholics Anonymous and his psychiatrist of twenty years. He wishes that he had started treatment sooner "but I did what I did."

Case Commentary: Self-Integrity

Mike's narrative was striking for its disorganized, non-chronological structure. As noted earlier, when someone is asked to tell their *Life Story*, two functional capacities come into play. First, we all have the lifelong task of organizing and integrating our *Life Story* for ourselves, which is a foundational component of our personal Identity. But then, when preparing to share this story with another, additional capacities are called upon. A small number of memories must be selected from the vast storehouse of information available, and they must be woven together into a meaningful, integrated narrative that can be sensibly communicated. People like Ann, who are fundamentally comfortable in their own skin, and comfortable with the life they have led, come across as relaxed, candid, and perhaps even transparent. When asked, Ann would probably present herself in a consistent way, as virtually the same person, each time.

For people like Mike or Natasha, however, the story is typically modified, depending on the audience. They are significantly conflicted about how honest and revealing they want to be. Because they are anxious and ashamed about many aspects of their lives, they are frantically trying to edit, curate and censor their story on the fly. This is a highly stressful cognitive and emotional task, one that is typically marred by one or more disturbances of communication. When the conversation veers too close to an overwhelming memory or uncomfortable feeling, they may suddenly shift topics, launch into an irrelevant digression, or defensively resort to numbers, technical jargon, or specious details.

In addition to these potential eruptions, the narrative can also be disrupted by the need to 'forget' important events, or even entire periods of life that are simply too painful or scary to tolerate. Just talking about an upsetting situation can reactivate some of the same disturbing feelings experienced at the time of its occurrence. If a person has systematically avoided remembering and processing these difficult events, the memory fragments will remain too highly charged for them to be integrated successfully into their personal Identity. The greater the number of these unintegrated fragments, the more disrupted the narrative will be. This is what we observed with Mike: the number of disconnections in his narrative were proportional to the traumas, the chaos, and the unstable relationships in his life. His mind seemed in turmoil much of the time.

Regarding EIR, Mike's Identity is riddled with inconsistencies and self-defeating expectations. He sees himself as fundamentally not Competent and is barely able to keep track of his medical appointments. Fortunately, he does not feel lack of Control because he can depend on the staff at his facility to manage most of his basic needs. His Connection with others is extremely impoverished. He has a high degree of Continuity in his Identity, but it is as someone who frequently sabotages himself. Considering Consciousness, he is quite unreflective and does not have much capacity or inclination to think about existential or spiritual matters. Mike had a difficult childhood, and a tough adulthood, and he is unable to make sense of most of his life. As illustrated by the recent relationship with his chess-playing teenage friend, he continues to repeat the same sort of impulsive mistakes. Mike is a tragic example of incomplete Identity consolidation and severely compromised Self-Integrity.

To consider a contrasting portrait, we resume our examination of the life of neurologist/author Oliver Sacks, especially as he describes himself in *Gratitude*, the collection of four essays forming his *Life Review*. (Such a *Life Review* is an important late-life opportunity to fill in the gaps and weave together the disparate strands of one's *Life Story*. Life makes more sense if we can assemble a coherent, honest, and inclusive autobiographical narrative.) At the time he wrote the first of these essays, Sacks was on the threshold of his eightieth birthday, and he felt himself to be in reasonably good health. He was somewhat incredulous that he was quite so old—he had been the youngest in his family, almost the youngest in a large group of cousins, and always the youngest in his high school class. But, as he had to concede, he had become one of the oldest people he knew.

In her aptly named book, *The Ageless Self,* Sharon Kaufman studied sixty individuals seventy years of age or older. She found that a large majority of these elders shared Sacks' stubborn self-perception of persistent youthfulness. (To challenge this distortion, for the final question in her interview, she would hold up a mirror in front of their face and asked them what they saw.) Based on her findings, we asked our *Aging Wisely* interviewees if they felt older or younger than their chronological age. Unless they were suffering from chronic pain or disabling physical problems, they almost all felt younger than their age. Many reported being repeatedly surprised by how old they looked.

Sacks recalled that his father had lived to the age of ninety-four and that he had declared that his eighties had been one of his most enjoyable decades. Sacks hoped for the same for himself—that this could be a time of freedom and leisure, a period of life liberated from the "factitious urgencies" of earlier times. He eagerly anticipated the opportunity to heed Freud's maxim "to love and to work." When the weather was perfect he would find himself spontaneously exclaiming that he was happy that he was not dead. (He contrasts this with the story of a friend who was walking with renowned playwright Samuel Beckett. When his friend exuberantly expressed his delight in being alive on such a fine day, Beckett dourly replied, "I wouldn't go as far as that.") At the time of this first essay, Sacks was preparing to write his autobiography, *On the Move: A Life.* He was feeling the urge "to bind the thoughts and feelings of a lifetime together," to consolidate his *Life Story*, to strengthen his Self-Integrity. Sacks emphasized his commitment to include everything, all the good and bad aspects of his multi-faceted life.

By the time he wrote the second essay, eighteen months later, Sacks' life had lurched precipitously in a radically unexpected direction. He had just learned that the cancer that he thought had been successfully treated nine years earlier had returned, and had riddled his liver with metastases. The remaining three essays of the book can be seen as an accelerated striving to fit the pieces of his life together, written by a profoundly honest and curious individual. Sacks had just published his autobiography a few weeks earlier and it came to about 400 pages. By comparison, the *Life Review* that he hastens to summarize in the *Gratitude* essays amounts to just thirty-four pages. The conciseness of this writing mirrored his attitude toward his life in general at that point—everything had to be focused, carefully chosen, and pared down to essentials. But, he insisted, there would still be time for fun, and even for some silliness.

One aspect of his initial reaction to his grim health prognosis was to feel a sort of detachment, as if he was looking at the landscape of his life from a lofty perspective. This is akin to the 'derealization' that traumatized patients often describe. This is a truly desperate maneuver by the mind, a frantic attempt to diminish psychic shock: 'this really isn't happening to me, this is unreal, surreal.' Such an automatic coping strategy gives the mind more time to adjust to a devastating new reality, and to internalize it, incrementally, in smaller doses. For someone like Sacks, it also afforded enough psychological distance to enhance his self-reflective capacity. He began to see the connections between different elements, and different eras, of his life. Memories and feelings flooded his mind. He wanted to emphasize the most purposeful activities: spending time with friends, seeing patients, writing, swimming, playing the piano, and traveling.

Although Sacks' predominant reaction was one of Gratitude, he did have some regrets. The regrets mentioned in the first essay were rather superficial: not learning a second language, not traveling more, wasting time, being too shy. By the writing of the subsequent essays, however, Sacks had gotten in touch with deeper, more disturbing regrets: he would not live long enough to see some fundamental scientific questions answered, and, most poignantly, because of his culture's homophobia, he had missed out on the chance to have a long-term intimate relationship or a family. (Starting in mid-adulthood, he had been celibate for thirty-five years.)

Sacks was a secular realist. He claimed to not harbor any belief in, nor wish for, an afterlife. Regarding his legacy, he hoped that his books would still speak to people after he was gone, and that friends would remember him. Before closing out the second essay, he allowed himself to delve more deeply into the anguish of loss. He admitted that he had become more conscious of the deaths of many of his contemporaries, and that each loss felt like a tearing away of part of himself, leaving holes that could not be filled. Grimly, he noted that there will never again be anyone quite like these wonderful individuals. We are all unique, he observed, and we each have to find our own path, live our own life, and die our own death.

In the third essay, Sacks engages deeply in autobiographical reconsideration. He is impressively self-reflective, perhaps as a result of his psychoanalytic treatment, as well as having written several times previously about his life. Sacks wonders if his wartime childhood isolation from his family had led him to some unusual psychological adaptations: "numbers became my friends...the elements in the periodic table became my companions." These were entities that could not be taken away from him, things that would never die. He titled the first of these four essays *Mercury* because he had a dream about a huge, pulsating globule of mercury, whose atomic number (each element has a unique atomic number, based on its number of protons) matched his impending age, eighty. At seventy-nine, he was still Gold, at eleven years of age he had been Sodium. At the time of the second essay, he had at his desk a chunk of Thallium, element #81, sent by his 'element friends' in England, and a Lead box to commemorate his eighty-second birthday. Inside the box was radioactive Thorium, element #90, beautiful but deadly. Sadly, he knew he would not live to see his Thorium birthday. He called these elemental mementos "emblems of eternity." Focusing on atomic numbers combined his love for mathematics and chemistry, and made him feel a part of something larger and more eternal, than himself. And it was a pleasant reminder of his superb education and his extraordinary intelligence.

On another occasion, Sacks had an even more profound transcendental experience while gazing up at a cloudless night sky that was teeming with stars. Sacks found himself transfixed by their remote beauty, but also plunged into contemplation of the infinities of time and space, and of his own very limited time. In the first essay, he wrote about having, at almost age eighty, a lived sense of history and an acquired capacity for taking the long view. He had seen promising scientific theories rise and fall. He could feel in his bones what a full century was like. But by the time Sacks wrote his final essays, his perspective had deepened and taken on a more existential cast.

As mentioned, Erikson, Tornstam, and others have written of the importance of this existential-transcendent consciousness, the striving to connect one's circumscribed life with the distant past and the unimaginable future, with the infinitesimally small and the boundless reaches of the universe. As with Sacks' reaction to the starry night, this can engender, simultaneously, the experience of insignificance, but also a god-like expansiveness. As Carl Sagan famously wrote, "The nitrogen in our DNA, the calcium in our teeth, the iron in our blood, the carbon in our apple pies were made in the interiors of collapsing stars. We are made of star stuff."

Dying can be a lonely process—it is not surprising that Sacks wished to remind himself that he was not alone. In these four brief essays he repeatedly inserted mentions of the deaths of others. His father died at ninety-four, friend W.H. Auden at sixty-seven (although Auden had thought that he would 'bugger off' at eighty). Francis Crick died in his late eighties and Ralph Siegel, a neuroscientist friend, "prematurely" at fifty-two. For his second essay, Sacks copied the autobiographical title, *My Own Life*, from his favorite philosopher, David Hume, who died at sixty-five. For the title of his autobiography, *On the Move*, he borrowed the title of a poem by deceased friend Thom Gunn. For someone as spectacularly original and creative as Sacks, this was a lot of borrowing—that connected him with departed companions.

Just after the second essay's publication, a novel cancer treatment was introduced that afforded Sacks a brief period of reinvigoration. He seized the opportunity to meet with friends, to see patients, to write, and to travel back to his birthplace in England. He was also determined to fulfill his plans to visit a lemur research center, where he could ponder the ancient common ancestors that we share with this curiously inquisitive primate. As he defiantly declared in the inscription of *Gratitude*: "I am now face to face with dying, but I am not finished with living."

Just a month later, Oliver Sacks wrote his final essay, entitled *Sabbath*—he would die just two weeks after its publication. When he had written the first of these four essays, two years earlier, he was hopeful that he would live as long as his father: another fourteen years. There is an old Talmudic adage: "Man plans, Gods laughs." Just eighteen months later he received his terminal diagnosis, and six months after that he was gone.

Although Sacks was unambiguously secular throughout his adulthood, his final essay is surprisingly religious, as the *Sabbath* title would suggest. He begins the piece by going back a couple of generations in his family, describing their pious devotion to Orthodox Judaism. Family legend had it that his maternal grandfather was so observant that he would wake up at night if the yarmulke slipped off his head. Sacks recalled his early religious experiences, especially the reverence his family felt for the holy Sabbath. In granular, loving detail he writes about the elaborate preparation for this weekly celebration: the scrupulous adherence to the religious prohibitions and rituals, the carefully choreographed group participation, and then, at last, the excitement of aunts and uncles and cousins crowding in to partake of the cherished traditional delicacies. These were deeply meaningful times of family unity and togetherness.

Sadly, all this was lost to Sacks when his parents so violently rejected him for his homosexuality. Thereafter, he was decisively non-religious. However, in the year just prior to his death, Sacks was invited to rejoin his family. First was an elderly aunt's birthday party. Then, it was a Sabbath celebration, hosted by a cousin, who just happened to be a Nobel Prize laureate. (In Buddhism, it is said that when the student is ready, the teacher will appear.) To his astonishment, both he and his gay partner were warmly welcomed to participate, and they were unreservedly embraced by the family. This eleventh-hour repair of tattered family connections added a final sense of completion to Sacks' already rich and full life.

Woven into Christianity and Islam, and also represented to a lesser degree in Judaism, is a mythology about 'The Last Judgment' or 'Day of Reckoning,' which was depicted on the Sistine Chapel ceiling by Michelangelo. According to this myth, every person, upon their death, is brought before a divine tribunal and held to account for their earthly deeds, after which they are consigned to either heaven or hell. This same notion also has a more secular, psychological manifestation, as an aspect of one's personal *Life Review*. At age forty-one, Sacks broke his leg in the mountains and thought he was about to die. Curiously, at that moment, he felt a powerful surge of Gratitude for what he had been given and for what he had given back—which was a sort of moral accounting. Four decades later, after announcing to the world that he was terminally ill, he received hundreds of letters of love and appreciation. This seemed to have convinced him "that [despite everything] I may have lived a good and useful life." This flood of uplifting correspondence seems to have tipped the scales of judgment in his favor.

Given Sacks' extraordinary career as a physician and author, and his wide circle of friends, it is indeed curious that his self-appraisal had been so tentative. His description would suggest that, prior to receiving these end-of-life messages, he had been uncertain about his moral standing, and about the value of his contributions to the world. At the end of the last essay, however, he seems to have unequivocally made up his mind in the affirmative. Acknowledging that he was writing these final few pages with his last reserves of strength, he declared that his thoughts, at this last juncture, were about "[w]hat is meant by living a good and worthwhile life and achieving a sense of peace within oneself. I find my thoughts drifting to the Sabbath, the day of rest, the seventh day of the week, and perhaps the seventh day of one's life as well, when one can feel that one's work is done, and one may, in good conscience, rest."

This passage conveys a sense of completion, a final judgment that he had indeed lived a life worth living, that his many contributions had justified and redeemed his existence, and had adequately compensated the world for all that he had been given. In the end, all the pieces had fit together.

The institutionalization of the Sabbath, in Judaism, Christianity, and Islam, embodies great psychological and even physiological wisdom. Establishing a consistent schedule for waking and sleeping, for working and resting, for practical engagement and spiritual reflection, has provided great benefit to our species. For people like Sacks with a strong work ethic, there can be a nagging conviction that there is always more work to be done, more people to be helped. Left to their own devices, such people might suffer from a persistent guilt that they have never done enough. This sense of unfinished business can torment. To prevent this sort of neuroticism, culturally sanctioned institutions such as the Sabbath provide ethical guidance, and can be powerfully reassuring. Similarly, at the end of one's life, to accept that what you have done is indeed enough, and to be given permission to let go, and to surrender to an eternal rest—that would be a great blessing indeed—as it apparently was for Oliver Sacks.

Observations and Conclusions

Sacks lived an extraordinary and unusual life. We utilized his *Gratitude* essays to model the work to be accomplished in the final developmental Tasks of Self-Integrity and EIR. So, how do his experiences and insights pertain to the rest of us? Sacks reminded us of Freud's dictum about a healthy life, that bears repeating: "to love and to work."

For Sacks, his life largely revolved around his work. For most people, however, the emphasis is much more on loving, on the relationships in our lives. But the same questions can be asked: Have we loved enough, and been loved in return? Have we forgiven others, and been forgiven ourselves? Have we honestly expressed our feelings and thoughts to those we loved? Conducting an honest *Life Review* can help us dedicate the time and energy necessary to grapple with these questions. And doing so may reconnect us with the parts of our lives that we have forgotten or neglected, and with the people who have been important to us.

Because we are now older and hopefully wiser than ever before, recollecting events from years ago may give rise to new insights. These insights may grant us a deeper understanding of how we became the person that we are at this ultimate stage. Fitting the puzzle pieces of one's life together can be a surprisingly powerful experience. This can be accomplished by journaling, memoir writing, or just telling your story to someone (unfortunately, few listeners are patient enough to want to hear it all). Any of these options might seem intimidating. There may be a worry that strong feelings might be triggered by this *Life Review*, and that might be overwhelming. In some cases, a professional counselor or therapist might be needed, but most people can just jump in and get started.

This completes our description of the five Healthy Habits (Gratitude, Resilience, Active Practices, Self-Acceptance, and Purpose), along with Connection and Self-Integrity. These seven factors are most highly predictive of aging wisely. Chapter 11 concludes with our final thoughts about which strategies and practices are most likely to enhance one's efforts to age well and wisely.

PART THREE
CONCLUSIONS AND BEGINNINGS

11

Knowing and Practicing Wisdom— Back to Basics

A s we cross the threshold of turning seventy and beyond, the path behind is long and the path ahead considerably shorter. For most of us, this stage of life is less burdened by daily urgencies and more generously provided with time to reconsider and reflect. It is an opportunity to notice the various patterns, themes, and inflection points in our life trajectory. Does it all seem to hang together despite all its complexities, paradoxes, and contradictions? Finding coherence and meaning in our *Life Story* can evoke a sense of wholeness, a confident feeling that our feet are solidly planted on the ground. Understanding where we have been, and what we have learned, can prepare us for the rest of the journey.

The road ahead, even under the best of circumstances, is fraught with challenges and stress. We previously shared the work of Hans Selye, the mid-century endocrinologist who helped educate our culture about stress, which he defined as any condition or event that compels an organism to adapt. As we listened to the *Life Stories* of our fifty-two elders, we learned about their capacities to respond adaptively to stress. These capabilities were a critical determinant of their overall health and happiness in old age. By considering their temperament and their childhood experiences, both good and bad, we see a picture of their early-life coping skills. We followed their stories through their school years, their careers, and their efforts to find partners and to build families, then on to their mid- and late-adulthood challenges. Each of them had dealt with Erikson's universal developmental Tasks and with additional stressors that were unique to their lives.

In this final chapter, we build on the paradigm of stress and adaptation, and then weave in some of our fundamental *Aging Wisely* insights.

Attitude Matters

Alia Crum, principal investigator of the Stanford University Mind and Body Lab, has studied how 'mindsets' affect how the body and mind respond to a wide variety of stressors. The myriad changes and losses of elderhood clearly constitute stress. These stressors force elders to respond, either adaptively or maladaptively. (Even the refusal to recognize a stressor, or the decision to not change a behavior, can be considered psychological responses.) The more an adaptation enables an individual to deal effectively with a changing environment, the healthier and happier they will be, going forward.

Crum's work underscores the consequences of one's mindset. If you see a stressor as something that you can master, and that doing so will make you stronger, you are adopting a 'stress-is-enhancing' mindset. Scott and Ben had elder role models who gave them hope that they could thrive in elderhood. For Scott, it was his father-in-law Jack, a Holocaust survivor. Jack was an inspirational social dynamo, full of energy, engagement, and a story or joke for every occasion. Ben remembers his robust and charismatic Granddad Paul, who was repeatedly told by his doctors that his health status was fifteen years younger than his age. If aging is a marathon, our ancestors ran a great race, so we believe that we can as well.

Conversely, if you consider aging to be an overwhelming stressor that will inevitably wear you down and defeat you, you are operating with a 'stress-is-debilitating' mindset, which will enfeeble you. Elders like Daniel (Chapter 5), who claimed that he never really had any goals in life, and that no male in his family had lived past their forties (so why make plans?), seem to be just biding their time, and waiting to die. Although well into his seventies, Daniel had made no new friends in years, his drinking buddies had abandoned him or died, and he had virtually no contact with family. He showed little evidence of Purpose, Gratitude, Self-Acceptance, or Self-Integrity. All his best days as an athlete, a handicapper, and a barroom eminence were behind him. His mindset was one of powerlessness in the face of the inevitable deterioration of aging.

Across numerous studies, Crum and her colleagues have demonstrated that a stress-is- enhancing mindset evokes a healthy response, while a stress-is-debilitating mindset damages us physically, mentally, and emotionally. For example, Crum studied the effect of briefly educating hotel housekeeping staff that their work cleaning rooms and making beds could be considered legitimate exercise, which satisfied the Surgeon General's recommendations for daily physical exertion.[54] This changed their mindset about their work. When assessed a month later, they had lost weight, improved their Body Mass Index (BMI), and even lowered their blood pressure readings. The control group, who had not heard the 'work is good exercise' presentation, showed no such health improvements.

In a second study, small incremental doses of peanuts were administered to kids to help them overcome their peanut allergies.[55] The group was again divided in half. The first group was reassured that the minor symptoms that they would experience after their injections would not be life threatening. The second group was told the same thing, but were also informed that the symptoms that they experienced were actually a *good* thing—because these symptoms would prove that the immunotherapy was working. This second group suffered less anxiety, made fewer emergency phone calls to the staff, and their blood tests showed that they had higher levels of immunoglobulin, which would protect them from future allergic reactions.

In these studies, it may not be that surprising that a brief educational presentation could have beneficial psychological effects on anxiety and hopefulness. But it is rather astounding that it also altered objective physiological variables, such as body weight, blood pressure, and immunoglobulin levels. Crum even found that the stress-is-enhancing mindset could predict which Navy SEAL candidates persisted longer and performed better in their training.

There are two essential aspects to a healthy stress-response mindset in elderhood:

1. *These stressors are not bigger than me: I can master them.* We can remind ourselves that we have already dealt with numerous challenges and traumas throughout our lives, and that we somehow found a way to survive, and maybe even thrive. Death is inevitable, but despair and hopelessness in our final decades are optional. We can choose our attitude.
2. *These stressors can make us stronger.* We have all met elders who embody wisdom, tranquility, and compassion. They have faced the inevitable losses of life and have kept their heads high. They are quietly heroic. Why should we not do the same?

We believe that Crum's research on mindsets has important implications for aging wisely. It is our hope that the ideas and *Aging Wisely* case examples have offered you some measure of inspiration, direction, and confidence. We know we have given you a lot to think about. As a final encompassing integration, we have organized *The Aging Wisely Project's* Healthy Habits as a series of interlocking attitudes and practices:

- *Gratitude* is an overarching attitude toward one's life. Life is an extraordinary gift, one that we did not earn. Theologically, the bestowing of an undeserved blessing is called Grace. Appreciating this is the first step towards Wisdom. Gratitude can be enhanced by keeping a Gratitude journal or by using some of the other Gratitude practices described in this book, and in other resources (see Suggested Reading list).

- *Purpose* gives shape and direction to what we will do with this gift of life. Realizing that self-centered hedonism, material acquisitiveness, and narcissism are shallow and ultimately unfulfilling is the second step toward Wisdom. Seeking to help others and make the world a better place is what sustains us and gives life value.

- *Resilience* is the next strength to build and maintain. Like the Buddha on the way to Enlightenment, we will face pain, suffering, loss, and our own mortality. Our task is to prevent despair and bitterness from crowding out our Gratitude and distract us from our Purpose. Ultimately, this is an affirmation of our existence. If you are struggling with this, consider re-reading the thoughts of Frankl (Chapter 5), Hone (Chapter 6), or Oliver Sacks (Chapters 9 and 10).

- *Active Practices* combine the joy of vigorous biopsychosocial engagement with the self-discipline needed to keep ourselves as strong and functional as long as possible. These practices acknowledge that we cannot take our capacities for granted, that we must continue to nurture our bodies and minds and souls. Connection with others is the most critical aspect of all. Reflect on and assess those areas that need more work (see Appendix for the self-assessment and journaling exercise), and perhaps review Chapter 8.

- *Self-Acceptance* is the final step towards Wisdom. In the biblical book of Genesis, after God created the world in six days, he stops to look at his handiwork and concludes that it is good. We are not God, and our work is never perfect. But to thrive, we need to feel that we are 'good enough.' Mistakes and poor decisions were undoubtedly made, but now it is time to let go of regrets and bitterness and appreciate what we have learned. Undertaking a thorough *Life Review*, especially if performed in writing, strengthens our Self-Integrity, which is the pinnacle of Self-Acceptance.

Establishing New Habits

After conducting an honest self-appraisal, you may realize that you need to strengthen one or more Healthy Habit. Old habits are hard to break, and new ones difficult to establish. In one study of New Year's resolutions, although 52 percent of the participants were confident of success, by year's end only 9 to 12 percent had made good on their resolutions.[56] There is quite a library of relevant research about how to choose and pursue behavioral goals, which we will summarize below. For more insights, watch Andrew Huberman's excellent video on this subject, "The Science of Making and Breaking Habits" on YouTube.[57]

Obviously, there is tremendous variety among us as unique individuals, and many choices to make in individual lifestyles, but the following recommendations may be helpful:

1. Building a new habit takes time and effort, so commit to only one project at a time (As Scott's grandmother used to say, "Don't bite off more than you can chew, you could choke."). Choose goals that are truly meaningful to you in order to sustain your motivation. For instance, Jon Kabat-Zinn cautions that building a mindfulness meditation habit takes forty-five minutes per day, six days per week, for eight weeks. Establishing any healthy new habit requires a serious commitment and a willingness to rework your daily schedule. Be prepared to resist all manner of self-sabotaging behaviors: avoidance, procrastination, self-doubt, and distraction.

2. Be as specific about your goal as possible, hopefully choosing something that is measurable. Write the goal down; handwriting engages several important brain regions. State your goal in action terms, as verbs: *what you plan to do*. How will you know you have accomplished it? Commit yourself to how much time you will allocate per week, and even per day. If it is a big goal, like learning Spanish or training for a marathon, divide it into three-month ('bite-sized') segments. Break the ultimate goal down into a series of intermediate, measurable goals. Celebrate and reward each incremental accomplishment; give yourself a treat after losing the first five pounds, or exercising twenty days in a month, or learning to play a simple song. Every three months, compare the progress made with your timetable, and modify

your goals or practice routine as necessary. Be kind to yourself and expect frequent ups and downs in your progress.

3. In general, if the goal is too difficult to achieve, you may get discouraged and give up quickly. If the goal is too easy, your brain will not mobilize its capacity for neuroplasticity and learning. Pay attention to what you are already doing, or what you like to do. If you can link new behaviors to an existing habit, such as brushing your teeth at a particular time of day, this can be extremely helpful. Choose a goal that offers some intrinsic rewards. If it is a new exercise routine, do you naturally prefer walking, or cycling, or swimming? Outside or inside? Alone, with a buddy, or in a group? While listening to music, or a podcast? If it is learning to play a musical instrument, what sort of music gives you pleasure? (One psychoanalyst we know spent six months learning to play a ragtime piano piece by Scott Joplin.) If you want to help others, can you use the skills or expertise that you previously developed during your career? Is it an activity that you actually enjoy doing? And who would you most want to help?

4. Choose the right time of day for your practice. Are you an early bird or a night owl? If it is a cognitively demanding task, there is research that suggests that, for many people, thirty minutes, three hours, and eleven hours after waking up are the prime times for attention and motivation.

5. Telling people that you are going to write a book or learn to play the guitar will elicit congratulations, which will prematurely gratify your brain's reward circuits, but accomplish nothing. This will, paradoxically, lessen your chance of success. Do not tell anyone about your goal before you actually get started. However, if you can find a no-nonsense 'compliance buddy' who will periodically hold you accountable for sticking to your schedule, that could be helpful.

6. Notice anything that can reduce 'friction' associated with the activity. Marketing data has found that people living no more than three-and-three-quarters miles from a gym will average about five visits per month, while those who live five miles or more will only go once a month. One female psychologist found that sleeping in her running clothes significantly helped her to get up and out for an early morning run. Having a buddy to meet, or a class that you are scheduled for in advance, can also make a big difference.

7. Avoid distractions or interruptions. If this is something you can do by yourself, choose a quiet setting and a time free from demands. Turn off all

electronics. If this is a more social goal, try to avoid unnecessary complications or diversions.

8. To enhance positive motivation, begin each session by taking one to three minutes to envision a positive outcome: what it will feel like when you accomplish your goal? This will stimulate your brain's dopamine reward circuits.

9. To strengthen your motivation to stop a bad habit, such as binge eating, focus on the consequences of failure—like having to take insulin shots or having to buy 'fat clothes.' This imagining of adverse outcomes triggers your 'fight-or-flight' adrenaline circuits, which can help get you through a short-term dip in willpower.

Aging Wisely Elders: In Their Own Words

In our early interviews, we asked elders if they had any advice for the next generation—what we got back was mostly banal platitudes. So, in subsequent interviews, we waited to hear if they would spontaneously offer some illuminating observations or advice, and many did. We have grouped these 'wisdom comments' into several categories:

- **Relationship Advice** (thirty-five comments). Prioritize family and relationships. Ask for help when you need it and offer to help others. Examine your own contribution to a problem before blaming others. Forgive others and do not hold a grudge. Be careful with your words and deeds. Get over your anger and do not argue to win. Admit your mistakes and make amends. Do not be judgmental or intolerant. Be kind and compassionate, share with others, and teach them. Be honest. If you lose a companion, find another. If you are a woman, do not depend on a man for support or happiness.

- **Resilience Advice** (thirty-two comments). Let go of the past and focus on the present. Keep going and take the good with the bad. Remember—this too shall pass. Do not waste time feeling sorry for yourself. As the Buddha says, "Pain is inevitable, suffering is optional."

- **Gratitude Advice** (nineteen comments). Be grateful. Love. Enjoy yourself and seek beauty. Remember, happiness is a choice.

- **Personal Growth Advice** (fifteen comments). Keep learning and growing. Be open and honest about feelings and relationships. Be proud of your accomplishments. Be curious and engaged. Grieve your losses, then move forward. Find Purpose, and lead by example. Take care of your health. Read the Bible or the Koran (or other spiritual or inspiring texts).

- **Self-Esteem Advice** (thirteen comments). Do not expect too much of yourself. Accept your limitations, be humble, and trust God. Forgive yourself. Use your gifts, work hard, and do your best. Be true to your beliefs.

Final Thoughts

We are fond of Nietzsche's metaphor: build the best sand castle you possibly can, even though you know that the tide will inevitably come in and wash it away. The end game is not for the faint of heart. Sam (Chapter 6) and his wife were exemplary in their determination to face his metastatic cancer and her progressive dementia with courage and honesty. They sat down with their kids and had a somber and tearful conversation about their end-of-life plans. They proceeded to design their funerals; update their wills and advanced directives; and designated powers-of-attorney. They meticulously documented investment account information and contact information for their accountant, investment advisor, and attorney, and all relevant online IDs and passwords. They also made their beneficiaries joint owners of investment and bank accounts to avoid complications with estate and probate issues.

Preparing for and executing plans like these requires a wholehearted acceptance of mortality, and a concern for those who will be left behind. Margreta Magnusson's *The Gentle Art of Swedish Death Cleaning: How to Free Yourself and Your Family from a Lifetime of Clutter* is written in this same spirit. Embracing the reality that you will never downhill ski again, or reread those books from college, or ride that racing bike with drop-down handlebars—this acceptance is what you need to start to declutter your house and spare your descendants that onerous task. Hold the garage sale while you are still around.

Another insightful book (with an equally off-putting title) is Katy Butler's *The Art of Dying Well*. This book is dedicated to empowering terminally ill patients, and their families, to understand the dying process and how to maintain as much control as possible. Rather than passively turning things over to the doctors or the hospice staff, perhaps you will decide to retain a death doula, organize a pre-death memorial service, add some aromatherapy, or bring in a musician. These insights all underscore recurrent *Aging Wisely* themes: knowledge enables you to understand your choices, and exercising your intentionality engenders a deeper sense of ownership and control over your body, your mind, your health, and your life.

We hope *The Aging Wisely Project* has elevated your awareness of the relevant late-life developmental Tasks and, particularly, the benefits of continually revising your elder Identity. Coping well with the myriad losses in late life—the 5 C's of EIR—is our ultimate challenge. We have also emphasized the pivotal significance of strengthening your Healthy Habits.

Thank you for walking this path with us. We hope this book has been insightful, informative, and even entertaining. For us, there is nothing more meaningful than loving and helping others. As Tenzin instructed, it is fundamentally important to live the life of your dreams—and writing a meaningful book has been a part of our dreams.

So, what about *your* dreams? Have you already realized them, or is there more to do in your elderhood? Perhaps our efforts have made you think a little more about your dreams and whether your current path will take you there. We hope that the ideas and the research presented here, by us and from others, and the *Life Stories* of your elder peers, will inspire and inform your journey ahead. Let knowledge and intentionality be your mantra for aging wisely.

Bon voyage!

Acknowledgments

A significant measure of the satisfaction and joy we have experienced through *The Aging Wisely Project* comes from the participation and support of all who helped make it possible. What began as a simple literature search, initiated by two old friends trying to learn how to age more successfully, evolved into a six-year effort involving many people and organizations.

First, we must thank all of the fifty-two elders who openly and willingly shared their *Life Stories* with us without expecting anything in return. We couldn't share every story with you in this book, but each one of them contributed to the insights and conclusions described herein. We were awed and inspired by the diversity and uniqueness of their experiences, and the resilience with which most had faced the challenges they'd encountered. We hope that these stories have helped illuminate the common adversities of elderhood, the coping skills needed, and the myriad ways that various individuals have adapted to the unique circumstances of their lives.

We want to thank the many individuals—friends, colleagues, and *Aging Wisely* elders—who were gracious enough to read through earlier versions of our manuscript and offer their insights on how to make it better. We tried to listen and to adopt suggestions where possible; the feedback undoubtably improved the final iteration of this project. Heartfelt thanks go out to Carmen Ashbaugh, Cindy Aspromonte, Tom Avery, Stephen Blum, Andrew Braun, Michael Burger, Susie Carol, Tamara Cohen, Ted Gaensbauer, Lynne Gillick, Sharyl Harston, Joan Heron, Cory Hines, Kathy Huckins, Lee Johnston, Ana Lash, Bob Lederer, Mary Ann Levy, Ester and Roy Lowenstein, Lucy Marcus, Patti McKinnnell, Jon Meredith, Larry Mortazavi, Dianne Moskowitz, David Nichol, Rob Socolofsky, Skip Spensley, Margy Stewart, Carol Tierney, Judy Whitbeck, Nancy Wright, and Greg Wolf for your efforts, cogent thoughts, and invaluable suggestions.

In the midst of the COVID-19 pandemic, institutional lockdowns, and public anxiety, the executives and staff at Kavod Senior Living (KSL), a Medicaid-qualified independent living facility in Denver, agreed to invite residents to volunteer for interviews with us. They reserved the conference rooms, set up the computers, helped residents get to their interviews on time, and made sure that the video conferencing worked smoothly during each two-hour confidential interview. Without their help, the demographic diversity of our interview sample could have been compromised. Special thanks to Michael Klein, Tracy Kapaun, and Mandie Birchem. And aside from our project, Scott's subsequent volunteer experience with KSL, including joining its Board of Directors, has been a gratifying and purposeful opportunity to serve the elder community in Colorado.

Many thanks to Stephen Blum and the Yale Alumni Association, Libby Reinhardt and the 1973 50th Reunion Committee, and Yale University for hosting our 2023 reunion weekend presentation. At that reunion, we met Ron Roel, learned about his 45 Forward podcast, and launched a gratifying collaboration with him. Two independent living facilities, KSL and The Everleigh Central Park (thanks to Bob Lederer and Carol Tierney), invited us to share our research findings with residents and community members. Similarly, Cory Hines and the Mt. Washington (Massachusetts) Council on Aging have hosted presentations over the past seven years. The Men's Group at the Park Hill Congregational UCC Church has also heard and responded to several of the early drafts of this manuscript. It was the enthusiasm and positive feedback from all these groups that helped us realize that we had a book worth writing.

We were initially overwhelmed by, and quite ignorant of, the publishing options and technologies available. Through a friend, and later a mentor, Denver author Debra Fine, we were referred to Morgan James Publishing, a publisher based in New York City. Beginning with Isaiah Taylor, then David Hancock and later Addy Normann, they made us feel like part of their family. The rest of the Morgan James team have not disappointed, and it has been a joy to work with them throughout the design, publication, and distribution processes. Talking with other Morgan James authors resulted in the introduction to our editor, Adam Cohen, who quickly and seamlessly became an integral member of *The Aging Wisely Project* team. We have been delighted by his contributions to the final manuscript and grateful for his ability to steady, rather than rock, our writing boat.

Special thanks go to Ben's daughters, Zoe Green, who, in addition to her new-mom responsibilities, has taken on the Webmaster role at *theagingwiselyproject.com*;

and, Katie Green, who ably assisted with spreadsheet management. Thanks also to Scott's son, Ben Fisher, for his detailed and diligent editing of an earlier version of this manuscript. Chris Clark did the heavy lifting on the statistical analysis of the interview data, which helped us bolster our intuitive insights with admirable scientific rigor. Mindee Forman and Mezzo Forte Digital provided essential expertise in developing our new and evolving website. We thank those of you, present and future, who have joined us to explore strategies for aging wisely. And we look forward to continuing this conversation with you.

Most importantly, we want to thank our life-partners, Carol Green and Bev Michaels, for their constant support and wise critique throughout this project. Despite the occasional defensive responses from one or both authors, they persisted in offering good counsel and heartfelt support. It is not for the faint of heart to research, write, edit, and publish a book. The ups and downs—frustrations, conflicts, delays, and unanticipated obstacles—repeatedly tested the very fiber of our beings. But, when the finish line came into sight, we were able to appreciate what we learned from this process, as well as how it has qualitatively deepened our half-century friendship and how it has given rise to a delightful number of new relationships. It is one of our personal aging wisely goals to build upon all this, as we move through this last, ultimate stage of life.

Ben Green and Scott Fisher
April 2024

A Personal Note from Ben

I grew up poor, pinching pennies, and that feeling never completely left me. Now, although I am not wealthy, I have more money than time. Time is indeed of the essence. My beloved Grandfather taught me to play bridge, and he cautioned me, "Don't go to bed with your aces." Initially, I blushed, thinking this was something sexual. I later realized that he was telling me to play whatever cards I had in my hand before they became worthless. That's not a bad guiding principle for our final years: make the most of what is possible, and don't waste your time with regrets, envy, self-pity, or grievances. Instead, embrace, as Joan Chittister entitled her book, *The Gift of Years*.

I want to thank my family, and especially my wife, Carol, for their patience and support. And, of course, my dear friend and co-author Scott—for persevering, and steadying, and being the best travel companion that I ever could have hoped for.

As the last strains of these carefully wrought concepts and lofty sentiments fade away, one is left to face the irreducible complexity of the journey ahead. What we have proposed here is immensely challenging to fully realize. At the end of the day, we must all make our peace with our remarkable human potentials, but also with our inherent fragilities. If, for instance, you meet up with me on the road in five or ten years, feel free to ask me how I'm doing with the dimming of my vision, the stiffening of my joints, the slowing of my cognition. I hope that I can respond with both a deep sigh *and* a smile. But, putting this manuscript out into the world, and continuing to offer lectures and postings and workshops, will make me feel that I've at least made an earnest effort to play the cards I've been dealt. Thank you, gentle reader, for having joined us in this endeavor.

A Personal Note from Scott

Ben and I began this effort in 2018 with minimal expectations. I thought it would be useful to learn what wisdom was out there about aging wisely and believed it would be more fun and provide more laughs doing it with my best friend. Those goals were achieved quickly and then *The Aging Wisely Project* gained momentum as we conducted our elder interviews. It became an inspirational process, listening to life stories and absorbing the wisdom of these elders as they recounted the challenges, successes, and disappointments of their unique lives.

Then, almost without realizing it, this project transformed into something much more for me. In a nutshell, I realized it had given me a renewed sense of Purpose as I entered my own elderhood and I was grateful for this opportunity. Not only had we validated the research of others, we had generated new ideas to share with you and the motivation to write this book gathered steam. We hope our discussion of Elder Identity Revision (EIR)—our proposed ninth developmental stage in life—generates serious debate and further research. And, *The Aging Wisely Project* has made me more aware of aspects of my life I am exceedingly proud of, and also more cognizant of mistakes I made and the consequences to others of those lapses when I was not my 'best self.'

I realize there is much hard work to do, both internally and in my relationships with others, if I am to wrap up this last stage of life well and be satisfied at the end of the day. But for me, the Tasks (EIR and the 5 C's) and the Tools (skills and attitudes) embodied in the GRASP acronym are meaningful guides for all of us who navigate the path to age wisely. With intentionality, and some consistent (and persistent) goal setting, they can help me make the most of my remaining time. I hope they offer the same assurance and assistance to you and the people close to you. Old age may not be for sissies, as Bette Davis said, but it can be meaningful and fulfilling even as we struggle with the inevitable losses.

Most importantly, I know that this last part of my journey will be better for sharing it fully with my wife Bev, with family, and with good friends. And, of course, with Gratitude and thanks to Ben—without him, *The Aging Wisely Project* journey would not have been possible.

About the Authors

BEN **GREEN, M.D.**, has been fascinated by the psychological development of humans since his time at Yale College. He worked as a hospital-based, and later office-based, psychiatrist for forty years, treating children and adults. Twenty years ago, he became a child and adult psychoanalyst and is currently a Clinical Associate Professor of Psychiatry at the University of Colorado Health Science Center. He has taught and supervised psychiatric residents for four decades. Dr. Green has served as President of the Colorado Child and Adolescent Psychiatric Society and the Denver Psychoanalytic Society. He also taught high school math in Congo-Kinshasa for a year and spent a year at Yale Divinity School. Dr. Green has had a long-standing interest in religion, humanistic-existential psychology, and issues related to aging, meaning, and mortality. He has delivered community lectures on these subjects for many years. Based in Denver, Colorado, Dr. Green is happily married and has three daughters and a recently born grandson.

SCOTT FISHER, M.A., is deeply interested in understanding the factors that motivate people and the different ways they achieve their career and life objectives. He holds a Bachelor of Science in Organizational Behavior and a Master's in Organization and Management from Yale University. Throughout his career, he has held various executive positions in different corporations and industries, leading human resources organizations to support rapid growth and employee engagement. As a consultant and executive coach for more than twenty-five years, he has worked with CEOs and their teams on strategy development and implementation, change management, culture assessment, and leadership development. He has also taught graduate-level strategic human resources management and change management courses to MBA students at the University of Colorado/Denver School of Business for twelve years. Scott currently resides in Denver, Colorado, where he enjoys playing golf (although he admits he's not very good at it) and spends time traveling and making the most of every day with his wonderful wife.

Appendix

The Aging Wisely Project Elder Interview Protocol

The Aging Wisely Project Self-Assessment

The Aging Wisely Project Statistical Analysis of Interview Data

The Aging Wisely Project Interview Sample Demographic Information

The Aging Wisely Project
Elder Interview Protocol

Introduction and Establish Rapport

We discussed: background to *The Aging Wisely Project*, confidentiality of personal identity, informed consent signature, interview format, and bathroom breaks. We reassured them that they didn't need to answer uncomfortable questions and that, as the interviewee, they were in control. We confirmed age and other demographic data. We informed them that we'd be asking open-ended questions to which there were no right or wrong answers—we just wanted to hear their story. We would try to manage the time so that we collect all the information we need for our research.

Developmental Narrative

1. **Life Story.** Here's what we generally said: Please tell us your *Life Story*, from your earliest memories, and organize your story in any way that you prefer. If we have questions, or need clarification, we will ask, but please proceed at a pace that is comfortable for you. We want to have a good give-and-take conversation, and hear your story in your own words, with as much detail as you wish to share with us.

2. **Attachment Figures.** From your earliest memories, who were the adults who took care of you; who were the people you could depend upon to keep you safe and take care of your needs? How would you describe these important people in your life?

3. **People in Childhood, Most Influential.** Tell us more about the people who were most influential in your life. In what ways were they important, what

did they teach you? Were they family members? Neighbors? Friends? Teachers? Coaches?

4. **High School Reputation.** How would your peers in high school have described you? How would you describe yourself at that age? Rebellious vs. compliant? What did you especially like about school: academics, sports, clubs, cliques, interests and extracurricular activities?

5. **Early to Mid-Adulthood.** Tell us about your college (if any), marriage/partnership, children, career, and any particularly important events. Celebrations? Significant losses? How did you cope with parental and other significant deaths?

6. **Reminiscences.** Do you think a lot about the past these days? Do you have significant regrets about the way your life has unfolded? How much of what happened involved luck? Bad choices? What characteristics or traits helped you the most? Which ones did not serve you well? If you could do things over, what would you do differently? Are there people you cannot forgive?

Life Today

7. **Starting the Day and Routines.** How do you start your day? Morning rituals? Has the COVID pandemic forced changes to your routine? Made the world feel more unsafe? Changed feelings about yourself or other people? Do you have daily, weekly, longer-range goals? What gets you energized? Who are the important people in your life today?

8. **Favorite Music, Reading Materials, Movies, TV.** How do you exercise your brain—games, puzzles, projects, social or community activities? Do you get bored often? Are there specific projects you are working on?

9. **Recurring Night Dreams.** How would you describe your sleeping habits? How often do you wake up during the night? If you have occasional or chronic insomnia, what do you do about it? If you have recurring dreams, what do you think those are about?

10. **Recent Pleasures.** What has made you smile recently? Laugh? What makes you happy these days? Do you have a Bucket List—what's on it? What do you look forward to doing?

11. **Recent Pain, Anxiety; Biggest Crisis, Response.** What has made you sad recently? Angry? Upset?

12. **Health Domains.** (a) <u>Medical</u>—What chronic medical issues are you managing right now? (b) <u>Medications</u>—identify all prescription and

over-the-counter medications. (c) <u>Physical Limitations</u>—Limitations in daily activities? Walking? Climbing stairs? Bathing/dressing? Lifting/carrying heavy things? Do you still drive? Other means of transportation? (d) <u>Cognitive</u>—Are you as sharp as you were a few years ago? Are there things you used to do well, but struggle with these days? Family history of dementia? Alcohol/drug use? (e) <u>Psychological</u>- Do you struggle with anxiety? Depression? Do certain types of events upset you when they happen? (f) <u>Financial</u>—How secure do you feel financially? Do you worry about having enough money? Have you taken care of legal issues like wills, Power of Attorney documents, burial or other estate matters? Talked with children and grandchildren about your end-of-life wishes? (g) <u>Exercise Routines</u>—What regular exercise do you do? How often? Strength? Flexibility/range of motion? Balance and coordination? Stretching, yoga? Other? (h) <u>Habits</u>—Are there other activities you engage in regularly that we should know about?

13. **Life Today Compared to Life at Time of Retirement.** What were your preparations, adjustments, transitions, and challenges regarding retirement? Energy level then vs. now? Friendships: old, new, and how are you coping with losses, sustaining/growing your social network? Marriage, partnership, significant people in your life—if you have a crisis, who can you get to help you?

Future Hopes and Potential Pitfalls

14. **Meaning and Purpose Now.** What projects are you working on? What keeps you energized?
15. **Hardest Person in Your Life to Lose.** Who, when and under what circumstances? What was especially hard about this loss? How do typically deal with these big losses? What helps you to move forward after these losses?
16. **Bucket List / Hopes**. What else do you want to accomplish? Need/want to do? Travel destinations and people to see?
17. **Anyone Hurt You.** Is there anyone who's hurt you so badly that it's hard to forgive them? Do you have a strong inclination to repair an important relationship? Are there people you need to reconnect with?
18. **Loneliness.** How often do you get lonely? What do you do? Does this bother you? How difficult is it for you to ask for help?

Current Support Systems

19. **Attachments.** When upset, who can you call? In a crisis, who's there for you?

20. **Current Living Situation.** Single family, multi-family, independent/assisted living? Anticipating any changes? In what sort of timeframe?

21. **Imagining Sickness, Disability, Dementia, Dying.** Do you think a lot or worry about being debilitated by a serious illness? Do you think much about dying? As we all get closer to the end, how do you deal with that?

22. **Religion/Spirituality.** Do you have strong religious faith? More spiritual than religious? Have you returned to your faith, or your religious community, as you've gotten older? How has your belief helped or hurt you in dealing with the big questions about life and death: Where do we come from? What happens after death? Heaven/Hell? Reunite with family and friends?

Self-image Today

23. **Person You Want to Be.** How close are you to being the person you want to be? Are there significant gaps between who you are and how you want to be? Are there things you can do to close that gap? How would you like to be remembered? What wisdom would you hope that others might have learned from you?

24. **Self-Perceived Age.** You told us how old you are—how old do you feel? Younger or older than actual age? Has your self-perception changed in the recent past?

25. **Anything Else.** Is there anything else you'd like us to know about you?

The Aging Wisely Project

Self-Assessment

Introduction and Guidelines

Throughout *The Aging Wisely Project*, we encouraged you to reflect on the elder growth and development issues identified in our research. This exercise presents a framework from which to continue that work and provides an opportunity to get to know yourself better. Findings by other researchers suggest that journaling stimulates personal insight. As you chronicle aspects of your life trajectory, be honest about your own behavior and the influence of others in your life. Each of us is a unique blend of genetic inheritance, the influence of other people, and how we have responded to the circumstances of our lives.

Obviously, these responses will remain confidential unless you choose to share them. However, talking with parents, siblings, partners, and friends can augment your own recollections. There is no time limit. You may work on these questions in any order. It may be helpful to take breaks to let your brain work at a leisurely pace—memories may bubble up that contribute to the richness of your narrative. And you may always revisit and modify your journal entries at a later date.

We suggest focusing on one question or issue in a single journaling session. Because it takes time, discipline, and repetition to develop a new habit, you might schedule regular quiet time for journaling on your phone, computer, diary, spiral notebook, paper calendar—where and how you do your journaling is up to you! Writing thoughts out by hand or typing them is your decision; do what's most comfortable and convenient for you.

Part 1 invites you to recall significant memories and experiences from your early life, with a focus on primary caregivers, family relationships, friends, and school. Then you are asked to reflect on how those childhood experiences have influenced your adult years. In **Part 2**, you will evaluate where you are currently in your life. You will score yourself on a simple three-point scale, ranging from 'requires improvement' (1), 'could be better' (2), or 'a definite strength' (3), on the **Tasks** of Elder Identity Revision (the 5 C's: Continuity, Control, Competence, Connection, Consciousness) and then the **Tools** embodied in our five Healthy Habits (Gratitude, Resilience, Active Practices, Self-Acceptance, Purpose). This helps to identify how you're doing with the critical challenges of elderhood and enables you to focus attention on the strengths to be leveraged and the deficits that need improvement. Then you are asked to consider your priorities and to begin setting goals, if you wish to make changes.

Note: In developing this journaling exercise, we gratefully acknowledge the pioneering work on Attachment Theory of John Bowlby and Mary Ainsworth; and, specifically, the developers of the Adult Attachment Interview (AAI): George, C., Kaplan, N., & Main, M. (1985). The Adult Attachment Interview; Unpublished, University of California at Berkeley. Other items were adapted from the elder interview protocol developed for *The Aging Wisely Project* by Ben Green and Scott Fisher.

Part 1: The Past—Childhood, Adolescence & Adulthood

1. Briefly describe your earliest childhood memories, with as much detail as possible, and with an emphasis on the quality of your relationships with parents, caregivers, and siblings. Overall, are these happy memories, or do they provoke feelings of sadness or anger?

2. Describe your overall relationship with parents (primary caregivers), first together and then individually. How would you describe your family and how it operated; what family dynamics issues seem especially positive to you? What things were problematic and had long-term consequences for you?

3. Identify five adjectives or phrases that *describe your relationship* with each caregiver (do not describe the person, e.g., tall or short, brown or blue eyes—instead describe the relationship, e.g., warm and loving, close or distant). Once you describe each relationship, note specific incidents or memories of caregivers that relate to each descriptor.

4. Digging a bit deeper, which caregiver were you closest to and why? Who comforted you when you were hurt, ill, or upset? What forms did this comforting behavior take?

5. Would you describe your early years as a good childhood? Did you feel loved and protected by the adults around you? Were you encouraged to explore your world safely and appropriately as your understanding and capabilities developed? How well or poorly did you learn to trust the people and the world around you?

6. Did you lose (through death, divorce or for other reasons) caregivers or important adults during childhood? How did you cope with this loss? Who helped and supported you during this difficult time? Did you eventually feel 'healed' and how long did that take? Do these losses still affect you today in significant ways?

7. Were any primary caregivers threatening or abusive toward you, either physically or mentally, or both? Were you the victim of any other form(s) of trauma during childhood? How did these experiences carry over into adulthood? Do they still affect your ability to trust others, or form and maintain close relationships? Did these experiences have negative effects on your self-image, or result in your dealing with chronic depression?

8. Would you describe your teenaged self as confident and engaged with peers and the world? How would high school friends have described you? Did you excel at anything in particular—academics, athletics, social groups, extracurricular activities?

9. How active were you in dating and with early sexual experimentation? Looking back, do you think you abused tobacco, alcohol, or drugs during this time? Did these experiences influence adult life positively or negatively?

10. How successful were you in establishing and maintaining close, intimate, and secure relationships with partner(s)? Do you have a life partner who loves and supports you, and who you love and support in return? How robust and well-developed is your network of friends and family connections? Are there people who would help you in a crisis?

11. Would you describe your chosen career(s) as personally satisfying? Financially rewarding? Would you describe yourself as a person who 'works to live,' or as someone who 'lives to work'? Would others describe you as a workaholic? Are your work accomplishments a source of pride or of disappointment? Would you describe yourself as 'perfectionistic'—does this

affect your quality of life? Do thoughts of impending or actual retirement scare you? What are you doing, specifically, to manage the transitions you expect in old age?

12. If you have children, how would you describe the overall quality of your relationships with them? Was parenthood a positive or a negative set of experiences in your life; and, if you did not have children, is that a significant regret? Describe special moments of pride in your children, or incidents of significant disappointment. Do you feel like you take undue credit or blame for these outcomes?

13. How would you describe your relationship with religious belief and faith? Did you grow up participating in a religious group or community? Were you always a believer? Have there been times in your life when you lost your faith, and why? Is religious practice an important part of your life today, and do you expect it to support and sustain you in your aging wisely journey?

14. Reflecting on your many and varied life experiences, are you concerned about specific things that might have a negative effect on you in your elder years? Are there regrets or burdens you need to let go of at this point? Are there people in your life that you cannot forgive? Does this detract from your enjoyment of life today? If so, what do you need to do to lessen or remove these obstacles to life satisfaction?

15. What other memories, incidents and experiences in your life have surfaced during this self-reflective journaling exercise? Note and mark them for future consideration.

Part 2: Present & Future—Establishing a Baseline for Your Aging Wisely Journey

As you shift your perspective from the past to the present, we invite you to rate how you would describe yourself *today* on this three-point scale:

1. Requires Improvement
2. Could Be Better
3. A Definite Strength

Below, rate yourself on the five critical **Tasks** of elderhood we call Elder Identity Revision (EIR). If you need a 'refresh' on definitions, please refer to Chapter 4 in this book, scan the QR code video link at the end of this Appendix, or visit www.theagingwiselyproject.com.

Task	Score	Additional Notes
Generativity	_____	
Self-Integrity	_____	
<u>**5 C's**</u>		
Control	_____	
Competence	_____	
Connection	_____	
Continuity	_____	
Consciousness (Overall)	_____	
- Self-Consciousness	_____	
- Existential Consciousness	_____	
- Transcendental Consciousness	_____	

After scoring yourself on the 5 C's, consider the following questions and continue your journaling efforts. As a result of this self-reflective work, you may decide to modify one or more scores and refine your priorities for improvement.

1. *Control.* Issues of Control focus primarily on changes in our physical and cognitive health and capabilities. What significant losses have you experienced, and how is it affecting your ability to do things, go places, and spend time on the things you love to do? Are you managing chronic medical conditions to the best of your ability? Are you getting the help you need from professionals, family, and friends to cope in the best ways possible?

2. *Competence.* Are there tasks you struggle with now that used to be relatively easy? As you learn that specific strengths or competencies—physical and/or cognitive—are waning, how has that affected your ability to manage your environment, your relationships, technology, and your quality of life? Are there challenges that you are avoiding because you don't want to face them (e.g., having to move from a long-time home to independent living or to an assisted living environment)? Will avoiding the issue make it go away? How

have these losses of Competence affected your self-image? Your self-confidence? Your ability and willingness to ask for help?

3. *Connection.* As we age, it is inevitable that the loss of important Connections in our life becomes increasingly significant. Who have you lost in the past several years from your social network and how has that affected you? How were these people important to you? Do you feel increasingly isolated? What are you doing to make new friends and acquaintances; vary or increase social activities; and develop new work, hobbies, or volunteer activities?

4. *Continuity.* To what extent do you consider yourself the same person you've always been? If you perceive significant changes looming on the horizon, what are they? Detail both the negative and the positive changes. How challenging has it been to maintain your core self-image as the losses of aging accumulate?

5. *Consciousness.* Dealing with issues of Consciousness can be challenging and complex, and we have divided this arena into three discrete categories. How would you describe your level of *self-consciousness*, your ability to understand yourself and your motivations? To what extent are your behaviors inconsistent with your thinking and inner thoughts? What kinds of activities might you be motivated to engage in to improve self-consciousness (e.g., yoga, journaling groups, or mindfulness training)?

How have you dealt with issues related to mortality (*existential consciousness*)? Do you think much about death and dying? Does the fact that death is closer depress you, or does it motivate you to get the most out of your remaining time? Have your feelings about religion, God, and/or spirituality changed, or do you expect them to change as you get older? Do you find yourself returning to religious observance, or wanting to return to it, as a way to get some answers to important questions about life and death? How content are you with your one-and-only life cycle?

Do you find yourself thinking more about issues of *transcendence* these days—links and connections with ancestors and your personal history in the context of your time and place in human history? Are you satisfied with the legacies you will pass on to children, grandchildren, and great-grandchildren? Are there parts of your *Life Story* you need to share? Is there more you can or need to do, like writing your memoir? Do you feel more, or less, connected with humanity in general, your place in the cosmos? To what extent do you feel your time on earth has been well-spent?

Now, use the same three-point rating process as you think about the **Tools** (skills and attitudes) or the Healthy Habits required to navigate your elder years successfully. Similarly, refer to Part 2 (Chapters 5 through 10) of *The Aging Wisely Project* for definitions and examples of these essential Tools, as well as the QR code at the end of this Appendix. Continue journaling with the questions following the assessment.

Tools (GRASP)	Score	Additional Notes
Gratitude	_____	
Resilience	_____	
Active Practices	_____	
Self-Acceptance	_____	
Purpose	_____	

1. *Gratitude.* Do you generally think of yourself as an optimist or a pessimist? Is life's glass half-full or half-empty for you? Are you a worrier? Do you spend too much time thinking about things that went awry in the past, or about things that could go wrong in the future? When you're dealing with a current crisis or challenge, are you aware of the things you are grateful for in your life? How can you improve your appreciation of life's small daily pleasures?

2. *Resilience.* Do you think of yourself as a strong person? Thinking about mistakes made in the past, was it difficult to recover from setbacks, and to move on productively? Are you a person who puts yourself in a position to be successful, or do you sometimes sabotage yourself and invite failure? Are there times when you wonder if it's worthwhile to go on? Do you relish the thought of the next challenge, known or unknown, or does change frighten you, and why? What might you do to strengthen your resilience and coping skills?

3. *Active Practices.* To what extent, within your capabilities, are you working to maintain or improve your physical and cognitive strengths? Do you regularly exercise; work on your flexibility, range of motion, and balance; and engage in enjoyable physical activities? What are you doing to keep yourself sharp mentally: reading and book club discussions, crossword puzzles and mentally stimulating phone apps, volunteer projects, classes, scrapbooking, gardening, cooking, etc.? Is there a new area of learning you'd like to explore, either through formal (e.g., Olli classes) or informal (e.g., surfing the internet) means? Is there a past interest to re-engage with, like the piano or that old guitar you haven't strummed for ages?

4. *Self-Acceptance.* How close are you to the person you want to be? Are there significant aspects of yourself you would change? Is it too late to make changes? Do you have significant regrets about things you did (or didn't do), people you've hurt or who have hurt you, other situations in which you were not your best self? What can you do to remedy these situations with the individuals involved? Do you think it's time to forgive yourself and stop beating yourself up? How difficult is this, and can you ask for help from family, friends, or professionals?

5. *Purpose.* When you wake up in the morning, do you feel energized by the things you want to accomplish that day? Are there things you look forward to doing in the next week, month, or year? Are you contributing to the welfare of others? What activities and projects generate a sense of Purpose and meaning in your life? Are there still things you need to do, people you need to see, places you want to visit and explore, both in person or virtually?

Additional suggestions: Remember that the most important thing is to be honest about your scores—the goal is to review where you are with these Tasks and Tools. We do not believe that totaling the scores up is meaningful. However, where you score yourself '3,' consider this a significant strength. How can you utilize this strength to even greater effect? How can you leverage this skill or attitude to improve yourself, help others, or improve the world?

Where you have scored yourself a '2,' consider this a neutral response, neither a strength nor a significant weakness. It may not be significant as you evaluate your journey to age wisely. Or it may be worth working on, depending on what you still need to accomplish in your life. There may well be room for improvement in a specific area, and it could serve you well to consider the benefits of strengthening a GRASP factor in the context of your goals.

If you have scored yourself a '1,' then you have identified a significant weakness or deficit in your approach to aging wisely. Given your individual circumstances, and what you hope to accomplish in your remaining years, some serious attention to these deficits may be warranted. If you don't improve the low-rated skills and attitudes embodied in the Tools, it may be more difficult to work on the elder Tasks you need to complete.

When working on setting goals for improvement, utilize the SMART acronym: Is the goal *Specific*? Can the end-result be *Measured*? Is the goal *Achievable* and *Realistic*? Have you established a *Time* or date by which it will be completed? Consider the **benefits** that will be yours when you achieve the goal. If the goal is to lose twenty pounds, then what are the benefits for accomplishing this goal? For example, you will feel and look better, improve your cardiovascular health, etc. Whose help do you need to accomplish this goal? Break down the goal into bite-sized tasks with clear deadlines.

Finally, investing time and energy in this journaling and goal-setting process involves a serious commitment. It's not easy and at times it may be discouraging. But it can also be quite motivating, and we encourage you to keep working at it! You may be upset by some of the issues that emerge during this self-reflective work. Enlist the help of family members and friends as 'coaches' to keep you focused and on target with your plan. Find an 'accountability buddy' who is working on aging wisely goals and then you can support each other. Consider working with a professional if negative feelings persist, depression ensues, or things just seem overwhelming.

Statistical Analysis of Interview Data

B ecause our primary interest was to determine which of the twenty-nine individual factors were most influential in determining the final *Aging Wisely* score (AW#), we asked our statistician to calculate the correlations between each of these individual factors and AW#. The nature of our five-point Likert scale scores guided him to use Spearman's Correlation Coefficients.

We invite you to challenge yourself by guessing which of the factors, perhaps your top five, that were most consequential in determining AW#. Which category of factors do you think was most predictive? Was it the elders' success with Erikson's and Vaillant's developmental Tasks, or how the elders came across during their interviews with us? Was it their mastery of Elder Identity Revision Tasks (defined as the 5 C's), or their success with the five Healthy Habits?

Here are the four general categories and the twenty-nine specific items for you to consider:

- **Erikson and Vaillant (Tasks)**: *Erikson*—Generativity and Self-Integrity; *Vaillant*—Guardianship and his Seven Protective Factors (no smoking, no obesity, no excessive alcohol, regular physical exercise, higher education, late-life partner, and good coping skills).
- **Elder Identity Revision (Tasks)**: Control, Competence, Connection, Continuity, and Consciousness (the 5 C's).
- **Interview Data Elements (What Elders Reported and What We Observed)**: Reliable Attachment Figure in adulthood, Healthy Grief, Sense of Humor, Frankl's Tragic Optimism (hopeful, but realistic), Mood (stable,

positive), Anxiety (well regulated), Energy (vitality, but not excessive), Cognition, Engagement (with interviewers), Candor, Openness (to experience, to new ideas), Narrative Coherence, Transparency (same on the inside as outside), and Youthfulness (for their age).

- **Healthy Habits (Tools)**: Gratitude, Active Practices, Purpose, Resilience, and Self-Acceptance (GRASP).

Have you made your choices? Actually, *all* of these variables were significantly correlated with AW# (at the 0.05 significance level). In general, Spearman correlations between 0.50 and 0.70 are considered 'moderate,' from 0.70 to 0.90 are deemed 'high,' and anything above 0.90 (approaching 1.0, the strongest relationship possible between variables) is considered 'very high.' The diagram below displays the correlations between each of these factors and the final AW#:

AW# CORRELATION COEFFICIENTS (1.0 IS HIGHEST)

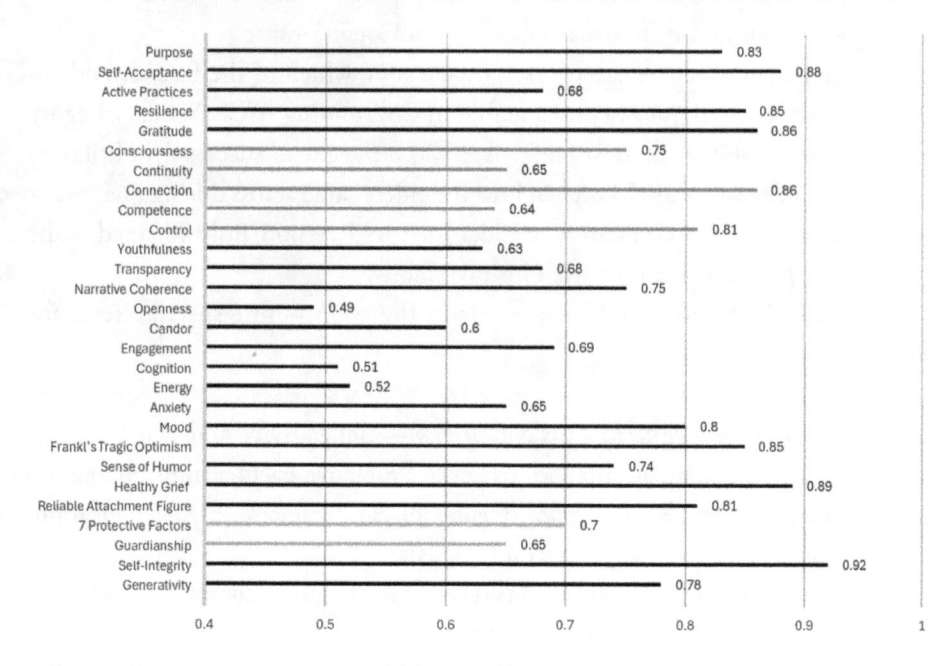

How accurate were your guesses? Were there any big surprises here for you? Erikson's Self-Integrity gets the gold medal for first place, and the thematically related item, Self-Acceptance (a Healthy Habit) was third. Our conclusion: *being comfortable in your own skin and well-integrated goes a long way toward aging wisely.* Our emphasis on attachment has been vindicated by top ten finishes for three attach-ment-related items: Healthy Grieving (second), which is strongly associated with stable, loving attachments, as are Connection (EIR Task) (fourth, tied) and having a Reliable (adult) Attachment (ninth, tied). All of the Healthy Habits were in the top eight except for Active Practices, whose correlation, as previously discussed, is diminished by those people who are trying to compensate for other lower-scoring aspects of their lives (good for them!). EIR also had two Tasks in the top ten: Con-nection and Control. Also of note is the power of Tragic Optimism (sixth, tied), another accurate insight by Holocaust survivor Viktor Frankl.

Some of our favored predictions were not confirmed by the statistical analy-sis: we had high hopes for sense of Humor, Openness, and Engagement with the interviewers, but all fell short of having the top-tier correlations. Mood, particularly during the interview, did make it to eleventh on the list, but Energy was far behind.

The second statistical analysis executed by our expert had to do with determining which combination of factors, taken together, were most influential. (For this analysis, we were looking at the variances, which are calculated by squaring the combined cor-relations.) The most efficient trio was Self-Integrity, Connection, and Resilience, which accounted for 99.4 percent of the total AW#. We note with some satisfaction that this included, respectively, one developmental Task, one EIR item, and one Healthy Habit (Tool). In fact, as noted in the Introduction to Part Two, 99 percent of the variance of the AW# can be achieved by any combination of at least three of the following six items: Self-Integrity, Connection, Self-Acceptance, Gratitude, Resilience, and Purpose.

We suggest thinking of the last four of these factors (Self-Acceptance, Gratitude, Resilience, and Purpose) as a four-legged stool, because they are so highly correlated with each other that if you have a high score in any one of them, you almost always get high scores in the other three as well. Not only is this interesting, it confirms a major insight from our fifty-two elders' *Life Stories*. Aging wisely can be accom-plished in myriad ways; different individuals may start out with different strengths, which they then use to develop others. For instance, one person might have a consti-tutional strength in the domain of Purpose which, over time, helps them to develop more Resilience, then Gratitude, and then Self-Acceptance. Another might start with an inborn predilection for Gratitude and then, subsequently, develop the other three. In general systems theory, the notion of equifinality describes how, in com-plex systems, the same 'final result' can be achieved via multiple pathways.

As a final note, the scores for our elders in their seventies, eighties, and nine-ties did not vary significantly by age. Obviously, there are significant physical and cognitive differences in the functional capacities of a seventy-year-old compared with a ninety-year-old. But, as Carstensen (Chapter 1) has observed, with improved coping skills and enlightened attitudes, elders can make up for significant losses or deficits in other functional areas.

More statistics, should you desire additional analysis, may be found on our website at www.theagingwiselyproject.com.

Interview Sample Demographic Information

Although our sample of interviewees is small, we strove to make it as representative of the U.S. population as possible. A number of the sources we drew upon acknowledged the imprecise nature of several of these estimates.

Aging Wisely Elders in 70s	*Aging Wisely* Elders in 80s	*Aging Wisely* Elders 90+
30 (58%)	14 (27%)	8 (15%)
Gender and Sexuality	***Aging Wisely* Sample**	**U.S. Over-65 Population**
Female	48%	55%
LGBTQ	6%	4%
Racial/Ethnic Diversity	***Aging Wisely* Sample**	**U.S. Over-65 Population**
Caucasian, non-Hispanic	72%	75%
Hispanic	11%	9%
African American	11%	9%
Asian American	4%	5%
Arab American	3%	0.8%
Native American	0.5%	0.6%
Socioeconomic Status	***Aging Wisely* Sample**	**U.S. Over-65 Population**
Lower	25%	22%
Middle	67%	73%
Upper	8%	5%

Sources: U.S. Census, Administration for Community Living (Department of Health and Human Services), Pew Research, Williams Institute (2010), and other sources. Demarcations of race, ethnicity, and income strata are imprecise. Note that most *Aging Wisely* lower-income individuals were living in communal settings, which probably diminished their level of adversity.

Suggested Reading

Applewhite, Ashton. *This Chair Rocks: A Manifesto Against Ageism.* United States: Networked Books. 2015.

Bechdel, Alison. *The Secret to Superhuman Strength.* New York: Houghton Mifflin Harcourt. 2021

Butler, Katy. *The Art of Dying Well: A Practical Guide to a Good End of Life.* New York: Scribner, Simon & Schuster. 2019.

Chittister, Joan. *The Gift of Years: Growing Older Gracefully.* New York: BlueBridge. 2008.

Erikson, E. H. *Childhood and Society.* New York: W.W. Norton & Company. 1950.

Esfahani Smith, Emily. *The Power of Meaning: Creating a Life That Matters.* New York: Crown Publishing. 2017.

Frankl, Viktor E. *Man's Search for Meaning: an Introduction to Logotherapy.* Boston: Beacon Press. 1962.

Gawande, Atul. *Being Mortal: Medicine and What Matters in the End.* New York: Metropolitan Books, Henry Holt and Company. 2014.

Goffman, Erving. *The Presentation of Self in Everyday Life.* Garden City, N.Y.: Doubleday. 1959.

Greene, Robert. *Mastery.* New York: Penguin. 2012.

Hone, Lucy. "The Three Secrets of Resilient People," TEDx Talk, Christchurch, New Zealand, September 25, 2019.

Huberman, Andrew. "The Science of Making and Breaking Habits." *YouTube.com,* accessed January 3, 2022. https://www.youtube.com/watch?v=Wcs2PFz5q6g.

Kabat-Zinn, Jon. *Full Catastrophe Living: Using the Wisdom of Your Body and Mind to Face Stress, Pain, and Illness.* New York: Bantam Books. 2013.

Karen, Robert. *Becoming Attached: First Relationships and How They Shape Our Capacity to Love.* New York: Oxford University Press. 1998.

Kaufman, Sharon R. *The Ageless Self: Sources of Meaning in Late Life.* Madison: The University of Wisconsin Press, 1986.

Keltner, Dacher. *Awe: The New Science of Everyday Wonder and How It Can Transform Your Life.* New York: Penguin Random House. 2024.

Leland, John. *Happiness Is a Choice You Make: Lessons From a Year Among the Oldest Old.* New York: Farrar, Straus and Giroux. 2018

Levinson, D. J. *The Seasons of a Man's Life.* New York: Random House. 1978.

Levinson, D. J. *The Seasons of a Woman's Life.* New York: Ballantine Books, Random House. 1996.

Magnusson, Magreta. *The Gentle Art of Swedish Death Cleaning: How to Free Yourself and Your Family from a Lifetime of Clutter.* New York: Scribner, Simon & Schuster. 2018.

Martin, Seligman. *Authentic Happiness.* London, England: Simon & Schuster. 2004.

Medina, John. *Brain Rules for Aging Well: 10 Principles for Staying Vital, Happy, and Sharp.* Melbourne, Australia: Scribe. 2018.

Pinker, Susan. *The Village Effect: How Face-to-face Contact Can Make Us Healthier, Happier, and Smarter.* New York: Spiegel & Grau. 2014.

Putnam, Robert D. *Bowling Alone: The Collapse and Revival of American Community.* New York: Touchstone. 2001.

Sachs, Oliver. *Gratitude.* New York: Knopf Random House. 2015.

Sachs, Oliver. *On the Move: A Life.* Waterville, Maine: Thorndike Press. 2015.

Schachter-Shalomi, Zalman. *From Age-ing to Sage-ing: A Revolutionary Approach to Growing Older.* New York: Hachette Book Group. 2014.

Seligman, Martin. "The New Era of Positive Psychology," TED Talk, July 21, 2008.

Vaillant, George. *Aging Well: Surprising Guideposts to a Happier Life from the Landmark Harvard Study of Adult Development.* New York: Little, Brown Spark. 2003 (reprinted).

Volf, Miroslav, Matthew Croasmun, and Ryan McAnnally-Linz. *Life Worth Living: A Guide to What Matters Most.* New York: The Open Field, Penguin Random House. 2023.

Waldinger, Robert J. and Marc S. Schulz. *The Good Life: Lessons From the World's Longest Study of Happiness.* New York: Simon & Schuster.

Waldinger, Robert. "What Makes a Good Life? Lessons from the Longest Study of Happiness," TED Talk, December 23, 2015.

Zweig, Connie. *The Inner Work of Age: Shifting from Role to Soul.* New York: Park Street Press, Simon & Schuster. 2021.

Citations

Introduction

1   David G. Blanchflower, "Happiness Economics," *National Bureau of Economic Research (NBER)* 2 (2008): 7–10.

2   Laura L. Carstensen, *A Long Bright Future: An Action Plan for a Lifetime of Happiness, Health, and Financial Security* (New York: Harmony, 2009).

3   Becca Levy, *Breaking the Age Code: How Your Beliefs About Aging Determine How Long and Well You Live* (New York: William Morrow, 2022).

Chapter 1

4   B. Beebe and F.M. Lachmann, "Infant Research and Adult Treatment: Co-Constructing Interactions," (London: The Analytic Press/Taylor & Francis Group, 2002).

5   Constance Gustke, "Retirement Plans Thrown Into Disarray by a Divorce," *The New York Times*, June 6, 2014, New York Edition.

6   Susan L. Brown and Matthew R. Wright, "Marriage, Cohabitation, and Divorce in Later Life," *Innovation in Aging* 1, no. 2 (September 2017).

7   Paola Zaninotto, Eleonora Iob, Panayotes Demakakos, and Andrew Steptoe, "Immediate and Longer-Term Changes in the Mental Health and Well-Being of Older Adults in England During the COVID-19 Pandemic," *JAMA Psychiatry* 79, no. 2 (Dec. 22, 2021): 151–159.

Chapter 5

8   Adam M. Grant, Elizabeth M. Campbell, Grace Chen, Keenan Cottone, David Lapedis, and Karen Lee, "Impact and the Art of Motivation Maintenance: The Effects of Contact with Beneficiaries on Persistent Behavior," *Organizational Behavior and Human Decision Processes*, 103 (May 2007): 53–67.

9   Hajdi Moche and Daniel Västfjäll, "To Give or to Take Money? The Effects of Choice on Prosocial Spending and Happiness," *Journal of Positive Psychology* 17, no. 5 (June 17, 2021).

10 Koichiro Shiba, Laura D. Kubzansky, David R. Williams, Tyler J. VanderWeele, and Eric S Kim, "Associations Between Purpose in Life and Mortality by SES," *American Journal of Preventive Medicine* 61, no. 2 (August 2021): e56–e61.

11 James W. Pennebaker, *Writing to Heal: a Guided Journal from Recovering from Trauma and Emotional Upheaval* (New York: New Harbinger Publications, 2004).

Chapter 6

12 Howard E. Alper, Leen Feliciano, Lucie Millien, Cristina Pollari, and Sean Locke, "Post-Traumatic Growth and Quality of Life Among World Trade Center Health Registry Enrollees 16 Years after 9/11," *International Journal of Environmental Research and Public Health* 19, no. 15 (August 2022): 9737.

13 Richard G. Tedeschi and Lawrence Calhoun, "Post-Traumatic Growth: Conceptual Foundations and Empirical Evidence: *Psychological Inquiry* 15, no. 1 (2004): 1–18. Barbara L. Fredrickson, "The Role of Positive Emotions in Positive Psychology: The Broaden-and-Build Theory of Positive Emotions," *American Psychologist* 56, no. 3 (March 2001): 218–226.

14 Martin E. Seligman, "Learned Helplessness," *Annual Review of Medicine* 23, no. 1 (February 1972): 407–412.

15 John-David Collins, Amanda Markham, Kathrine Service, Seth Reini, Erik Wolf, and Pinata Sessoms, "A Systematic Literature Review of the Use and Effectiveness of the Computer-Assisted Rehabilitation Environment for Research and Rehabilitation As It Relates to the Wounded Warrior," *Work* 50, no. 1 (2015): 121–129.

16 Laura L. Carstensen, *A Long Bright Future: An Action Plan for a Lifetime of Happiness, Health, and Financial Security* (New York: Harmony, 2009).

Chapter 8

17 Robert Waldinger, "What Makes a Good Life? Lessons from the Longest Study of Happiness," TED Talk, December 23, 2015.

18 Sonja Lyubomirsky, Kennon M. Sheldon, and David Schkade, "Pursuing Happiness: The Architecture of Sustainable Change," *Review of General Psychology* 9, no. 2 (2005): 111–131.

19 George Vaillant, *Aging Well: Surprising Guideposts to a Happier Life from the Landmark Harvard Study of Adult Development* (New York: Little, Brown Spark, 2003 reprinted), 345.

20 James A. Coan, Hillary S. Schaefer, and Richard J. Davidson, "Social Regulation of the Neural Response to Threat," *Psychological Science* 17, no. 12 (2006): 1032–1039.

21 E.E. Werner, "Risk, Resilience, and Recovery: Perspectives from the Kauai Longitudinal Study," *Development and Psychopathology* 5, no. 4 (Fall 1993): 503–515.

22 Bryan D. James, Robert S. Wilson, Lisa L. Barnes, and David A. Bennett, "Late-Life Social Activity and Cognitive Decline in Old Age," *Journal of International Neuropsychology* 17, no. 6 (November 2011): 998–1005.

23 Ryota Kanai, Bahador Bahrami, Rebecca Roylance, and Geraint Rees, "Online Social Network Size Is Reflected in Human Brain Structure," *Proceedings of the Royal Society B Biological Science* 279, no. 1732 (April 2012): 1327–34.

24 Lynne Giles, Gary Glonek, Mary Luszcz, and Gary Andrews, "Effects of Social Networks on 10 Year Survival in very old Australians: The Australian Longitudinal Study of Aging," *Journal of Epidemiology and Community Health* 59, no. 7 (July 2005): 547–579.

25 John Medina, *Brain Rules for Aging Well: 10 Principles for Staying Vital, Happy, and Sharp* (Melbourne, Australia: Scribe, 2018), 22.

26 Candyce H. Kroenke, Laura D. Kubzansky, Eva S. Schernhammer, Michelle D. Holmes, and Ichiro Kawachi, "Social Networks, Social Support, and Survival after Breast Cancer Diagnosis," *Journal of Clinical Oncology* 24, no. 7 (March 1, 2006): 1105–1111.

27 Fabia de Oliveira Andrade, Lu Jin, Robert Clarke, Imani Wood, MaryAnn Dutton, Chezaray Anjorin, Grace Rubin, Audrey Gao, Surojeet Sengupta, Kevin FitzGerald, and Leena Hilakivi-Clarke, "Social Isolation Activates Dormant Mammary Tumors, and Modifies Inflammatory and Mitochondrialial Pathways in the Rat Mammary Gland," *Cells* 12, no. 6 (March 21, 2023): 961.

28 Robert Waldinger and Marc Schultz, *The Good Life: Lessons from the World's Longest Scientific Study of Happiness* (New York: Simon & Schuster), 259.

29 Robert Waldinger and Marc Schultz, *The Good Life: Lessons from the World's Longest Scientific Study of Happiness* (New York: Simon & Schuster), 257.

30 Gillian Sandstrom and E.W. Dunn, "Is Efficiency Overrated? Minimal Social Interaction Leads to Belonging and Positive Affect," *Social Psychological and Personality Science* 5, no. 4 (May 2014): 437–442.

31 Gemma Curtis, "Your Life in Numbers," *Creative Commons* (September 29, 2017).

32 Julianne Holt-Lunstad, Timothy B. Smith, Mark Baker, Tyler Harris, and David Stephenson, "Loneliness and Social Isolation as Risk Factors for Mortality: A Meta-Analytic Review." *Perspectives on Psychological Science* 10, no. 2 (March 2015): 227–237.

33 Richard Fry, "The Share of Americans Living Without a Partner Has Increased, Especially Among Young Adults," Pew Research Center (October 11, 2017).

34 Richard Weindruch, Roy L. Walford, Suzanne Fligiel, and Donald Guthrie, "The Retardation of Mice by Dietary Restriction: Longevity, Cancer, Immunity, and Lifetime Energy Intake," *Journal of Nutrition* 116, no. 4 (April 1986): 641–654.

35 David Snowdon, *Aging With Grace: What the Nun Study Teaches Us About Leading Longer, Healthier, and More Meaningful Lives* (New York: Bantam Books, 2002).

36 Denise C. Park and Evan T. Smith, "Facilitation of Cognition in Older Adults: Traditional and Non-Traditional Approaches to Inducing Change," *Medical Research Archives* 10, no. 10 (October 2022).

37 Shirley Leanos, Esra Kürüm, Carla M. Strickland-Hughes, Annie S. Ditta, Gianhu Nguyen, Miranda Felix, Hara Yum, George W. Rebok, and Rachel Wu. "The Impact of Learning Multiple Real-World Skills on the Cognitive Abilities and Functional Independence in Healthy Older Adults," *Journals of Gerontology, Series B, Psychological and Social Sciences* 75, no. 6 (June 2, 2020): 1–13.

38 William J. Cromie, "Aging Brains Lose Less Than Thought," *The Harvard Gazette,* October 3, 1996.

39 Stefanie H. Freeman, Ruth Kandel, Luis Cruz, Anete Rozkalne, Kathy Newell, Matthew P. Frosch, E. Tessa Hedley-Whyte, Joseph J. Locascio, Lewis Lipsitz, and Bradley T. Hyman, "Preservation of Neuronal Number Despite Age Related Cortical Brain Atrophy in Elderly Subjects Without Alzheimer's Disease," *Journal of Neuropathology and Experimental Neurology* 67, no. 12 (December 2008): 1205–1212.

40 Erin Blakemore, "Blind People's Brains Rewire Themselves to Enhance Other Senses," *Smithsonian Magazine* (March 23, 2017), https://www.smithsonian-mag.com/smart-news/blind-peoples-brains-rewire-themselves-enhance-other-senses-180962653/.

41 Holly Elser, Erzsébet Horváth-Puhó, Jaimie L. Gradus, Meghan L. Smith, Timothy L. Lash, M. Maria Glymour, Henrik Toft Sørensen, Victor W. Henderson, "Association of Early-, Middle-, and Late-life Depression with Incident Dementia in Danish Cohort. *JAMA Neurology* 80, no. 9 (September 1, 2023): 949-958.

42 Anne Case and Angus Deaton, "Without a College Degree, Life in America Is Staggeringly Shorter," *New York Times*, October 3, 2023.

43 Janice K. Kiecolt-Glaser, Timothy J. Loving, Jeffrey R. Stowell, William B. Malarkey, Stanley Lemeshow, Stephanie L. Dickinson, and Ronald Glaser, "Hostile Marital Interactions, Proinflammatory Cytokine Production, and Wound Healing," *Archives of General Psychiatry* 62, no. 12 (2005): 1377-1384.

44 John Medina, *Brain Rules for Aging Well: 10 Principles for Staying Vital, Happy, and Sharp* (Melbourne, Australia: Scribe, 2018), 65–85.

45 Ellen Langer, "The Young Ones," The Langer Mindfulness Institute, http://langermindfulnessinstitute.com/the-young-ones/.

46 World Health Organization, "Physical Activity Fact Sheet," October 12, 2021.

47 John Medina, *Brain Rules for Aging Well: 10 Principles for Staying Vital, Happy, and Sharp* (Melbourne, Australia: Scribe, 2018), 34.

48 Howard S. Friedman and Leslie L. Martin, *The Longevity Project: Surprising Discoveries for Health and Long Life from the Landmark Eight-Decade Study* (New York: Hudson Street Press, 2011).

49 Pew Research Center, "Modeling The Future of Religion In America," September 13, 2022.

50 Dacher Keltner, *Awe: The New Science of Everyday Wonder and How It Can Transform Your Life* (New York: Penguin Press, 2023).

Chapter 9

51 Robert A. Emmons and Michael R. McCullough, "Counting Blessings Versus Burdens: An Experimental Investigation of Gratitude and Subjective Well-Being in Daily Life," *Journal of Personality and Social Psychology* 84, no. 2 (2003): 377–389.

Martin E.P. Seligman, Tracy A. Steen, Nansook Park, and Christopher Peterson, "Positive Psychology in Progress: Empirical Validation of Interventions." *American Psychology* 60, no. 5 (July-August 2005): 410–421.

52 Amie M. Gordon, Emily A. Impett, Aleksandr Kogan, Christopher Oveis, and Dacher Keltner, "To Have and to Hold: Gratitude Promotes Relationship

Maintenance in Intimate Bonds," *Journal of Personality and Social Psychology* 103, no. 2 (August 2012): 257-274

53 Joshua Brown and Joel Wong, "Gratitude Changes You and Your Brain," *Berkeley Greater Good Magazine* (June 6, 2017).

Chapter 11

54 Alia Crum, "Science of Mindsets for Health Performance," Huberman Lab, *YouTube.com*, accessed January 23, 2022, https://www.youtube.com/watch?v=dFR_wFN23ZY.

55 Lauren C. Howe, Kari A. Leibowitz, Margaret A. Perry, Julie M. Bitler, Whitney Block, Ted J. Kaptchuk, Kari C. Nadeau, and Alia J. Crum, "Changing Patient Mindsets About Non-Life-Threatening Symptoms During Oral Immunotherapy: a Randomized Clinical Trial," *Journal of Allergy and Clinical Immunology: In Practice* 7, no. 5 (May-June 2019): 1550-1559.

56 "New Year's Resolution Statistics (2023 Updated)", Discover Healthy Habits (August 30, 2023 revised), https://discoverhappyhabits.com/new-years-resolution-statistics/.

57 Andrew Huberman, "Goals Toolkit: How to Set & Achieve Your Goals," Huberman Lab, *YouTube.com*, accessed August 28, 2023, https://youtu.be/CrtR12PBKb0.

A free ebook edition is available with the purchase of this book.

To claim your free ebook edition:

1. Visit MorganJamesBOGO.com
2. Sign your name CLEARLY in the space
3. Complete the form and submit a photo of the entire copyright page
4. You or your friend can download the ebook to your preferred device

Morgan James
BOGO™

A **FREE** ebook edition is available for you
or a friend with the purchase of this print book.

CLEARLY SIGN YOUR NAME ABOVE

Instructions to claim your free ebook edition:
1. Visit MorganJamesBOGO.com
2. Sign your name CLEARLY in the space above
3. Complete the form and submit a photo
   of this entire page
4. You or your friend can download the ebook
   to your preferred device

Print & Digital Together Forever.

Snap a photo

Free ebook

Read anywhere

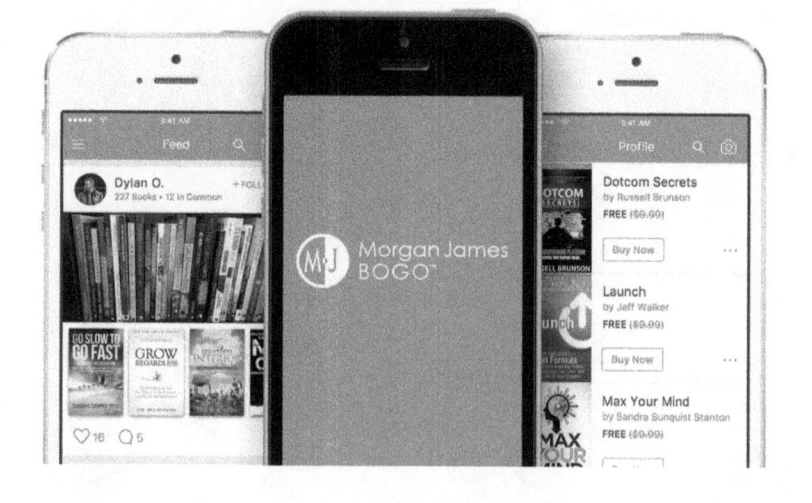

Printed in the USA
CPSIA information can be obtained
at www.ICGtesting.com
JSHW081012170824
68284JS00002B/13